Acknowledgements

I want to thank many who have contributed to my professional and personal life. Some of those include:

Lt. Issac H. May & Lulie	Margaret McLarty
Ted Taylor (Iron Man)	Ceil Perry
Trudy Gandy & Mark!	Bill and Beth Lathum
Mindy & David Costello	Kenny and Jamie Kilgore
George Wynn	Jeff Molenburg
Dr. James T. Draper	"McTom" in Idaho!
O. E. Perry	Krista Judson in Boulder!
Johnny & Erin Walton	Koyoko Fukui in Pebble Beach
Richard & Rhonda Harris	Robert Talbott in Carmel
Ginny & Maegan Brown	B. C. Hogan (from me & my dog!)
John & Zelma Gandy	Jeri & Mike Wray and Vida Hughes
Mark & Tricia V.	Bob Thomas
Wanda Greer	Lewis Lobo in Spain
Ro & Janice Gonzales	Bruce Grant; Mary Taylor
William Howard	Jerry Perry; Jim & Carolyn H.
My friends at Perry County	Teri D., Steve G., David L., Carl L.
My friends at Trustmark	Bill M., Bob M., Barbara R.
Luther, Kitty, & Andy Adkins	Denny Yost
Cami (here's one for history)	Mom & Dad
Don Davis (get to work)	Jim & Ann Brown and Nan
Sheri Rice	Russell Steele & Barry Alpart
Cythia Fetty	Russ & Monique Marshall
My friends at Digital Print	My friends at IBM worldover
Susan Rheames	Dee (big sister)
Jim Woodward (at Dell)	Zelma & Sam Donsing
"Bear" & Renee Brundrett	Butch McCardle
Dr. Samuel L. Gladney & staff	Aunt Jean & Uncle Carrol
Gene & Faith Aikens	Johnnie & Beverly Armstrong
Gaylerd and Mary Wineriter	Maria & Doug Davis
Kurt Grigsby & Bill Smith	Karen Lowell & Teri
My friends at Glenview	Gary Hegna

Francis Tucker (many thanks)
My friends at FBCE
Sharron & Don Guild
My friends at Merrill Lynch
My friends at Fidelity
My friends at the SSB
Sonny and Anita May
My friends at FTP Inc.
My friends at Uniden
My friends at ComputerWorld
Meadow Lark Lemmon
President Russel Dilday (SBTS)
Charles Sylvester
Friends in the IEEE
My friends at SPIE
Raliegh Curter
Louis Inacio in Portugal
Bill Taylor (remember the wreck)

Cleve, Stan, Nancy, Joyce, B. J.
Bill K., Colleen, Mike H.
Tom B., Herb C., Andrew C.
David P., David G., Gail B.
Steve K., Jack Hsu, Kim P.
Joey M., Mary F., Mark V.
Ellen L., Aaron K., Gary S.
Penny N., Tim H., Tina P.
Jerry W., Jerry S., Cathy K.
Gary Y., Dave B., John D.
Jim R., Larry J., Larry U.
Mike S., Johnjay L., Neil L.
George R., Ernie L., Alan M.
Glynn B., Kay C., Jerry W.
The IIJ crew
Jay at Harold's
Judge and Rene Sugg

Dedication

This book is dedicated to my wife who sacrificed so much for it to be possible.

Contents

Acknowledgements iii
Preface xi

1. A Primer on Integration 1
   1.1 Network Layers from a Practical Perspective 1
   1.2 LAN Network Devices 5
       Gateway 5
       Router 6
       Bridge 6
       Repeater 6
   1.3 Aspects of Networking Technology 6
   1.4 Conclusion 10

2. A Perspective on Integrating TCP/IP into SNA 11
   2.1 Orientation to TCP/IP and SNA 11
   2.2 The Machine and the Human Dilemma 12
   2.3 A User Perspective of TCP/IP and SNA 12
   2.4 Why Integrate TCP/IP into SNA 13
       Forces Driving Integration 13
       Maximizing Investment 13
   2.5 A TCP/IP and SNA Technical Brief 14
   2.6 Specific Aspects of Integration 17
   2.7 Conclusion 20

3. TCP/IP Fundamentals: Part 1 21
   3.1 TCP/IP History 21
   3.2 TCP/IP Components 22
       Application Layer Components 22
       Transport Layer Components 25
       Network Layer Protocols 25
       Data Link Layer Protocols 26
       Media Implementations 26
   3.3 TCP/IP Addressing 26
       IP Addressing 27
       Ports 28
       Sockets 28
   3.4 The Internet 29
   3.5 The internet 29

- 3.6 ETHERNET's Role with TCP/IP 30
- 3.7 Conclusion 31

4. TCP/IP Fundamentals: Part 2 33
   - 4.1 TELNET 33
     - What is TELNET? 33
     - A Raw TELNET 34
     - TN3270 Client Application 34
     - How is TELNET Used? 35
     - What are Valid TELNET Client Commands? 35
     - Helpful Hints Using TELNET 36
   - 4.2 What is FTP? 36
     - What Basic Functions Can FTP Perform? 37
     - Popular FTP Commands 38
   - 4.3 SMTP 39
     - Common SMTP Commands 39
   - 4.4 The X Window System 39
     - What is X? 39
     - Origins of X 40
     - X Components 42
     - The Function of X 43
   - 4.5 Conclusion 44

5. SNA Fundamentals: Part 1 45
   - 5.1 Breaking the SNA Ice 45
   - 5.2 A Perspective on Hardware 45
     - The Turning Point 46
     - Hardware Architectural & Timetable 46
     - Hardware Architectural Characteristics 47
   - 5.3 Understanding the Numbers 48
     - Processors 48
     - Terminals 49
     - Printers 50
     - 3174 Establishment Controller 50
     - 3720 and 3745 Communication Controllers 50
     - 3172 Interconnect Controller 50
   - 5.4 A Perspective on Operating Systems 51
     - Multiple Virtual Storage (MVS) 51
     - Virtual Machine (VM) 52
     - Virtual Storage Extended (VSE) 54

		5.5	A Perspective on Communications Software 54
		5.6	Conclusion 56

6. SNA Fundamentals: Part 2 57
    6.1 SNA in the 1970s 57
            SNA in the 1980s 64
            Systems Application Architecture Announcement 64
            SNA and Products From 1990 Through 1992 66
    6.2 Traditional SNA Layers 66
            Physical Control 67
            Data Link Control 67
            Path Control 67
            Transmission Control 68
            Data Flow Control 68
            Presentation Services 68
            Transaction Services 68
    6.3 IBM's Networking Blueprint 69
    6.4 SNA and APPN in Brief 71
    6.5 SNA Building Blocks 73
            Types of SNA Nodes 73
            Network Accessible Units 75
            Types of Physical Units 75
            Types of Logical Units (LU) 76
            Types of Sessions 77
            Types of Links 77
    6.6 SNA Definitions: A Practical Approach 79
            Defining Nodes 79
            The Logon Mode Table 80
            Defining Applications to VTAM 80
            Activation and Deactivation 80

7. When is a TCP/IP LAN Needed? 83
    7.1 A Historical Snapshot 83
    7.2 When a LAN is Needed 84
    7.3 Determining Which LAN is Best 85
    7.4 Need Evaluation 86
    7.5 Synthesizing Evaluation Results 87
    7.6 Selecting a Protocol 88

	7.7	Components Required to Build a TCP/IP Network	89
	7.8	Component Purchases	91
	7.9	Creating a LAN	92
	7.10	Conclusion	93
8.		Integrating Remote TCP/IP LANs into SNA	95
	8.1	A Perspective on Remote TCP/IP LANs	95
	8.2	Factors Beyond Integration	97
	8.3	Factors of Integration	98
	8.4	Integration by Gateway	99
	8.5	Conclusion	101
9.		Integrating Local TCP/IP LANs into SNA	103
	9.1	Typical Departmental Problem	103
	9.2	A Real Department Computing Problem	104
	9.3	Solution A to the Problem	106
	9.4	Solution B to the Problem	108
	9.5	Conclusion	109
10.		How to Achieve Integration	111
	10.1	What is Integration Anyway?	111
	10.2	Integration and Network Devices	112
		Gateways	114
		Routers	116
		Bridges	119
		Repeaters	120
	10.3	Viable Methods for Integration	120
	10.4	Integration by SNA Host	121
		Considerations of TCP/IP on an MVS Host	121
		Hardware and Software Requirements	122
		Customization Considerations	123
		User Perspective	124
		A Perspective on SNALINK	125
	10.5	TCP/IP Offload Feature	126
	10.6	Integration by Workstation Gateway Software	127
	10.7	Integration by a Hardware Gateway	130
	10.8	Conclusion	132

11.	Concluding Thoughts on Integration	135
	11.1 Disparities	135
	11.2 Basic Integration Requirements	136
	11.3 Block Mode and Character Mode	137
	11.4 Navigating Operating Environments	140
	MVS	140
	UNIX	143
	11.5 Reality 101	143
12.	Beyond Integration	145
	12.1 The Concept of Network Management	145
	12.2 IBM's NetView	147
	12.3 Network Device Mangement Support	148
	12.4 Simple Network Management Protocol (SNMP)	150
	SNMP Introduction	150
	SNMP Overview	150
	The Structure of Management Information	151
	The Role of ASN.1	152
	12.5 Managing Integrated Networks	152
	TCP/IP Management From NetView	152
	Gateway Management	154
	SNA Management From TCP/IP	155
	12.6 Conclusion	155

Acronyms		157
Glossary		161
Appendix A	Port Numbers	181
Appendix B	RFCs	183
Appendix C	UNIX File Structure	185
Appendix D	MVS File Structure	189
Appendix E	VM File Structure	193
Appendix F	VMS File Structure	197
Appendix G	Helpful Resources of Information	199
Appendix H	Vendor Listing	201
Appendix I	MS-DOS To UNIX Command Cross Reference	203
Appendix J	VMS To UNIX Command Cross Reference	205
Appendix K	vi Quick Reference	207
Index		209

Preface

This book is designed for individuals planning to integrate TCP/IP and SNA, currently involved in the process of integration, supporting an already integrated environment, or needing further information on the topics as listed in the table of contents. The following is a crisp summary of the goal in each chapter.

Chapter 1 — This chapter orients the reader to integration by providing network layers from a practical perspective, introduces network devices, and presents a wholistic view on networking technology.

Chapter 2 — This chapter presents a broad picture of TCP/IP and SNA networks, provides a technical brief, explains both from a user perspective, and answers why integrate them.

Chapter 3 — This chapter provides a beginning point for those new to TCP/IP. A concise history is presented, and an overview of TCP/IP components and basic addressing schemes used in TCP/IP is given. A brief look at the role of ETHERNET is also provided.

Chapter 4 — This chapter takes a user to the next step in TCP/IP. It is oriented towards users and the prominent TCP/IP applications. The X protocol is presented in a clear and understandable manner.

Chapter 5 — This chapter helps individuals new to SNA break the ice. A snapshot of SNA evolution is provided. Terms, numbers, and concepts are demystified. IBM's hardware architecture characteristics are presented for those new to SNA; then IBM's three major operating systems (MVS, VM, & VSE) are discussed. A brief look at communication software is also provided.

Chapter 6 — This chapter provides the next step for users needing additional information on SNA. SNA versions are quickly explained, the layered architecture is discussed, and IBM's latest networking blueprint is presented. A brief look at SNA and APPN is provided. The chapter also includes a topical perspective on SNA.

Chapter 7 — This chapter addresses the question of when a LAN is needed. Included are how to determine which LAN is best in different situations, need evaluation, and how to synthesize need evaluation results. Factors to consider when selecting an upper layer network protocol are listed, components required to build a TCP/IP LAN are listed, component purchasing is addressed, and a basic check-list is provided to be used during LAN creation.

Chapter 8 — This chapter focuses upon factors to consider when attempting to integrate remote TCP/IP networks into SNA. A typical scenario is presented, issues for consideration are included, and what integration is not is also discussed. Factors beyond technology are pointed out as well.

Chapter 9 — This chapter explores how to integrate a local TCP/IP network into an SNA environment. Typical computing problems are presented and two possible solutions are provided to solve this integration need.

Chapter 10 — This chapter explains how integration is achieved. A deeper look into network devices is presented. Viable methods for integration are discussed, and a deeper look at how to integrate TCP/IP and SNA is presented. Vendors who supplied pertinent information about products solving integration problems are presented. A brief example of some products is presented to show how integration is actually achieved.

Chapter 11 — This chapter summarizes disparities between TCP/IP and SNA and basic integration requirements. Block and character mode operations are explained at length and navigating operating environments is also explained.

Chapter 12 — This chapter explores network management. IBM's NetView, network device management, and SNMP are explained. Managing integrated networks is also highlighted.

CHAPTER 1
A Primer on Integration

Integrating networks means taking dissimilar network protocols and assimilating them in such a way that interoperability is achieved. This presupposes understanding devices, concepts, and terminology in both environments. This is especially true when attempting to integrate Transmission Control Protocol/Internet Protocol (TCP/IP) into Systems Network Architecture (SNA).

This chapter highlights prerequisites facilitating the understanding of integrating TCP/IP into SNA. Some of the information in this chapter may be familiar to the reader, however the context as presented here may be different.

Section 1.1 discusses networks from a layered perspective. The International Standard Organization's model is used to explain network layers in practical terms. Section 1.2 explains networking devices. Devices commonly used in integration are presented and explained. Section 1.3 discusses types of networking technology. In addition, network topology is explained. Section 1.4 provides a synopsis of the chapter as a whole.

1.1 NETWORK LAYERS FROM A PRACTICAL PERSPECTIVE

The International Standard Organization (ISO) created a model for evaluating networks (or modeling networks) in the late 1970s; they called it the Open Systems Interconnect (OSI) reference model. This model is prevalent in many publications including magazine articles, books, and other technical resources. This section presents the OSI model and a practical twist used to augment the purely conceptual approach commonly associated with it. Here the model is presented by layer, relating layers to components and concepts common to everyday operation. A practical explanation is presented, not purely theoretical.

Understanding the OSI model network layers and where protocols, functions, and components fit respectively is helpful because it can be used as a baseline to understanding TCP/IP and SNA architectures. Consider the OSI model in figure 1.1, depicting its seven layers and their names as ascribed by the ISO organization.

Chapter 1

Layer #	
7	Application
6	Presentation
5	Session
4	Transport
3	Network
2	Data Link ⟩ Token Ring
1	Physical

Figure 1.1

Layer one is the physical layer. From a component perspective, this is typically an interface card, or port, in a host. At this layer data is represented by voltages or light pulses. This layer (typically represented by an interface card) is responsible for generating the voltages or light pulses and transmitting them onto media for transmission. This is the lowest layer within a node (a node being a general term used to refer to a device on a network or in a stand-alone position). A few examples of interfaces represented at this level include:

- RS-232
- RS-449
- V.35

Depending on the protocol implemented at layer two, different interface cards may be included in the aforementioned list. An example would be a token ring interface card. Here the token ring interface card serves network layers one and two. On the other hand, if Synchronous Data Link Control (SDLC) is implemented, it could use an RS-232 or V.35 port.

Layer two is the data link layer. It serves two basic functions. First, it serves the function of establishing, maintaining, and gracefully ending a logical connection of two interface cards. An example would be a token ring interface card. The token ring card establishes and maintains a "logical data link" between two or more token ring interface cards.

The data link layer has two sublayers: the Media Access Control (MAC) and the Logical Link Control (LLC). The MAC sublayer is next to the physical layer. It is responsible for framing data, then passing it to the physical layer for transmission across the media. The LLC sublayer is responsible for the establishment, maintenance, and termination of the logical link between two nodes. Figure 1.2 depicts these sublayers in their relation to the physical layer.

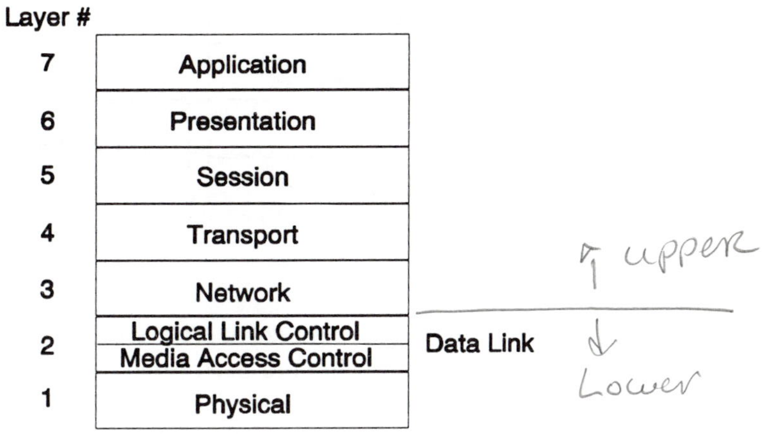

Layer #		
7	Application	
6	Presentation	
5	Session	
4	Transport	
3	Network	
2	Logical Link Control / Media Access Control	Data Link
1	Physical	

Figure 1.2

A list of data link level protocols applicable at layer two include:
- ETHERNET
- SDLC
- Token Ring
- Fiber Distributed Data Interface (FDDI)
- 802.3 (Similar to, but not identical to ETHERNET)
- Enterprise System Connection Architecture (ESCON)
- 802.4 (Token Bus)
- HDLC
- Parallel Channels
- ESCON

Layers one and two are considered lower level protocols, whereas layers three and above are considered upper level protocols. Consider figure 1.3 as an example of this.

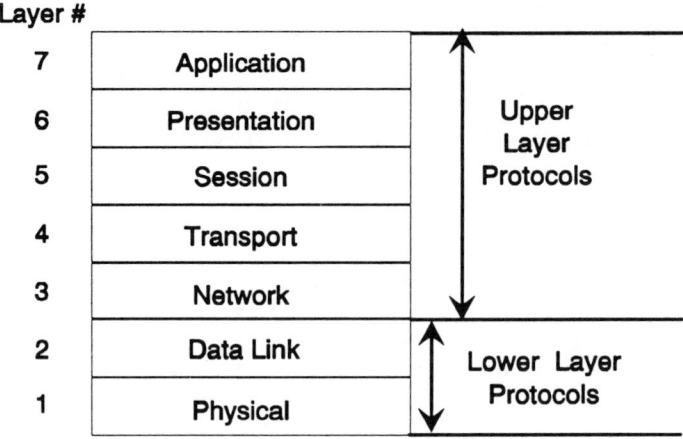

Figure 1.3

Layer three is the network layer, and here software begins to play a role. Routing, flow control, and messages relating to routing are performed here. For example, in a TCP/IP network, the IP addressing scheme is implemented at this layer. This addressing scheme can be implemented in the /etc/hosts file on UNIX based systems. This file consists of network and host addresses. This layer is not always implemented in software; sometimes it is implemented in firmware, but this is usually contingent on the particular network device, such as terminal servers.

Upper layer protocols begin at layer three. The following include some examples:

- SNA
- TCP/IP
- SPX/IPX
- NetBios

Knowing which lower level protocol is supported by a specific upper level protocol is important. Most upper layer protocols define which lower level protocol they support. Traditionally, SNA has supported Parallel Channels, SDLC, Token Ring, and ESCON. TCP/IP on the other hand does not specifically define which lower level protocols must be used because it is versatile. Some restrictions do apply to TCP/IP with respect to lower level protocols. For example, TCP/IP does not use SDLC; but TCP/IP can be routed through SDLC in an SNA network.

Layer four is the transport layer. Here lies the "transport" layer protocol responsible for getting data from the destination to the target host. End-to-end control between a target and a destination node is controlled here. Transport layer protocols are generally characterized as being connection oriented or connectionless oriented. They are also characterized as being reliable, in the sense they perform retransmissions if a negative acknowledgement is received; whereas they are considered unreliable if they do not perform retransmissions. Examples of transport level protocols are: Transmission Control Protocol (TCP) and User Datagram Protocol (UDP).

Layer five is the session layer. This layer provides network functions necessary for the initiation, activation, termination, and release of sessions (logical connections). Synchronization, transaction program control, and the type of data transfer is specified here.

Layer six is the presentation layer. Here data is formatted, message syntax is determined, and a data stream protocol is selected. Functionally, this layer selects a presentation syntax and encrypts data (if desired).

Layer seven, in the OSI model, consists of three parts:

- User Element—Represents the end points of the user information.
- Application Services—Examples recognized by OSI include X.400 (message services), X.500 (directory services), File Transfer and Management protocol (FTAM). Others exist and can be vendor or protocol suite specific.
- Common Application Services—Protocols that can select the type and structure of conversations between users. This also provides control protocols: for example, recovery, commitment, and concurrence.

1.2 LAN NETWORK DEVICES

Over the past decade LANs have grown in all parts of the world. Organizations from nonprofit institutions, universities, governmental agencies, and even corporations have experienced exposure to LANs. As the number of LANs grew, so did the number of devices used with them. Frankly, an entire book could be devoted to LAN devices, but the purpose here is to focus on those networking devices commonly encountered when integrating networks, particularly TCP/IP and SNA. Some of these devices include:

Gateway: The most complex network device. Gateways have traditionally operated at all layers in two networks. Gateways convert all layers of one network into all required layers of another type network. In the recent past some gateways have been viewed as operating at network layer 3 and above. The bottom line is: gateways make communication possible between two different network protocols. For example, TCP/IP and SNA. No other commonly known networking devices do this. Whether or not a gateway functions at all layers between two heterogeneous networks is a moot point; the fact is that upper layer protocol conversion is the forte of gateways.

Router: This device works at the third layer within a network, which is the network layer. Its basic purpose it to get data from one network to another. Multiprotocol routers exist; they support more than one type network for routing purposes. Literally, routing is its function.

Bridge: A bridge can connect networks of "like" protocols at layers one and two, or a special type bridge can connect networks of "unlike" protocols; for example, ETHERNET and token ring. A "remote" bridge will connect networks in physically different locations.

Repeater: This device operates at the physical layer in a network. Here, at the physical level, data is represented in binary format reflected in electrical voltages or photo pulses. Repeaters do what their name suggests; they repeat signals. Hence, the length of a network can be extended.

1.3 ASPECTS OF NETWORKING TECHNOLOGY

First, two types of networking technology clearly exist when examining lower level network protocols. These are:

- Broadcast technology—which is connectionless at a data link layer
- Connection oriented technology at a data link level

Examples of each of these would be ETHERNET and token ring, respectively. A broadcast type technology functions like a room full of individuals all wanting to ask a question. Here questions are blurted out, without the courtesy of raising a hand, so to speak. Obviously, in this type environment it is merely a matter of time before two or more individuals speak at the same time. When two or more (nodes) do speak at the same time, in broadcast network technology terms, a collision occurs. When such an event happens, all parties stop and wait a random amount of time, then proceed to speak again.

Advantages and disadvantages of this type networking technology is fairly straightforward. Nodes do not require "permission" to speak. On the other hand, as the number of nodes increase on the same network the number of possible collisions increase proportionally. Consequently, the odds of obtaining a defined theoretical throughput in this type environment is not good.

An example of a connection oriented technology, at a data link level, would be token ring. This type technology requires a node to possess a "token" (permission to speak) before attempting to communicate with a destination node. This environment can obtain higher throughput levels than a broadcast technology, if for no other reason than it does not have the overhead of collisions, etc. to take up media bandwidth.

Both type data link technologies are good in their own right. This author is not attempting to make a judgement call on one or the other, but simply to state facts as have been observed and understood through explanation of these technologies from reputable sources who understand the internals of each technology.

Technology implementations (topologies) include:

- BUS
- Ring
- Star
- Peer

Bus topologies are typically drawn and appear as figure 1.4.

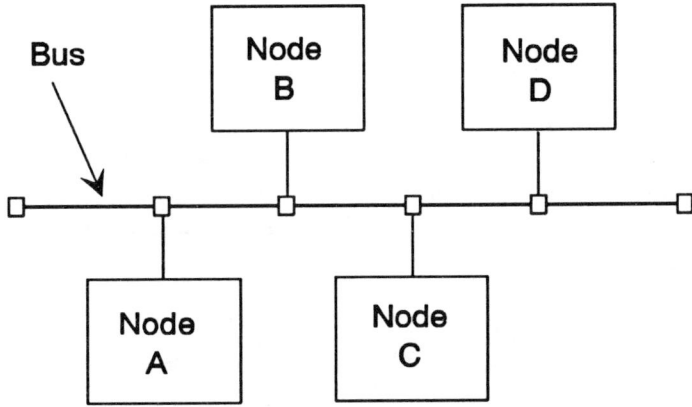

Figure 1.4

In reality, a bus topology looks more like a cable lying, not in a straight line, but in a fashion that poses the least resistance. Notice a bus topology has nodes that tap into the network backbone via what is known as transceivers.

Ring technologies are deceptive. Figure 1.5 is a typical drawing of a ring based network (usually token ring).

Chapter 1

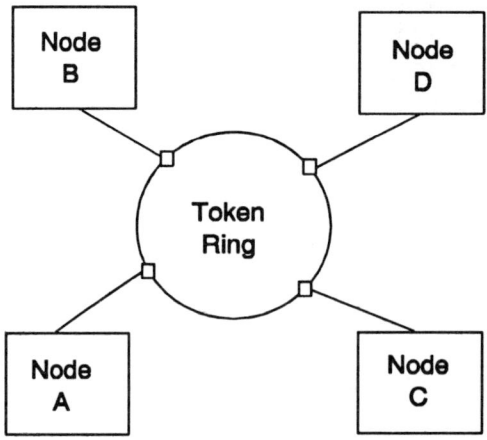

Figure 1.5

However, ring implementations do not appear as they are usually drawn in most presentations. Most diagrams of token ring networks show a ring with nodes attached to it. This type presentation only addresses the type of data link implementation, not its physical appearance. In real life, based on physical appearance, a token ring network appears like figure 1.6.

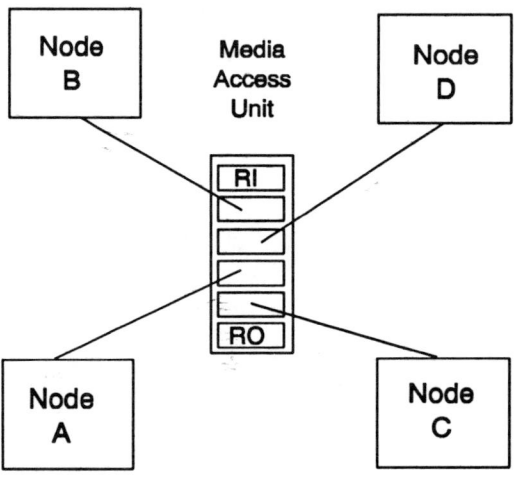

Figure 1.6

Here a device called a Media Access Unit (MAU) is the common link between all connecting nodes. This figure does not depict a ring, but rather something closer to a star arrangement. Do not be dismayed, the actual ring is inside the MAU!

The previous explanation concerning token ring environments is also true for Fiber Distributed Data Interface (FDDI) environments. The exception is that in FDDI, two rings exist.

Star implementations are also known as a hub type environment. Figure 1.7 depicts a hub implementation.

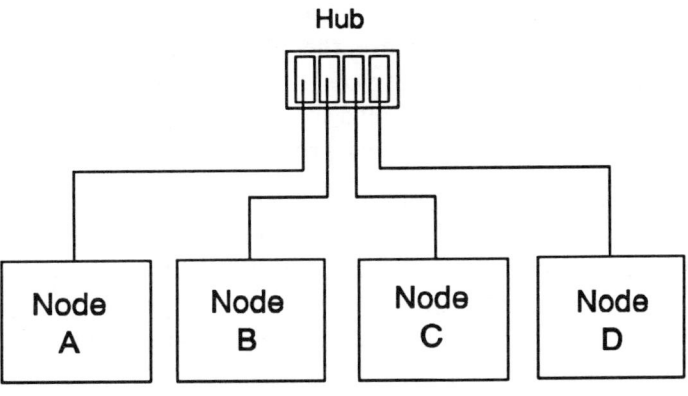

Figure 1.7

Peer oriented technology has more to do with software architecture and implementation than any physical layout. Peer technology, like Client/Server technology, is so at the upper layers within a network, not the lower layers. However, in some instances peer technology must be supported by the underlying hardware architecture or it will not operate. Client/Server technology, however, almost always references environments where a client program initiates (something) and the server program serves the request of clients. This *is* client/server technology in brief.

Networking technology can be discussed in light of lower level protocols being implemented and based on the inherent characteristics in the physical implementation. Networking technology can also be discussed in light of upper level protocols. However, upper layer protocol characteristics can be isolated (functionally) from their underlying counterparts. Contingencies exist between the two, but in many instances they are not necessarily imposed.

Merging upper and lower level protocols is achieved by understanding how the total networking environment was designed to operate based on its original design intent. Some latitude can be obtained and even seamless integration may appear possible between two heterogeneous technologies like TCP/IP and SNA, but falling short of understanding basic fundamentals of each environment can result in failure of integration altogether.

1.4 CONCLUSION

The OSI model presented in this chapter is used as a baseline to evaluate TCP/IP and SNA in subsequent chapters. It is merely used as a starting point; both TCP/IP and SNA are different than the OSI model, but in order to explain these networking architectures it helps to have a reference point for comparison and contrast. In addition, different types of LAN devices were explained. Of all these, the gateway is the device used to integrate TCP/IP into SNA. Other networking devices may make up a part of a networking environment, but only gateways are designed to convert all layers of one type network protocol into another (different) type network protocol.

The topic of networking technology addresses how communication is achieved at the upper and lower layers in a network. In addition, networking technology also explores how a particular network protocol is implemented. Physical implementation sometimes differs from the logical implementation. Different network protocols may have physical implementation contingencies, but this does not impede integration of two dissimilar network protocols such as TCP/IP and SNA.

CHAPTER 2
A Perspective on Integrating TCP/IP into SNA

This chapter provides a broad picture of TCP/IP and SNA. Section 2.1 provides basic information about the two environments. Section 2.2 presents a look at integration beyond the technical aspects. Section 2.3 provides insights to both environments from a user perspective. Section 2.4 answers the question, "Why integrate TCP/IP into SNA?" Section 2.5 provides a brief technical overview of both networking environments. Section 2.6 focuses upon specifics of integration. And section 2.6 concludes by summarizing specific highlights in the chapter.

2.1 ORIENTATION TO TCP/IP AND SNA

TCP/IP and SNA are dominant networking protocols today. Both have existed for numerous years. TCP/IP has its roots in the Department of Defense (DOD) dating back to the 1970s and was given broad support in 1983 when the Defense Advanced Project Research Agency (DARPA) stated that any computer connected to the Advanced Research Projects Agency Network (ARPANET also known as the Internet) must use TCP/IP. This had far reaching implications because of the number of computers involved.

Furthermore, because of its origins TCP/IP is considered public domain; hence many vendors have "created" TCP/IP protocol stacks to operate on different computers. In its early years TCP/IP was found in places such as universities, government agencies, research departments, nonprofit entities, and other predominantly noncorporate businesses; however, some TCP/IP was in corporations.

On the other hand, SNA is IBM's proprietary networking architecture. It was introduced by IBM in 1974. Since then IBM has maintained and significantly enhanced SNA. Since SNA is IBM's proprietary architecture, IBM has charted its development course.

Just as many entities used TCP/IP as a networking technology, so much of the corporate world uses SNA to accommodate their needs. For example, industries such as banking, insurance, etc. have been predominantly SNA oriented.

Today, both protocols have significant presence in the worldwide marketplace. Until the mid 1980s, these two networking environments were implemented without much effort to integrate them to create a total Enterprise Networking Solution.

2.2 THE MACHINE AND HUMAN DILEMMA

Integrating TCP/IP into SNA is a two-fold dilemma: First, TCP/IP and SNA are architecturally different. Second, individuals in the marketplace have tended to concentrate their talents in either one or the other environment. Generally, professionals working in TCP/IP environments concentrate on that technology. Conversely, professionals working in SNA environments concentrate on that technology.

Not too many years ago professionals began attempting to integrate TCP/IP within SNA and they began to realize each respective group of professionals lacked a deeper understanding of the other technology. Each networking technology is complex enough to spend a lifetime mastering it, and attempting to integrate the two requires understanding both equally well.

2.3 A USER PERSPECTIVE OF TCP/IP AND SNA

Transmission Control Protocol/Internet Protocol (TCP/IP) is a networking protocol. It has historically been considered a Local Area Networking (LAN) technology, generally occupying one physical location, but technically able to operate over multiple locations. TCP/IP is a client/server technology, meaning that communication (logons for example), file transfers, and electronic mail utilize this client/server relationship. Understanding client/server within TCP/IP is easy; just remember clients always initiate and servers always serve a client's request. TCP/IP has been traditionally LAN based simply because of its origins and early implementations. This, however, does not have to be the case.

Systems Network Architecture (SNA) is also a networking protocol. It has historically been considered a Wide Area Networking (WAN) technology, occupying more than one physical location. SNA is not based on a client/server technology, rather it provides services such as communication (logons for example), file transfer, and electronic mail via menu (panel) driven software and protocols specifying how certain services are to be performed. Adequate understanding of how services are performed in SNA requires knowing SNA structure to some degree, including grasping the terminology and concepts that reflect the hardware and software components. SNA does not have to be strictly a WAN in physical implementation: it can be implemented on a smaller scale in terms of size.

Key to integrating TCP/IP into SNA is realizing the two networking protocols are architecturally different. They have little in common from an architectural standpoint, hence the term integration. TCP/IP and SNA are not plug-n-play so to speak.

2.4 WHY INTEGRATE TCP/IP INTO SNA?

A commonly asked question is, "Why does TCP/IP need to be integrated into SNA anyway?" Besides the fact that technical obstacles must be overcome, there are other reasons.

Forces Driving Integration

Rapid growth of TCP/IP based LANs in the past few years in many corporations and organizations created TCP/IP network islands. At the same time many corporations and organizations maintained an SNA network as the backbone, traditionally carrying much of the computing weight. With TCP/IP based LANs coming into existence so rapidly, many users and IS professionals began realizing the isolation between TCP/IP and SNA. This alone has been a driving force to integrate TCP/IP into SNA. This example typifies marketplace needs that have crystallized. The result is realizing that SNA and TCP/IP networks are needed in the same organization.

One such need began to be immediately obvious, that is, the need for bidirectional communication (logons) between SNA and TCP/IP networks. A logon (generally called a remote logon) is the most basic form of user communication between the two networks. In addition, bidirectional file transfer capabilities are needed if a user wants to move a file from an SNA network to a TCP/IP network and vice versa, and the same is true for electronic mail. Determining what services are needed to accomplish the integration of TCP/IP into SNA depends on the source network (be it TCP/IP or SNA) a user is operating upon and the user need within the target network.

Maximizing Investment

Another factor driving the integration of TCP/IP into SNA is the desire to maximize current investment in resources without duplicating equipment. Consider corporate acquisitions and mergers between corporations of all sizes. This alone has forced technical considerations to the forefront over the past decade. The proliferation of such heterogeneous networks (specifically TCP/IP based networks) is an issue now that corporations, regardless of size, can no longer disregard. A hypothetical situation provides sufficient reasoning to support this concept.

For example, if a hypothetical company "A" acquires companies "B" and "C," there is no assurance that companies "B" and "C" will have compatible network equipment that can be incorporated into acquiring company "A." Odds are company "B" and "C" will not be totally compatible with company "A." Herein lies the dilemma: What should be done with the investment in hardware, software, data, and trained employees of acquired companies "B" and "C"? Does one discard the investment simply on the basis that it is different than the company which made the acquisition? Most individuals faced with decisions like this look for ways to integrate existing hardware, software, data, and personnel, to realize the synergy that can be obtained through the combined resources. In short, they look to integrate TCP/IP into SNA thus achieving maximum leverage of all resources.

2.5 A TCP/IP AND SNA TECHNICAL BRIEF

A more detailed view of each network architecture illustrates the diversities at a foundational level. Consider the following characteristics of TCP/IP:

- TCP/IP software is nonproprietary. Any vendor wanting to develop TCP/IP software or a specific TCP/IP application can do it. A recommendation is to obtain the Defense Data Network (DDN) Architecture manuals as a reference point. (Other TCP/IP standards manuals exist.)
- Data representation is ASCII, by default. (Meaning that each character, number, function key or whatever is represented by a defined arrangement of 128 distinct binary values; this is called a character set.)
- Traditionally, TCP/IP based networks have been categorized and implemented physically as Local Area Networks (LANs).
- TCP/IP software has applications/capability including:
  - TELNET. This provides remote logon capabilities.
  - File Transfer Protocol (FTP). This provides file transfer capabilities.
  - Simple Mail Transport Protocol (SMTP). This provides a mechanism for electronic mail.
  - X protocol is also a part of the TCP/IP software. This provides distributed windowing support through TCP/IP, specifically TCP.
  - Other applications/capabilities are available with TCP/IP. These listed above are quite common and just examples.
- Its method of communication is based on a client/server architecture, meaning clients "initiate" something. For example, a remote logon or file transfer is initiated by a client. A server "serves" the request of a client.
- Communication between nodes on TCP/IP based LANs is generally considered asynchronous.

- TCP/IP is character oriented. (This means it is similar to a TTY (teletype) function, where a character, number, or function key is pressed and it is immediately set to the host processor. This is in stark contrast to how SNA works, as will be explained later.)
- TCP/IP's popular LAN based implementation is based on ETHERNET. ETHERNET is a data link level protocol utilizing broadcast technology. (To eliminate a common misunderstanding, ETHERNET is not a cable, but the ETHERNET specification does identify media requirements. Consequently, TCP/IP can be implemented over Token Ring (TR), Fiber Distributed Data Interface (FDDI), as well as other media.)
- Typical media used in a TCP/IP based network can be:
  - COAXIAL cable (referred to as thick or thinnet, depending upon the size)
  - Twisted Pair cable
  - Fiber Optic cable

Consider a more detailed look at the characteristics of SNA:

- SNA is proprietary; it is designed and owned by IBM. Some IBM clones exist such as AMDAHL, Hitachi, and a few others in the mainframe arena. However, IBM owns and steers the development of SNA.
- Data representation is traditionally Extended Binary Coded Decimal Interchange Code (EBCDIC). This is in contrast to ASCII. EBCDIC is a character set, defined by IBM with the introduction of the S/360, representing alphabetic, numeric, function keys, and other special characters. It is based on a possible arrangement of 256 distinct binary values. Not all the 256 binary values are assigned in the sense they are in use, but the possibility for a 256-character set exists. Included in the EBCDIC character set are definitions for specific representations in Arabic, Cyrillic, Greek, Hebrew, Katakana, etc., thus accommodating multinational language by design.
- The concept of data streams exists in SNA. Data streams consist of end user data that are formatted for the destination of the end point; this is achieved by control fields contained within the data stream. Data streams are a defined format of continuous streams of transmitted data in binary or character format. SNA data stream examples:
  - 3270 is the data stream in a hierarchical based SNA environment. It has been, traditionally, the dominant data stream in SNA.
  - 5250 is the data stream used in IBM's AS/400 and previous S/38 and S/36 line of computers. This data stream was developed by a different division within IBM than the 3270 data stream and bears little similarity.

- LU6.2 is a type of Logical Unit (an LU is an end point used in addressing) that has been the focus for developing peer oriented protocols. The LU6.2 provides Advanced Program-to-Program Communication (APPC) support. The primary function for APPC is support for distributed processing.
- General Data Stream (GDS) is a data stream, using structured fields, that precedes a mapped conversation of user data in a communications data stream.
- SNA Character String (SCS) is a data stream made up by EBCDIC control codes with end user data. An example of its use is LU type 1 printing.
- Intelligent Printer Data Stream (IPDS) is simply a data stream that defines page layout to be printed on an all-points-addressable printer.
- Information Interchange Architecture (IIA) is actually a collection of data streams that define how information is exchanged between applications in specific instances.
* Historically, SNA based networks have been categorized and implemented physically as Wide Area Networks (WANs), occupying multiple locations.
* SNA (controlled by IBM) is an architectural definition of how operation occurs. It defines protocols, operation, and data handling from a physical layer to the upper layer defining network management.
* Some hardware architectures defined by SNA:
  - S/390
  - ESA/370
  - 370/XA
  - AS/400 and others
* Some software architectures defined by SNA:
  - MVS/ESA
  - VM/ESA
  - VSE/ESA
  - MVS/XA
  - VM/XA
  - OS/400 and others
* SNA supports software subsystems for:
  - Interactive development
  - Databases
  - Telecommunication Access Methods
  - Other software subsystems as well

- SNA users make selections for a desired function mainly via panels (also called menus) implemented by software packages. For example, to send mail a user would perform the function via a panel.
- SNA communication between hosts is typically synchronous; however, with Enterprise System Connection Architecture (ESCON), communication is asynchronous.
- SNA is block oriented with regard to data transfer. Actually, it means the transfer of a single block (sometimes a line) of text from a terminal to the host; this occurs after an Attention Identifier (AID) key is pressed. This is in contrast to character mode in an ASCII based host.
- SNA utilizes data link protocols such as:
  - ESCON
  - Parallel Channels
  - Synchronous Data Link Communication
  - Token Ring
  - FDDI
- Media used in an SNA based network can be any one of the following types:
  - Fiber Optics
  - BUS and TAG cables (copper stranded cable)
  - Twisted Pair cable and other specified cable types

The most fundamental aspects of TCP/IP based networks and SNA based networks are different. How data is represented: ASCII versus EBCDIC; how communication operates: asynchronous character oriented versus synchronous block oriented; how application programs are used: client/server architecture versus menu driven applications; and even network management operations are based on different architectural principles.

TCP/IP and SNA are different because of their original design intent. They were not designed by the same individuals, nor did they have the same design goals. Originally, their inventors did not envision their integration, but over the past few years TCP/IP and SNA integration has become eminent.

2.6 SPECIFIC ASPECTS OF INTEGRATION

Integrating TCP/IP into SNA presents challenges, but they can be overcome. Identifying the obstacles is key. Examples of some obstacles that occur when integrating TCP/IP into SNA include:

Chapter 2

- Resolving TCP/IP and SNA protocols. This must be done to achieve integration. How this is resolved is determined by where the software and hardware are located. Three popular ways of achieving this include:
  - On the TCP/IP host (see figure 2.1)
  - On the SNA host (see figure 2.2)
  - On a gateway between networks (see figure 2.3)

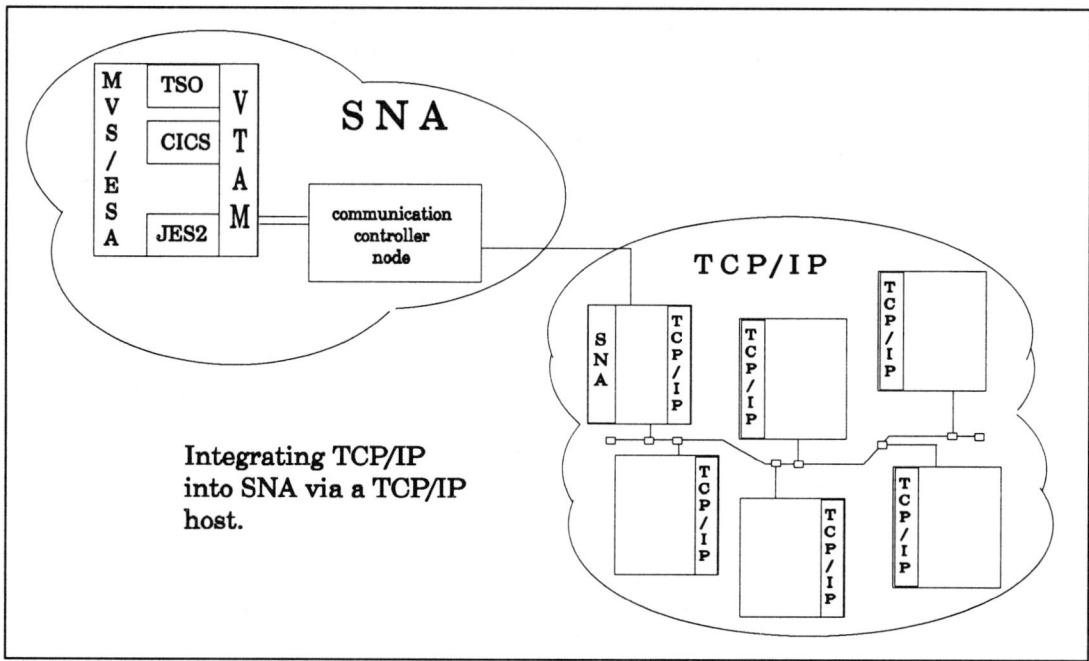

Figure 2.1

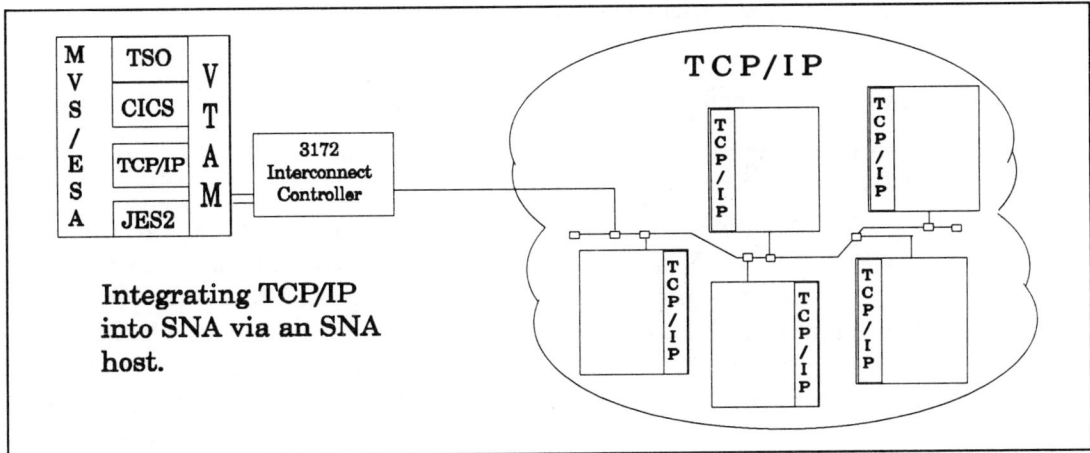

Figure 2.2

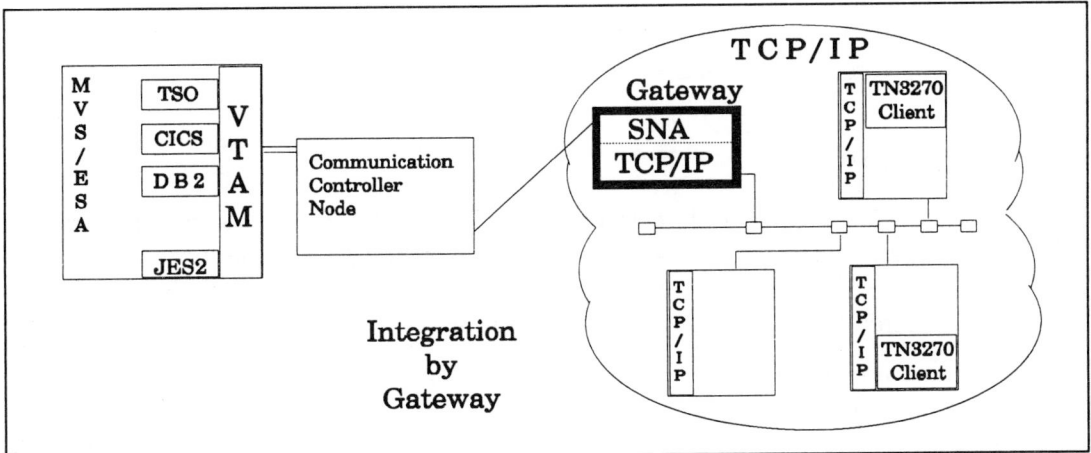

Figure 2.3

- Terminal emulation must be addressed. This is a two-fold consideration: First, if remote logons are initiated from a TCP/IP based LAN, the ASCII data stream must be converted into EBCDIC. Depending on the type of remote logon initiated (a raw TELNET client or a TN3270 client) from a TCP/IP based host, and the equipment involved, will determine where the ASCII to EBCDIC translation will occur; three possibilities exist:

- On the TCP/IP based host (refer to figure 2.1)
- On the SNA host (refer to figure 2.2)
- On a gateway between the networks (refer to figure 2.3)

Second, if a remote logon is initiated from an SNA host to a TCP/IP LAN based host, EBCDIC to ASCII translation must also occur.

- Integrating TCP/IP into SNA typically means users will perform file transfers between TCP/IP LAN based hosts. If so, understanding file structures of the source and target machines is required. File structures on UNIX, VMS, and DOS based hosts are different than those on MVS, VM, VSE, and AS/400 based hosts. Also, understanding where files are stored by default during file transfers between a TCP/IP based host and an SNA based host is needed.

- If remote logons from an SNA based host to a TCP/IP based host and intent of using the target machine's editor exists, then a basic understanding of the target machine's editor is needed, not to mention the keyboard mapping considerations of the SNA terminal and how they relate to the editor on the TCP/IP based host.

- Security clearance and appropriate privileges on the target machine are also required. This is true with SNA and TCP/IP based hosts.

2.7 CONCLUSION

Although TCP/IP and SNA architectures are different, integration can nevertheless be achieved. Focusing on the technical issues that integration poses, one must concentrate on two primary issues: how to integrate TCP/IP into SNA and what components of TCP/IP are desired for integration within an SNA network.

The integration process is better described by defining where the TCP/IP is located. The TCP/IP protocol suite can be loaded on an SNA host, or TCP, UDP, and lower level protocols can be offloaded to an IBM 3172 Interconnect Controller (this is known as the TCP/IP offloading feature). Integrating TCP/IP into SNA can be achieved by third-party vendors via gateways and unbundled TCP/IP applications.

Determining components required to integrate TCP/IP into SNA can best be illustrated by example. If an SNA host user wants to initiate an outbound TELNET client session to a TCP/IP based LAN host, and this is the only need (no file transfers needed or electronic mail, etc.), then implementing only a TELNET client on an SNA host would meet this specific need from an application standpoint. Because of the richness of support provided by TCP/IP, not all services are used in every implementation, hence further exploration into the matter of integrating TCP/IP into SNA is encouraged.

CHAPTER 3
TCP/IP Fundamentals: Part 1

Transmission Control Protocol/Internet Protocol (TCP/IP) is a set of protocols and applications that work together, comprising the upper layers of a network. TCP/IP has been shrouded in misunderstanding about its origins, related entities and organizations, and implementations. It evolved over two decades and is not owned by any vendor or professional organization such as a standard making body.

This chapter presents a basic technical overview of TCP/IP and related topics. Section 3.1 provides a concise history of the origins of TCP/IP. Section 3.2 explains TCP/IP components based on the layers where these components are located in the TCP/IP protocol suite. Section 3.3 gives a correlation between network layers and associated TCP/IP names and or addresses that apply. Also, TCP/IP addressing is discussed including: IP addressing, address classifications, ports, and sockets. Section 3.4 is a brief discourse on the Internet. Section 3.5 contrasts an internet with the Internet presented in section 3.4. Section 3.6 explores ETHERNET's role with TCP/IP. Section 3.7 summarizes focal points presented in the chapter.

3.1 TCP/IP HISTORY

TCP/IP origins are in a governmental organization called the Advanced Research Project Agency (ARPA) dating back to the '60s. ARPA, a Department of Defense (DOD) agency, conducted research and experiments in search of a solution to provide interoperability between different computer equipment. ARPANET was the result and was operational in 1969. ARPANET eventually expanded across the country and formed the main network of what began to be called the Internet.

The Defense Advanced Research Project Agency (DARPA) succeeded ARPA in 1971, thus ARPANET was under their domain. DARPA focused on research and experiments using packet-switching technology emphasizing satellite and radio technology for transport mechanisms.

In 1975 the Defense Communications Agency (DCA) took responsibility for ARPANET operation. About this time a new set of networking protocols had been proposed. These protocols laid the foundation for TCP/IP, and by 1978 TCP/IP had become stable enough for a demonstration. TCP/IP contributed to the growth in the number of networks located around the country and consequently an increase of networks connected to ARPANET.

In 1982 DOD created the Defense Data Network (DDN) and designated it as the focal point for distributed networks comprising the Internet. Shortly after this (in 1983), DOD stated acceptance of TCP/IP as the protocol that nodes should use to connect to the Internet. This statement of acceptance of TCP/IP ignited explosive growth of TCP/IP networks because now a recommended network protocol existed with the sole intent to permit interoperability between different vendor computers. TCP/IP continued to grow in universities, government organizations, and other places providing many people with de facto exposure to TCP/IP.

Local Area Network (LAN) growth in the '80s contributed to additional growth of TCP/IP. LANs were easily installed and could be expanded as requirements increased. TCP/IP growth profited from mergers and acquisitions that swept the business community. To a certain degree TCP/IP seemed to be the natural "link" that could bring together different companies' computer systems, and by the end of the '80s TCP/IP had become a dominant networking force throughout the world.

3.2 TCP/IP COMPONENTS

Application Layer Components

TCP/IP was architected machine independent and is a client/server technology at the application layer. A client initiates (invokes) an application, and servers serve the requests of clients. Because of TCP/IP's design, TELNET (the application for remote logons) has a client and server, just as FTP (the application used for file transfers) and SMTP (the application used for E-Mail). Notice figure 3.1 where TELNET, FTP, SMTP, and other services reside at the application level.

A Brief of the TCP/IP Protocol Suite

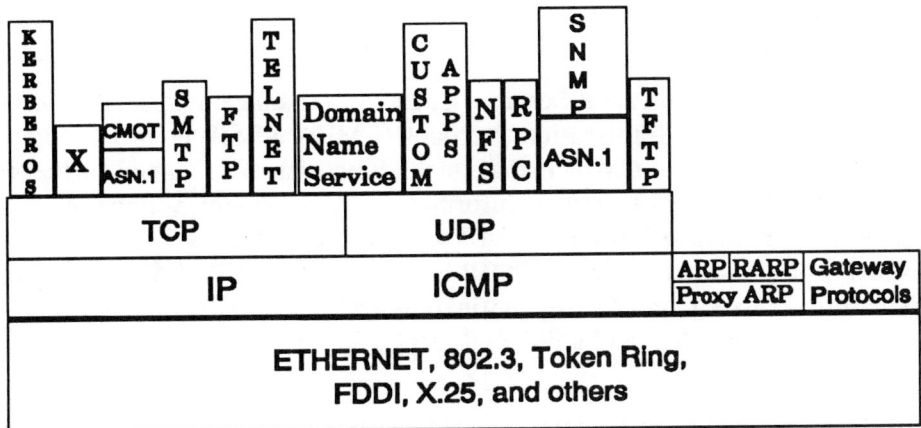

Figure 3.1

Other application layer components exist. X is a protocol and provides a distributed window environment. It permits request responses between X client applications and an X server. X includes the ability of an X client executing on one machine to operate against an X server on another machine thus enabling a distributed windowing environment. Some X basic components include:

- X Server—A program providing display services on a terminal supporting graphics at the request of an X client application.
- X Client—A program using the services provided by an X Server.
- X Window Manager—This program helps in resizing windows, modifying windows, and relocating windows.
- X Library—This contains the interface for application programming. It consists of C language subroutines. One function of the XLIB is to convert X client requests into X protocol requests.
- X Toolkits—This is a software library providing high level facilities for implementing buttons, menus, etc.
- Widgets—A widget is an X window, additional data, and procedures used to perform operations on that data.

Kerberos is a security protocol used with TCP/IP and operates by an authentication server, and by a "ticket" granting server. For example, a client requests a "ticket" to meet the "ticket" granting server, thus achieving authentication. Once authentication is achieved the "ticket" is presented to the "ticket" granting server giving the client the ability to use a particular service.

Common Information Management Service (CMIS) is a management service offered by the Common Management Information Protocol (CMIP). CMIP is an OSI method of network management. When CMIP management functions are mapped to the TCP/IP suite of protocols it is called Common Information Management Service over TCP/IP (CMOT). When it is mapped to the TCP/IP protocol suite it uses TCP for a transport connection. Figure 1 illustrates how CMIP operates over TCP. CMIP uses Abstract Syntax Notation 1 (ASN.1), a language defined by Internet standard documents. ASN.1 is a language for writing clear and uniform datatype definitions used in the management function.

Simple Network Management Protocol (SNMP) uses UDP (to be discussed in greater detail later) for a transport mechanism. It uses "traps" to report events including variables pertaining to the status of a host and "agents" that are processes in a host which get and set specific requests and additionally send trap messages. As of this writing, SNMP is very popular for TCP/IP management.

Remote Procedure Calls (RPCs) are programs permitting applications to call a routine executing a server; in turn the server returns variables and return codes to the requester. Simply, it is a mechanism implemented to support distributed computing via a client/server model.

Network File Server (NFS) is a collection of protocols produced by SUN Microsystems and uses a distributed file system allowing multiple computers supporting NFS to access each other's directories transparently.

Trivial File Transfer Protocol (TFTP) uses UDP; it has no security such as FTP that utilizes TCP as a transport mechanism. It is a very simple means of file transfer and not robust when compared to FTP.

Domain Name Service, also called the Domain Name System (DNS), is a distributed database system of IP addresses and aliases. It resolves addresses of hosts in order to establish contact with the target host. DNS was created to solve the problem of maintaining a host file on each host participating in a TCP/IP network. The host file consists of IP addresses and aliases, and each time a host or network is added or taken away the host file would need changing. DNS was designed to forego the constant updating of each host file on every host.

Transport Layer Components

Two different transport mechanisms are part of TCP/IP, Transmission Control Protocol (TCP) and User Datagram Protocol (UDP). TCP is connection oriented, providing retransmissions and reliable data transfer. It manages data passed down to it from the application layer from the perspective of maintaining a reliable transport mechanism.

UDP is connectionless oriented; it does not provide retransmissions or guarantee reliable data transfer. UDP is used by custom written programs for specific purposes. These programs are individually responsible for insuring reliable data transfer (checking to see if the data arrived at the destined location) and retransmissions (repeating a transmission of data due to a loss caused by problems at a transport level).

Network Layer Protocols

Internet Protocol (IP) transports datagrams across a network. A datagram consists of the data from the application layer and the transport level header and trailer information. IP exists at network layer three. It uses a 32-bit addressing scheme whereby the network and host are identified. IP was originally designed to accommodate routers and hosts produced by different vendors.

Internet Control Message Protocol (ICMP) provides messages concerning the status of nodes. These messages may reflect an error that has occurred or simply the status of a node. ICMP provides a way for certain commands to be issued against a target host to determine the status of the host, such as Packet Internet Groper (PING). ICMP is required to implement IP because of how the two are intertwined in the routing and response mechanisms.

Address Resolution Protocol (ARP) determines the physical address (sometimes called a hard address) of a node given that node's IP address. ARP is the mapping link between IP addresses and the underlying physical address, for example, the ETHERNET address. It is via ARP that a logical connection (BIND) occurs between the IP address and the hard address.

Reverse Address Resolution Protocol (RARP) enables a host to discover its own IP address by broadcasting its physical address. When the broadcast occurs another node on the LAN answers back with the IP address of the requesting node. Hence, it is commonly called reverse ARP.

Gateway Protocols are a collection of protocols, that is, the way routers communicate. A variety of them exist; an example would be Routing Information Protocol (RIP). RIP is a basic protocol used to exchange information between routers. Again, this is a misnomer now because gateways are network devices performing a specific function which is not routing.

Data Link Layer Protocols

TCP/IP does not define data link level protocols. The reasoning behind this is rooted in TCP/IP's original design intent. As stated in chapter 1, TCP/IP can use different types of data link layer protocols including:

- ETHERNET
- Token Ring
- Fiber Distributed Data Interface (FDDI)
- X.25

Media Implementations

TCP/IP can be found implemented in multiple types of media. For example, if TCP/IP is implemented with ETHERNET, media could be coaxial cable or copper stranded cable. TCP/IP can also operate with fiber optic media. If TCP/IP is implemented using X.25, then satellite, microwave, or serial telephone type lines may be the media used.

3.3 TCP/IP ADDRESSING

Before examining specific TCP/IP addressing schemes, consider the correlation of network layers and how they relate to a TCP/IP names and/or address:

Layer	*TCP/IP Name(s) and/or Address*
User applications	Assigned end user identification
Internet applications	Well-known ports
Transport layer	TCP and/or UDP
Network layer	Internet addresses
LLC sublayer	Local Source Access Point addresses
MAC sublayer	Media Access Control addresses
Physical	Interface Boards

IP Addressing

It is easier to understand TCP/IP addressing by approaching the concept as it relates to a specific host. All TCP/IP based hosts use a 32-bit IP address to uniquely identify themselves and the network they exist upon and operate with. This address contains three components: the significant bits identifying the address classification, the portion identifying the LAN, and the portion identifying the host. IP address classifications include:

- Class A
- Class B
- Class C
- Class D
- Class E

Class A addresses are typically large networks, class B medium-size networks, class C small networks, and class D addresses are used for multicasting, sending a message to a group of hosts connected to the Internet. Class E is virtually unused and considered experimental.

Address classes are important for two reasons. First, if network (X) is connected to the Internet, then (X's) network and host address is assigned by an organization managing Internet. If network (Y) is an organization's or business's internet, the network administrator assigns both network and host addresses.

Address classes provide a way for assigning more networks and fewer hosts, the same amount of networks and the same amount of hosts, and fewer networks and more hosts. Locally administered internets use either class A, B, or C. The addressing scheme uses dotted decimal notation. Knowing the first three digits is enough information to deduce its class. For example, the following first three digits are associated with the class:

- Class A addresses start with a number between 0 - 127
- Class B addresses start with a number between 128 - 191
- Class C addresses start with a number between 192 - 223
- Class D addresses start with a number between 224 - 239
- Class E addresses start with a number between 240 - 255

Figure 3.2 illustrates the IP addressing scheme and the correlation of network and hosts addresses.

Chapter 3

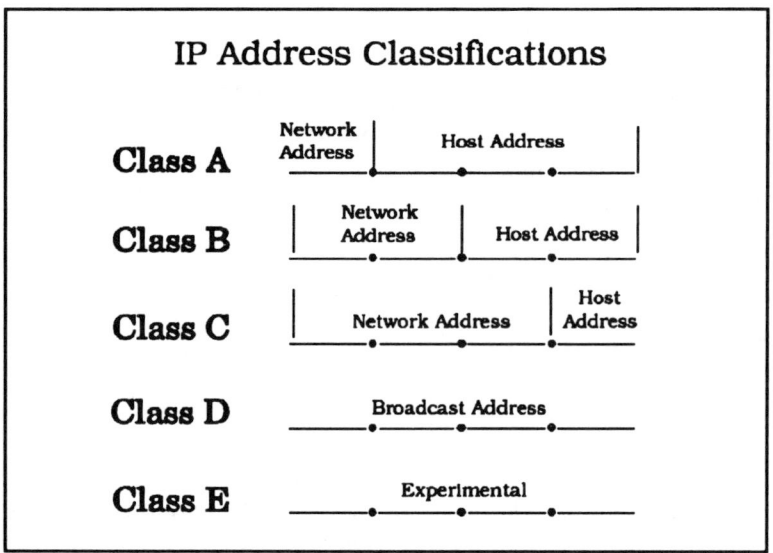

Figure 3.2

Ports

TCP and UDP addressing use well-known ports. They are published by the Internet Assigned Numbers Authority and are preassigned to identify widely used applications, called well-known services. For example, TELNET is assigned to TCP port number 23; FTP is assigned to TCP port number 20 and 21 (one is used for FTP data, the other is used for file transfer). Another example is SMTP; it is assigned to TCP port number 25. Examples of UDP well-known ports are: Domain Name Server (DNS) resides at port number 53, Simple Network Management Protocol (SNMP) network monitor uses port number 161, SNMP traps use port number 162.

Other port numbers exist and are used by TCP and UDP, respectively. Port numbers that are not defined as well-known ports may be used by custom applications, which is typical of applications using the UDP transport protocol. Port numbers can be changed, and in the UNIX environment, a file called /etc/services is used to administer port numbers.

Sockets

Sockets are the combination of an IP address and the port number appended to it. The socket is that abstract end point used for communication. The socket concept comes from Berkeley based UNIX systems. The socket, in Berkeley UNIX, is an I/O based concept and an end point in the communication process.

3.4 THE Internet

The word "Internet" (big I) has been a point of confusion in the marketplace. The word "Internet" was the name used to refer to ARPANET with other networks connected to it. The Internet has grown, and ARPANET remained the main network of the Internet until the late '80s when it was replaced by the National Science Foundation Network (NFSNET). The primary purpose for the change was the need to incorporate high-speed links in various places.

The Internet has a greater role than military usage, but DOD maintains coordination of it. The DDN Network Information Center (NIC) maintains what are known as Request for Comments (RFCs). These are protocol descriptions, ideas, and other comments from individuals interested in the Internet, and in a real sense this is part of what makes TCP/IP public domain. Individual RFCs have a state and status assigned to them. RFC states include:

- Standard
- Draft
- Proposal
- Experiment

RFC's status include:

- Required
- Recommended
- Elective
- Limited Use
- Not Recommended

3.5 THE internet

An internet (little i) is a locally administered LAN utilizing TCP/IP for its upper layer protocols. It does not have all of the restrictions and requirements the Internet must abide by because it is a "local" network. But, an internet does have restrictions and requirements in order for it to be functional.

Many globally connected internets connect to the Internet. Special restrictions apply to internets connected to the Internet. Typically, the connection of individual internets to the Internet must be accomplished by having a multihomed host, a host attached to two or more LANs. A multihomed host connecting an internet to the Internet has a local internet address and an Internet address assigned to it so it can be known by both networks.

3.6 ETHERNET'S ROLE WITH TCP/IP

ETHERNET is a term often used in conjunction with TCP/IP. It is a data link level protocol and a broadcast technology. ETHERNET is implemented in computer systems and devices by firmware on a network interface card (NIC). The name ETHERNET came from a theoretical electromagnetic material named "luminiferous ether." This material was considered a universal element holding together the universe and its parts! The leap of reason was an "ETHER"-net could be a link to bind all components connected to the network.

The Xerox corporation started a research facility in Palo Alto, California, in 1970, called Palo Alto Research Center (PARC). Commissioned with the task of charting a course towards what Xerox thought would be an electronic office in the 1990s, PARC devoted time, talent, and teams to envision where Xerox would make its next market since it already had a strong foothold in copying machines, etc.

In 1973 PARC had a team working on networking computers, printers, and other devices. Specifically, a man by the name of Robert Metcalfe worked with a team to find a way to speed up the link between computers and printers on the network. They created a way to connect computers and printers on a network whereby higher speeds could be achieved than that used in the past. This is what would become known as ETHERNET. Prior to ETHERNET the technology of the day required fifteen minutes to transmit and print a page with a resolution of 600 dots per inch. The first implementation of ETHERNET cut this fifteen minute time period down to seconds; it was a major breakthrough and got a lot of attention. This version of ETHERNET was later known as experimental ETHERNET and had a data transfer rate of approximately 2.6 megabits per second. Time passed, and in 1982 Digital Equipment Corporation, Intel, and Xerox presented Version 2.0 ETHERNET, which specified 10 megabits per second data transfer rate, among other specifications.

ETHERNET and TCP/IP are different technologies, but together they create an effective LAN. ETHERNET is a protocol and operates at layers one and two in a network. TCP/IP is a suite of protocols and operates at networks layers three and above. ETHERNET has a 48-bit addressing scheme and uses it to communicate with other ETHERNET NICs. TCP/IP uses IP's 32-bit addressing to identify networks and hosts. ETHERNET and TCP/IP can operate together because of a protocol that is a part of TCP/IP, namely Address Resolution Protocol (ARP). ARP maps ETHERNET addresses to IP addresses and vice versa.

By the end of the '80s, ETHERNET, like TCP/IP, could be bought off the shelf at computer stores. ETHERNET and TCP/IP's maturity as a technology and their inexpensive price make them a good match for a networking solution. These characteristics and others have contributed to the dominance of TCP/IP based ETHERNET LANs.

3.7 CONCLUSION

TCP/IP is a mature networking protocol dating back to the 1970s. Its proliferation among universities, government institutions, and organizations of all types has contributed to its dominance in the marketplace. TCP/IP is best defined as an evolving network protocol with core components capable of networking heterogeneous hosts. TCP/IP's power lies in the following:

- It can operate on different vendor computers.
- Remote logons, file transfers, and electronic mail are three major applications it provides.
- Its IP addressing scheme makes connecting multiple networks relatively easy.
- It offers two distinct transport mechanisms.
- It has a relatively low overhead from the standpoint of amount of software code required to provide a particular function.
- It is relatively inexpensive.
- A broad base of technical people have experience with it.
- It can operate with multiple data link level protocols and different types of media.

TCP/IP is based on a client/server relationship at an application layer. This client/server technology makes its applications fundamentally user friendly. Other components make up TCP/IP including network management and a distributed windowing mechanism. TCP/IP also employs a flexible addressing scheme.

Associated with TCP/IP are the Internet and the internet. The (big I) Internet is comprised of the NFSNET and other networks connected to it making a virtual network spanning the globe. The (little i) internet is what is implemented in locally administered environments. Institutions, businesses, organizations, and even individuals can connect to the (big I) Internet.

A term frequently heard when TCP/IP is discussed is ETHERNET. Created at PARC, refined by Digital, Intel, and Xerox, ETHERNET has become the common data link level protocol used with TCP/IP networks. A broadcast technology and capable of being implemented over different types of media, ETHERNET has permeated the marketplace. It is mature and inexpensive, and this has also contributed to its success.

Together TCP/IP and ETHERNET are a good choice to provide LAN services. Both accommodate the novice and the network technocrat. Together they provide not only networking basics but also the foundation to exploit advanced networking techniques including distributed databases, network management, and even file systems. Their proven effectiveness continues to make them a network of choice for many implementers.

CHAPTER 4
TCP/IP Fundamentals: Part 2

This chapter focuses on popular TCP/IP applications. It provides information on how to use common TCP/IP applications. Section 4.1 explains what TELNET is, the concept of a raw TELNET, a TN3270 application, how TELNET is used, valid TELNET commands, and helpful hints when using TELNET. Section 4.2 explains what FTP is, the basic functions which can be performed with FTP, valid FTP commands, and a list of popular FTP commands. Section 4.3 explains what SMTP is, how to use SMTP, and common SMTP commands. Section 4.4 presents the X window system for users (not programmers); it also explains what X is and the origins of X (which helps to understand why it does what it does). X components are depicted by a layered approach and their functions are explained. Section 4.5 concludes with a crisp summary about TCP/IP from a user perspective.

4.1 TELNET

If you are new to the TCP/IP protocol suite, you may be asking What is TELNET anyway? What does it really provide? How do I use it? What are the commands used with it? These questions are common for those first using TELNET and these questions, among other issues, are addressed in this section.

What is TELNET?

TELNET is typically written in upper case; however, it is found in lower case in various publications as well. There is no "correct" way of writing the term. This author has observed that different articles and books on the topic have different styles.

TELNET is an application and a protocol. From an application standpoint, TELNET provides the ability for a user to invoke it and perform a remote logon with another host. Consider figure 4.1

Chapter 4

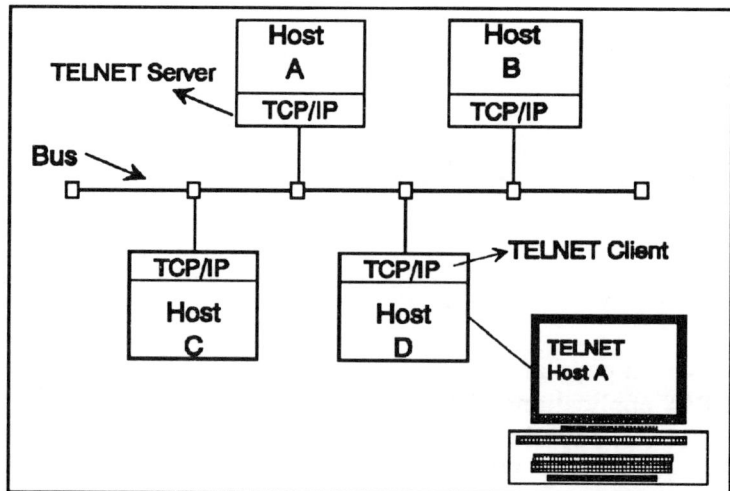

Figure 4.1

A Raw TELNET

Figure 4.1 depicts a user invoking a raw TELNET client from the TCP/IP protocol stack on host A by entering TELNET at the operating system prompt. The term raw TELNET client refers to the TELNET client found in TCP/IP protocol suites natively. Along with entering TELNET, the user includes the target host name desired to establish a logical link between the two systems. Once this is achieved, the user who initiated the TELNET command sees the logon prompt for the remote "target" system. Now the user can sign on to the target system and perform tasks just as if he or she were physically attached to it.

TN3270 Client Application

A TELNET protocol is defined and exists. If an individual with required knowledge wishes to design a program based on TN protocol, this can be done. The most common program written using TN protocol is an emulator application providing data translation services between ASCII and EBCDIC and vice versa.

TELNET has an ASCII based data format by default, and it does not fit into SNA which is dominated by a 3270 data stream. Hence, converting ASCII data into a 3270 or a 5250 data stream is required. With the data stream dilemma between TCP/IP networks and SNA networks, this fundamental question of data translation must be resolved. How do users on a TCP/IP based LAN have the TELNET ASCII data converted into the SNA requirement? Two possible solutions exist.

First, a TN3270 client application can be used like a raw TELNET to gain entry into the SNA environment, but a TN3270 client application performs data translation. The

TN3270 client application translates the native ASCII data into a 3270 data stream (or 5250) before it leaves the LAN host, thus resolving the conflict in data representation. Some individuals refer to this as ASCII to EBCDIC translation and vice versa.

Second, if a raw TELNET client is used to establish a session between a TCP/IP based host and an SNA host, then data translation must occur at the target host or a gateway between the SNA environment and the TCP/IP environment. Regardless which method is used, both provide the user with a remote logon capability. This is the purpose of TELNET.

How is TELNET Used?

TELNET consist of both a client and a server; these make up TELNET. A client always initiates a session and a server always answers the request of a client; this is true for TELNET, FTP, and SMTP. So, to use TELNET, a command must be entered to invoke the TELNET client. The command to invoke the TELNET client from the TCP/IP suite is TELNET. Assuming TCP/IP has been installed properly and normal setup occurred, entering the TELNET command invokes the TELNET client from the TCP/IP protocol stack installed on the host which the user is operating from.

If the TELNET command is entered without a target host name, alias, or internet address, the following prompt appears:

```
telnet>
```

This command is generated from the TELNET client on that host.

What are Valid TELNET Client Commands?

Valid TELNET client commands can be entered after the TELNET command has been entered. If a user does not know valid commands to execute against a telnet> prompt, then a question mark can be entered (?) and a list of valid TELNET commands will be displayed. A list of valid TELNET client commands and a brief explanation of each is listed below:

- close—This closes a current connection if one is established.
- display—This command will display the operating parameters in use for TELNET. Because these parameters can be changed, they are site dependent.
- mode—This command indicates whether entry can be made line-by-line or one-character-at-a-time mode.
- open—This command is required prior to the target host name in order for session establishment to occur.
- quit—This command is entered to exit the telnet> prompt, thus existing TELNET.

- send—In certain instances special characters may need to be transmitted. This provides the means to accommodate some of these characters.
- set—This command is used to set certain parameters to be inforced during a TELNET session.
- status—This command provides information regarding the connection and any operating parameters in force for the TELNET session.
- toggle—This command is used to toggle (change) operating parameters.
- z—This command will suspend the telnet> prompt.
- ?—This command prints valid TELNET commands that can be entered against the telnet> prompt.

Helpful Hints Using TELNET

Using TELNET is fairly straightforward. After breaking through the initial newness of the technology, it is not difficult for users. Learning TELNET is easier when one understands basic TELNET operation, TELNET commands and what they do, and how to log on to another host appropriately.

Since TELNET is part of the TCP/IP protocol suite it does work with other components in the suite. For example, it attempts to establish a remote logon with a target host, but if it is unsuccessful, a response is displayed on the terminal such as "host unreachable." This example is indicative of problems not necessarily related to TELNET. In this example, the "host unreachable" message comes from the Internet Control Message Protocol (ICMP) component discussed in chapter 3. Here, destination host is not reachable by the TELNET client. The obvious question is, why? In this example a couple of possible reasons would be viable. It could be the host is unreachable because of a break in the physical cable connecting the hosts together. Or, it could be that the host is located on another segment of the network that is, for some reason, inaccessible at the moment. Other possibilities exist.

Whatever the case, when messages such as these appear when attempting to use TELNET they are most often generated from the ICMP portion of the TCP/IP suite. It would be helpful to familiarize yourself with common messages and understand their meaning. It can prove to be a valuable troubleshooting tool.

4.2 WHAT IS FTP?

File Transfer Protocol (FTP) is an application that enables files to be transferred from any host to any other host that supports TCP/IP. Actually, a file is not transferred in the sense it is removed from a system; a file is copied from the source to the destination host. The original file is neither moved nor changed.

FTP is considered a user application and is fairly easy to use. It too has a client and server which constitute the FTP application. The FTP client is used to initiate a file transfer and the FTP server is used to serve FTP client requests.

FTP is part of the TCP/IP protocol suite like TELNET. Any host that has a TCP/IP protocol suite on it has FTP (consisting of both a client and server). FTP is a powerful file transfer program.

What Basic Functions Can FTP Perform?

Before listing and explaining some FTP commands consider the power FTP offers through its functions. The following list is an overview of basic functions available with FTP.

Basic FTP functions:

- The ability to copy a single file from one host to another
- The ability to copy multiple files from one host to another host
- The ability to list all accessible files in a target host
- The capability to create and/or remove directories in a target host
- The ability to identify the current directory in a target host
- The ability to append a local file to a file located in a remote (target) host
- The ability to append a file from a local host to a file located in a target host

In addition to these functions, a FTP client can have commands executed against it. When the prompt below is present, an FTP client has been invoked:

    ftp>

FTP Command Listing

The following lists valid FTP commands:

!	cr	macdef	proxy	send
$	delete	mdelete	sendport	status
account	debug	mdir	put	struct
append	dir	mget	pwd	sunique
ascii	disconnect	mkdir	quit	tenex
bell	form	mls	quote	trace
binary	get	mode	recv	type
bye	glob	mput	remotehelp	user
case	hash	nmap	rename	verbose
cd	help	ntrans	reset	?

Chapter 4

cdup	lcd	open	rmdir
close	ls	prompt	runique

This list is typical of ftp commands which could be obtained from most FTP client prompts. FTP is the command used to invoke the ftp client. Normally, it has a host name or address associated with it. For example, FTP RISC6000. But, if no name or address is included, the following will appear:

```
ftp>
```

Popular FTP Commands

All following commands are issued against the FTP client prompt.

- open—initiates an ftp session with a target host. Normally, a valid host name or address is supplied.
- user—prompts for a user id, then password.
- quote—displays the operating parameters of the target host.
- get—used to copy the contents of a file from the target to the source host. If no filename is entered with the get command, a prompt asking for a filename on the target (remote) host will appear.
- put—copies the contents of a file from the target host to the originating host where the ftp command was invoked.
- ls—lists the files in the working directory of the target host. It is like performing a directory listing command against the directory of the target host.
- mkdir—permits a user to create a directory on the target host.
- ascii—places ftp in a mode where file transfers will be performed in ASCII.
- binary—causes file transfers to be performed in binary mode.
- close—used to terminate the ftp session between an ftp client and the ftp server.
- quit—terminates the ftp client.

Other valid ftp commands exist; however, the commands just explained constitute the frequently used ftp commands.

When performing file transfers, messages appear on the display at different times. For example, after a user has established an ftp session, the ftp> prompt is present. If the user enters "get" and a valid filename on the target host, then messages will be displayed stating the status of the connection, the internet and port address, the name of the file being received, the size of the file, and the time it took for file transfer (copying) to take place.

4.3 SMTP

Simple Mail Transfer Protocol (SMTP) is part of the TCP/IP suite of protocols. The concept of sender and receiver is used with SMTP and is parallel to the client/server relationship used in TELNET and FTP.

SMTP operation is straightforward. Once the "sender" starts a mail transaction with a receiver the following sequence is executed: The originator of the message is identified, the destination (receiver of the mail message) is identified, the message is sent, and indication of message status is displayed to the sender.

Common SMTP Commands

SMTP has a limited number of commands because sending a message is not that complex. Some commands that can be executed against SMTP follow:

- mail—invokes SMTP.
- send—causes a message to be delivered directly to the designated recipient if the intended receiver is currently logged on.
- soml—causes message delivery direct to the recipient's display, assuming the recipient is logged on; if not, the message is treated as mail and stored in the recipient's mailbox.
- help—asks a recipient for a list of commands supported by the mail system on the host to which he/she is attached.
- turn—entered by the mail sender to request the recipient to become the sender rather than the receiver.
- saml—performs two functions. First, it delivers a message to the intended receiver's mailbox. Second, if the intended recipient is logged in, it will deliver the message to the user's display.

Other SMTP commands exist, and they can be obtained by entering help at the mail prompt.

4.4 THE X WINDOW SYSTEM

The most misunderstood part of the TCP/IP suite is probably X. This section presents a brief explanation of what X is, where it came from, its basic components, and what it does.

What is X?

X is not a graphical user interface (GUI); neither is it a window system similar to Microsoft Windows Version 3.1. X is an asynchronous software protocol used to transmit bit-mapped data across a network and can be implemented with a variety of operating systems and hardware operating platforms. X is not a transport level protocol, but it utilizes TCP as its transport mechanism. Figure 4.2 shows the location of X in relation to other parts of network components.

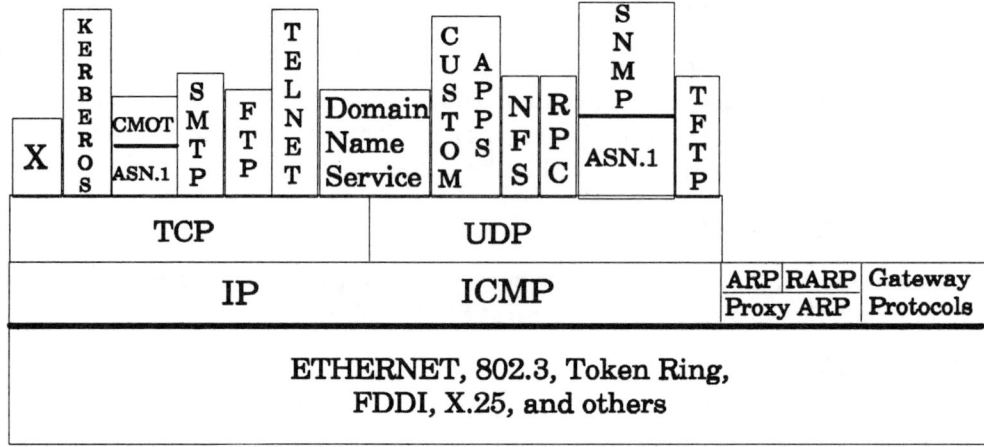

Figure 4.2

X divides application software (like TN3270 emulation applications) from display (server) software. The former is used for a specific purpose such as logging onto an SNA host and performing data translation on the host from which the TN3270 application is executed. The software application is the client (such as the TN3270 application mentioned here). Software that controls the display is the server. Since display software is separate from application software, applications (also called clients) can operate locally or on any host on the network. This is achieved through the configuration of X software, hosts, and application programs resulting in a distributed windowing environment.

The X server program is responsible for two-dimensional drawings on a display. Actually, a server is responsible for everything on the display directly or indirectly. Drawings, however, are the result of events generated from a client application, and the server passes messages it receives from a user to the interacting client. Hence, X's event driven architecture.

In short, X provides components that make a windowing system possible. It is generally called the X window system.

Origins of X

X is not as old as many think. Its birth can be dated back to the early '80s at MIT's computer science laboratory. Specifically, it grew out of a group concentrating on programming languages being developed for distributed computing. This development project involved a number of people working on different programs. Those who have programmed in any language understand that "bugs" (errors in the code) are part of any development project. An individual working on this project focusing on distributed computing concluded that a windowing system would be ideal to expedite working through program bugs. This is how the idea of a windowing system began.

If program bugs were not enough problems, these scientist and researchers were developing programming code for a distributed computing environment (DCE). DCEs were charting new waters at the time, and to complicate matters further they were up against an environment of heterogeneous computers which had fundamental problems with basic communications. Numerous vendors had computers and related devices of all types at MIT. One of the focal points at the time was an intense work group devoted to developing a heterogeneous environment where all computers and devices could communicate with one another in a practically seamless fashion.

Those working on the distributed computing environment project began researching, attempting to determine if anyone (institution, agency, etc.) had explored this concept of a windowing system in a heterogeneous environment before. They discovered work had been done on a windowing system at Stanford. The work at Stanford had been named "W," correlating the abbreviation with windows. For information sake, the associated time frame was approximately 1984.

After working with individuals at Stanford, some at MIT pursued this windows environment and acquired a copy of the "W" software. The copy of windows software from Stanford focused on DEC equipment, but those at MIT were interested in a distributed window environment because of the heterogeneous equipment at MIT. After initial modifications were made to the "W" software from Stanford, MIT's researchers decided to rename it "X."

By 1985 X software had been refined and brought through six versions. By mid-1986 X was at version 9. In 1986 SUN MicroSystems announced a product called Network eXtended Windowing Systems (NEWS). This announcement added fuel to the fire of X growth because it was so close to X from MIT. In 1987 MIT held an X conference; eleven companies attended and began joint work on X with MIT. The X Consortium (as the eleven companies were dubbed) began taking shape and was formally announced in 1988. X is now at version 11 release 5. In short order X took the LAN marketplace by storm. It was a perfect (close to perfect) match for the UNIX operating system and the TCP/IP protocol suite because it offered a friendly interface for the UNIX operating system and provided distributed windowing support. Combined with UNIX, TCP/IP, and LAN growth throughout the 1980s, X seemed to meet windowing needs well. Add to these factors contributions from computer, networking, data and telecommunication companies and the result is the proliferation of X.

X Components

X itself was created with a layered concept; however, the majority of references to X do not explain it in this way. X was intended to have maximum portability, and in order to achieve this a layered approach was required. Figure 4.3 depicts X layers, their functions, and associated programs and components.

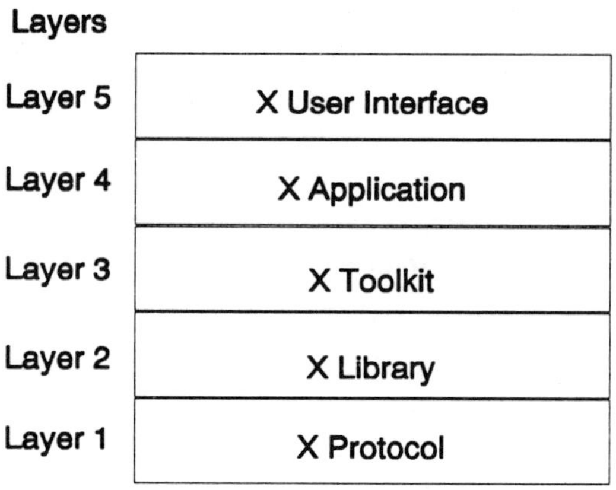

Layers

Layer 5	X User Interface
Layer 4	X Application
Layer 3	X Toolkit
Layer 2	X Library
Layer 1	X Protocol

Figure 4.3

The following chart associates X layers to function and associated programs.

Layer	Function	Associated Program/Function
Layer 5	User Interface	SUN's OPENLOOK
		OSF's Motif
		NeXT computer
Layer 4	Application	Window Manager
		olwm
		mwm
Layer 3	Toolkit	Xt
Layer 2	X Library	Xlib
Layer 1	X Protocol	components of X software

The topmost layer (what the user interacts with) is the User Interface layer. This layer consists of interfaces such as OPENLOOK from SUN MicroSystems, Motif from the Open Software Foundation (OSF), and NeXT from the NeXT computer corporation, for example. These interfaces prescribe the look and feel of the interface.

Layer 4 is the X application layer. The window manager operates at this layer. As the chart following figure 4.3 indicates olwm is the acronym for OPENLOOK Window Manager and mwm is the acronym for Motif Window Manager. A window manager in X actually controls the display. It makes multiple, simultaneous "windows" on one display possible. The window manager provides functions such as being able to resize a "window," invoke pop-up menus, etc. Technically, a window manager itself is a client application running against an X server. Because X was designed for maximum flexibility, it can support different window managers as long as they follow the basics of X protocol. Hence, different window managers exist, notably from SUN MicroSystems, OSF, and NeXT.

Layer 3 represents the X toolkit. Multiple toolkits are possible. A toolkit is a collection of high-level programs (routines) created from lower level programming in the Xlibrary. Frequently, toolkits are referred to as Xt. Toolkits provide programmers with specific functions that can be used such as menus, scroll bars, etc. Specific routines in a toolkit are commonly referred to as widgets. The benefit of having toolkits is that a programmer does not have to start from nothing when creating an X client application.

Layer 2 is the Xlibrary. The Xlibrary is a collection of C language subroutines. The Xlibrary is frequently referred to as Xlib. These routines are the lowest level programming aid in X. Some Xlibrary subroutines provide functions such as drawing, responding to mouse events, and responding to keyboard events to name a few. X version 11 Xlibrary is considered the industry standard and is the base for future enhancements.

Layer 1 is the X protocol. This protocol supports asynchronous, event driven, distributed windowing environments across heterogeneous platforms. When used with TCP/IP, X uses TCP as a transport mechanism and resides atop the TCP portion of the transport layer.

The Function of X

X provides windowing capabilities across heterogeneous operating systems, hardware platforms, network protocols, and network implementations (topologies). It appears different because of the versatility in support built into X for user interfaces and window managers. But, at the lower layers (or closer to the core) of X, adherence to X protocol and Xlibrary routines exists.

Seemingly, X's most prevalent implementation is an interface for the UNIX operating environment. Even though X is not as user friendly as many would like, it is somewhat friendlier than UNIX and other environments it operates within.

4.5 CONCLUSION

TCP/IP users typically interface with the applications presented in this chapter such as: TELNET, FTP, SMTP, and X from a window perspective. TELNET is the application that provides remote logon capabilities. FTP provides file transfer capabilities; however, in actuality files are copied, not "transferred." SMTP provides users with EMAIL capability. The X window system provides users with a graphical interface for interaction. Typical applications used with X are 3270 applications providing emulation capabilities for accessing an SNA environment. Most TCP/IP application commands are easy to understand. The X window system is complex, but once its component functions are understood it becomes a helpful graphical interface tool.

CHAPTER 5
SNA Fundamentals: Part 1

This chapter provides a basic foundation for understanding some aspects of Systems Network Architecture (SNA). Section 5.1 explains how to break the SNA ice. Section 5.2 presents a brief historical perspective on IBM's hardware—where they were and where they are today. Fundamental architectural characteristics of each architecture are provided. Section 5.3 helps demystify the numbering system associated with the world of SNA. Various hardware devices are presented and their fundamental purpose explained. Section 5.4 provides insight to three of IBM's popular operating systems. Section 5.5 examines SNA communication software in brief. Section 5.6 concludes by reiterating chapter highlights.

5.1 BREAKING THE SNA ICE

Systems Network Architecture (SNA) is IBM's proprietary networking architecture. It has become a dominant networking technology worldwide. It consists of its own set of terms and concepts IBM defined and has refined since 1974. SNA, as originally conceived, is a layered network architecture. Ironically, this layered approach to networking predates the International Standard Organization (ISO) seven-layer model for networking by approximately three years.

Understanding SNA is tricky. Since IBM literally created the "wheel" so to speak, they wrote the book including hardware and software components, terms, and concepts. For some, it is difficult to learn because of its structure, but it is this structure that makes it easy for others to learn. SNA is based on hardware and software components, and consequently it can be analyzed from a hardware and a software perspective.

5.2 A PERSPECTIVE ON HARDWARE

IBM's hardware architectural lineage is traceable and clearly definable. IBM's first big gamble, according to popular opinion, was the System 360 (S/360) architecture announced in 1964. This announcement was considered a gamble of significant proportions because

Chapter 5

IBM was attempting to bring together different systems designed to perform specific tasks and put these diverse system offerings under the umbrella of one architecture.

In the 1950s IBM became increasingly aware of strains placed on the company because its endeavor to support different technologies resulted in diverse computer systems—an ala carte approach. For example, IBM's efforts in the 1940s and 1950s produced systems (product lines and different models) such as the following:

- 701—Focused on raw calculating speed.
- 702—Emphasized ease of handling characters.
- 650—Offered comparatively low costs and focused on general computations.
- 1401—Offered multiple components making it an attractive choice for those needing card readers, printers, the processing unit, tape units, and disk drives.
- 604—This was an electronic calculating punch card system and was considered to be a high speed machine.

IBM had other systems during the 1940s and 1950s, but the point is IBM realized they were spread thin and began to focus upon developing a single system accommodating a variety of needs and providing a growth pattern for customers so migration from one system size to the next would have nominal impact. Compared to diverse predecessors that posed significant constraints for customers needing to upgrade to accommodate business growth, this new approach was revolutionary. Herein was the impetus for a single hardware architecture.

The Turning Point

The S/360 architecture was envisioned to be the vehicle customers could use to minimize expenditure while maximizing results. This architecture provided the means for upgrading processors to a more powerful model with nominal impact on programs and related areas formerly impacting expenditure and day-to-day business operations. A quick review of IBM's architecture and related timetable provides insight to the architectural growth IBM has provided its customers since 1964.

Hardware Achitectural & Timetable

The hardware architectural lineage and the associated time frames include:

- S/360   1964
- S/370   1971
- 370/XA   1981
- 370/ESA   1988
- S/390   1990

Hardware Architectural Characteristics

A brief synopsis of the hardware architecture characteristics provide enough insight to reveal the evolution in technology through the past 28 years. For example, the S/360 was the first break with IBM's past that supported multiple hardware architectures. The S/360 provided a single architectural line providing growth potential with little disruption, a wide range of supporting peripheral equipment, and consolidation of IBM's internal efforts to support one architecture. In short, it was IBM's effort to leverage the power of synergy.

S/370 was architecturally designed with the following:

- Virtual storage
- Dual processors
- 24-bit addressing
- An expanded instruction set beyond the S/360 providing enhanced processing ability
- Support for three types of channels (data paths):
  - selector
  - byte
  - block multiplexer
- The concept of channel ownership by the CPU
- Maximum storage amount of 16 Mb

370/XA was architecturally designed with the following:

- A distinct channel I/O subsystem, whereas previous architectures had the channel subsystem built into the processor component cabinetry
- Channels not owned by a particular CPU
- Dynamic I/O reconnection
- 31-bit addressing scheme
- Maximum storage amount 2 gigabytes
- An architecture that supported both S/370 mode (24-bit addressing) and/or XA mode (31-bit addressing)

370/ESA was architecturally designed with the following:

- A storage hierarchy where data is staged in the following order:
  - CPU
  - CPU cache

Chapter 5

- central storage (main storage)
- expanded storage
- Direct Access Storage Device (DASD) cache
- DASD
- tape or other means of archiving
- A System Control Element (SCE) responsible for routing data throughout the hierarchy
- Data Facility Storage Management Subsystem (DFSMS), a collection of software programs used to provide a user friendly interface for storage management
- 16 terabytes addressing capability
- A linking program function built into the hardware providing automatic stack and unstack functions

S/390 was architecturally designed with the following:

- An initial line of 26 processor models either air or water cooled, known as the ES/9000 Series
- Built around Enterprise System Connection Architecture (ESCON). Simply put, IBM's fiber optic I/O system
- The 3172 Interconnect controller accommodating various LAN implementations
- An enhanced version of VTAM supporting LAN implementations and remote system links
- The introduction of SystemView, an enhanced method of system management and a new system management product design structure

In conclusion, each new architecture brought new features, functions, and products (typically hardware and software alike). The idea driving this approach was having common threads throughout different generations of hardware, thus giving the needed link to make the next architectural leap without totally re-creating programs, arranging data, etc. In short, each architectural generation has taken advantage of state-of-the-art technology and brought it to the marketplace in a useable fashion.

5.3 UNDERSTANDING THE NUMBERS

Processors

Many times confusion arises over numbers associated with SNA hardware architecture/components. Deciphering numbers as they relate to processors is easy if one understands the structure.

The following shows the numbering system structure used to identify processors and their underlying architecture.

First, processors are based on an architecture. The most popular architectures are:

- S/370
- 370/XA
- 370/ESA
- S/390

Second, processors are categorized by series; for example:

- 4300
- 9300
- 3090

Third, each of the series have models. For example, the 4300 series of processors have approximately a dozen individual models. An example of models in the 4300 series of processors are:

- Model 4341
- Model 4381

Another example from the 3090 series would be the following models:

- Model J
- Model S

In summary, numbers have meaning. Knowing the architectures, processor series, and models is enough information to deduce additional information.

Terminals

IBM's large systems are based on what is called a 3270 data stream. This is a type of format and protocol used with most large IBM processors. Consequently, 3270 type terminals exist. Actually, the number 3270 indicates an entire family of devices built around the specifications accommodating the 3270 data stream. Other data streams exist, but the 3270 data stream is dominant. An example of a 3270 type terminal could be the 3278. This type terminal has four models, differing in characteristics. The 3278 incudes four models:

- model 2
- model 3
- model 4
- model 5

Each of these have specific characteristics, but they all have the 3270 data stream in common.

Other numbers reflecting terminals exist such as the 3179G. This is a graphics terminal, but it too operates on a 3270 data stream.

Printers

IBM offers a variety of printers for its large processors. Some types of printers include: Line, Thermal, Laser, Band, and others. Normally, these are integrated via a controller of some type. Different numbers are associated with printer types; they do not necessarily follow a particular series or family order.

3174 Establishment Controller

This device succeeds the 3274 cluster controller. Both the 3174 and the 3274 are devices to which 3270 type terminals and printers attach. Consequently, the 3174 is an integral part of the 3270 Information Display System. The 3174 consists of different models, each having special offerings/features providing a range of products for customers to select from. Fundamentally, the 3174 is a communications processor with models supporting network management functions, a variety of physical layer connecting interfaces, 3270 data stream support, among other SNA related functions.

3720 and 3745 Communication Controllers

These devices, also known as front-end processors (FEPs), support data link protocols like SDLC, Token Ring, Parallel Channel, and others. The model dictates the capabilities of the device. Both use a Network Control Program (NCP) and support other programs providing additional functionality.

3172 Interconnect Controller

The forte of the 3172 is its versatility. It supports a variety of data link level protocols, such as:

- ETHERNET
- 802.3
- 802.5
- 802.4
- Parallel Channel
- FDDI

Additionally, it can function in an offload processing mode with TCP/IP operating upon it rather than upon the host to which it is connected. It can also function as a remote channel-to-channel controller as well. The versatility and architecture of the 3172 make it a powerful addition to the enterprise hardware line.

5.4 A PERSPECTIVE ON OPERATING SYSTEMS

IBM designed and created numerous software packages through the past 28 years, but the focus here will be on operating systems. In the beginning (around the 1964 timeframe) there was diversity! There still is for the most part, but IBM's operating systems today can be narrowed to three; these include Multiple Virtual Storage (MVS), Virtual Machine (VM), and Virtual Storage Extended (VSE). Before examining the parallel between the hardware and software architecture, consider a brief description of the aforementioned operating systems, respectively.

Multiple Virtual Storage (MVS)

MVS is an operating system. Its name describes its characteristics. MVS means it has built within itself the capability to accommodate multiple users, performing multiple tasks, all simultaneously (or at least it would appear that way to a user). If virtual storage is a new concept for you, then do not feel alone. It is not mysterious nor above your ability to understand. First of all, let us address each word, singularly.

Virtual anything means it appears to exist, but in reality does not. It is a concept, not a tangible thing. It appears to exist and to be real because of functionality, but it does not.

Storage on the other hand is real, meaning it is tangible. Large IBM systems such as those being addressed in this book consist of basically two types of storage; they are:

- Memory—also known as core memory, or better known as real memory. (I have often wondered what was unreal memory.) This type memory is volatile and generally considered internal.
- Storage—a type of media such as disks, reel tape or cartridge tape drives, or some other method that is generally held as not being volatile and generally considered external.

Admittedly, other names for storage exist, but for the most part those names depict an implementation of memory. For example, expanded storage is made up of the same components that core or real memory consist of, but the functionality of expanded storage is different than core or real memory. As I have said many times, memory is memory; what differs is how it is implemented and the addressing scheme used to do so.

Now, without creating a section on storage, consider this: Data and programs are tangible. If true, then where are these in light of virtual storage since we know virtual storage cannot exist? Data and programs are either in internal (real) storage or external storage, such as a disk drive, or they are in between (even if for only a millisecond). Technically, data or programs are in virtual storage when part is in internal storage, part in external storage, and/or in route to one or the other. By definition all of data or a program could be in internal or external storage and actually be classified as being in virtual storage. This is possible because moving data or programs from one place to the other entails either paging (moving a part of data and/or storage) or swapping (moving all data and/or storage to external storage). Virtual storage is achieved via processor speed, the amount of internal storage, and the amount of external storage available. These three ingredients go together to make virtual storage possible.

Because of the implementation of virtual storage, MVS provides users with the illusion they each have there "own" machine. Additionally, MVS means a multiple number of "tasks" are supported concurrently. MVS components include an I/O Supervisor, like a "traffic cop" of I/O for example; a number of utilities that make operations such as copying data sets (files) possible; a number of system utilities that make updating software fixes possible; and of course actual software code that interacts with hardware and microcode (IBM's name for firmware).

MVS is a huge operating system, but it was designed to operate with some of the largest hardware IBM ever architected. In light of this, its size is not a negative issue with respect to overhead. MVS is complex; therein lies its beauty. Complexity, if designed appropriately in operating systems, can translate into power, and MVS is powerful.

MVS is also generally considered a production type operating system; that is in contrast to being a software development oriented type operating system. It has been the work horse supporting large software subsystems for years and with each release becomes more powerful and refined.

MVS System Product (SP) began with the S/370 hardware architecture as its foundation. Subsequent releases of MVS, such as MVS/XA, included support to exploit 370/XA hardware architecture. Likewise, MVS/ESA exploited the ESA/370 architecture, and the latest release exploits the S/390 architecture.

Virtual Machine (VM)

The VM operating system had a different design intent than MVS. Whereas MVS supported multiple users performing multiple tasks simultaneously, VM took that one step beyond. VM literally has the power to simulate multiple machines, supporting multiple users and performing multiple tasks simultaneously. If you are new to VM, you are probably asking, why?

VM was designed with a slant towards a need to support multiple operating systems, possibly each performing distinct functions and providing the ability to isolate each

SNA Fundamentals: Part 1

operating system from the other. Conceptually, a general diagram depicting this would appear as figure 5.1.

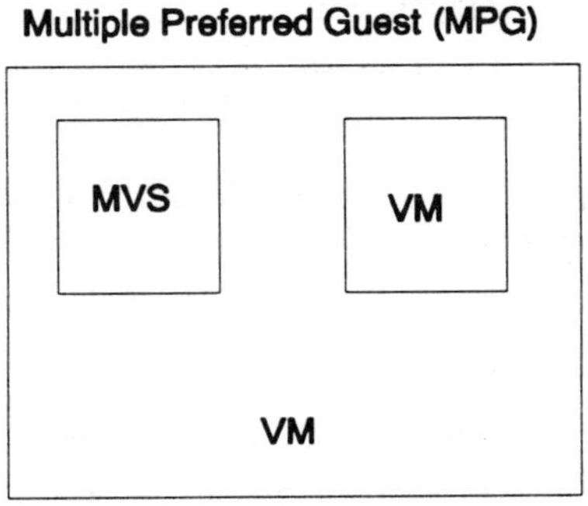

Multiple Preferred Guest (MPG)

```
+-------------------------------+
|                               |
|   +--------+      +--------+  |
|   |        |      |        |  |
|   |  MVS   |      |   VM   |  |
|   |        |      |        |  |
|   +--------+      +--------+  |
|                               |
|              VM               |
+-------------------------------+
```

Figure 5.1

Assume a software development company exists and has the need to provide its developers with multiple operating system support because they are designing, writing, and testing code for distinct operating systems. How can this need be accomplished? One way is to purchase as many different hardware systems as required to support the number of operating systems needed for development and/or testing purposes. This quickly becomes costly and one would seek another way to try and solve this problem. This is where VM offers its services.

VM has the capability of permitting Multiple Preferred Guest (MPG) operating systems to execute simultaneously. This means that MVS can operate under the control of VM. It also means that VM can operate under the control of VM. Likewise, other operating systems are supported as MPGs. This also means each guest operating system can operate its respective software subsystems simultaneously and independently of any other MPGs operating under VM.

This scenario is advantageous because any given MPG could crash and would not affect other guests running under the VM control. From a software development standpoint this is advantageous, for obvious reasons. VM like MVS has numerous software subsystems that can operate under its control. VM does not require MPGs; that capability is just a feature of VM. VM like MVS has its base component, the System Product (SP). VM/XA and VM/ESA are also available which match the aforementioned hardware architectures. Other components and IBM licensed products exist and relate to the VM product, however they are not the focus of discussion here.

Chapter 5

Virtual Storage Extended (VSE)

VSE, known also as Virtual Storage Extended/Advanced Function (VSE/AF), is the smaller of the three operating systems listed, but size should not be deceptive because VSE is robust. VSE got its name from DOS/VSE, an earlier product. It has the reputation in the marketplace of being flexible, reliable, and user friendly.

IBM has enhanced VSE to operate with its ESA architected machines, thus putting VSE on the same footing as MVS and VM from the standpoint of support. This author is aware of one reliable study indicating some 30,000 VSE installations worldwide. This installation base size is significant in anybody's terms.

VSE has traditionally been viewed as a production based operating system and smaller than MVS. It has been considered ideal for situations requiring robustness in moderate-size environments.

5.5 A Perspective on Communications Software

Two major components make up the communications software in large systems. First, there is the Virtual Telecommunications Access Method (VTAM). This is a telecommunications subsystem that operates on the previously discussed hardware architectures and operating systems. Pictorially, it would appear like figure 5.2

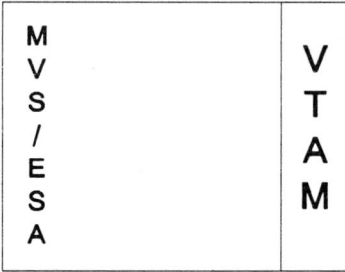

Figure 5.2

VTAM is the focal point of an SNA network. In essence, all entities, be they terminals, printers, programs, or other devices outside the processor, must be defined to VTAM in order for them to operate. Likewise, software subsystems and any applications running inside the processor must be defined to VTAM. In a simplified explanation, VTAM is the mediator matching requests, such as logging onto an application, to the service (subsystem or application) requested. It provides a needed common denominator between devices such as terminals, printers, etc., and software operating inside the processor. It also plays a role in the communication function between software executing in one system communicating with software executing in a different system.

All software operating in a processor must be defined to VTAM for operation. Figure 5.3 depicts a host with an operating system, VTAM, and other software subsystems.

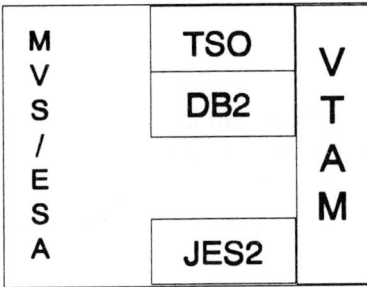

Figure 5.3

Figure 5.3 shows MVS/ESA as the operating system and VTAM as the telecommunication subsystem. TSO is IBM's Time Sharing Option. It has three modes of operation and is considered an interactive subsystem. For example, it has an editor and users can create programs under this editor. DB2 is IBM's relational database subsystem that operates in an MVS environment. JES2 is IBM's Job Entry Subsystem; this is a spooling subsystem for jobs to be printed, written to disk, or waiting to be executed.

Second, the Network Control Program (NCP) running on the communication controller node serves to control attached lines and terminals, provide a mechanism for error control, and perform the routing of data throughout the network. Figure 5.4 shows the relationship of the NCP in respect to other components in the network.

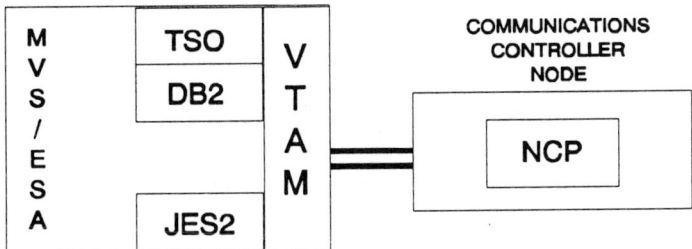

Figure 5.4

Chapter 5

IBM has software related to the NCP that performs specific tasks. For example, a program called the NCP Packet Switched Interface (NPSI) provides the programming requirements needed to support an X.25 network. Another example is the System Support Program (SSP) which is a collection of supporting programs and utilities that aid in the generation, loading, and dumping of an NCP.

5.6 CONCLUSION

IBM developed hardware and software architectures in parallel over the past 20 years. Though not parallel timewise, hardware and software development has been merged together to provide the foundation of SNA. Even though the architectures changed, the goal of maintaining continuity and room to grow remained the driving force behind development.

The architectures presented in this chapter are the foundation of hardware that IBM manufactures. The hardware (processors, terminals, printers, enterprise controllers, interconnect controllers, and communication controller nodes) can be mixed and merged into a variety of arrangements to meet the needs of a customer. Series of processors can be added to and augmented so that a right-sizing can be achieved.

IBM software is also contingent to the hardware architecture. Because the software architecture is parallel with the hardware architecture, and the microcode is structured horizontally and vertically, a sense of portability and resource maximization can be achieved.

IBM created many terms specific to the IBM environment, and outside of this environment they can be confusing. In the next chapter, additional terms and concepts will be explained to build a deeper understanding of SNA from a conceptual perspective.

CHAPTER 6
SNA Fundamentals: Part 2

Systems Network Architecture (SNA) past, present, and future is discussed in this chapter. Terms and concepts are explained and specific details pertinent to integration are also presented to lay the foundation for understanding SNA from a perspective of integration.

Section 6.1 presents basic strides made beginning with the first few versions of SNA and tracks significant advancements until now. Section 6.2 explains SNA's traditional layered architecture. Section 6.3 explores IBM's recently introduced blueprint for future networking. Section 6.4 presents basic differences between SNA and APPN. Section 6.5 explains SNA building blocks from a topical perspective. Section 6.6 lists and explains basic terms, concepts, and components frequently encountered when integrating TCP/IP into SNA.

6.1 SNA IN THE 1970s

SNA's first version was primitive when compared to today's standards. It was a strictly hierarchical implementation. Consider figure 6.1.

Chapter 6

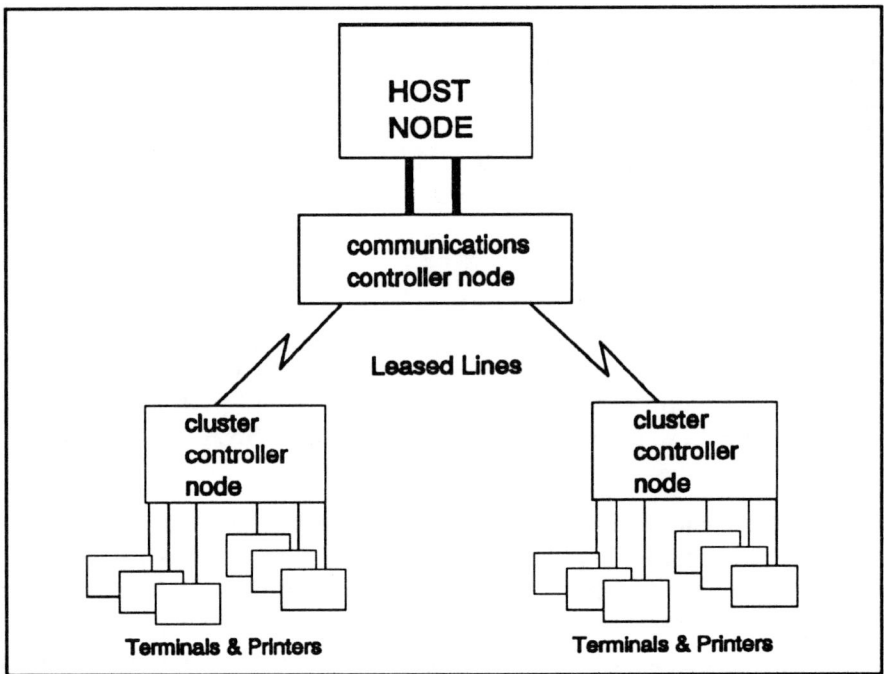

Figure 6.1

SNA, as announced in early 1975, seemed to be the first real public commitment and was the next logical step in its evolution. This version of SNA implemented a star type arrangement of communications controller nodes. This provided the capability for a remote communications controller node. But, with the introduction of a star based communication controller node environment came an interesting irony. In a scenario where a remote communications controller node was located, only non-SNA devices were supported in the remote location. See figure 6.2

SNA Fundamentals: Part 2

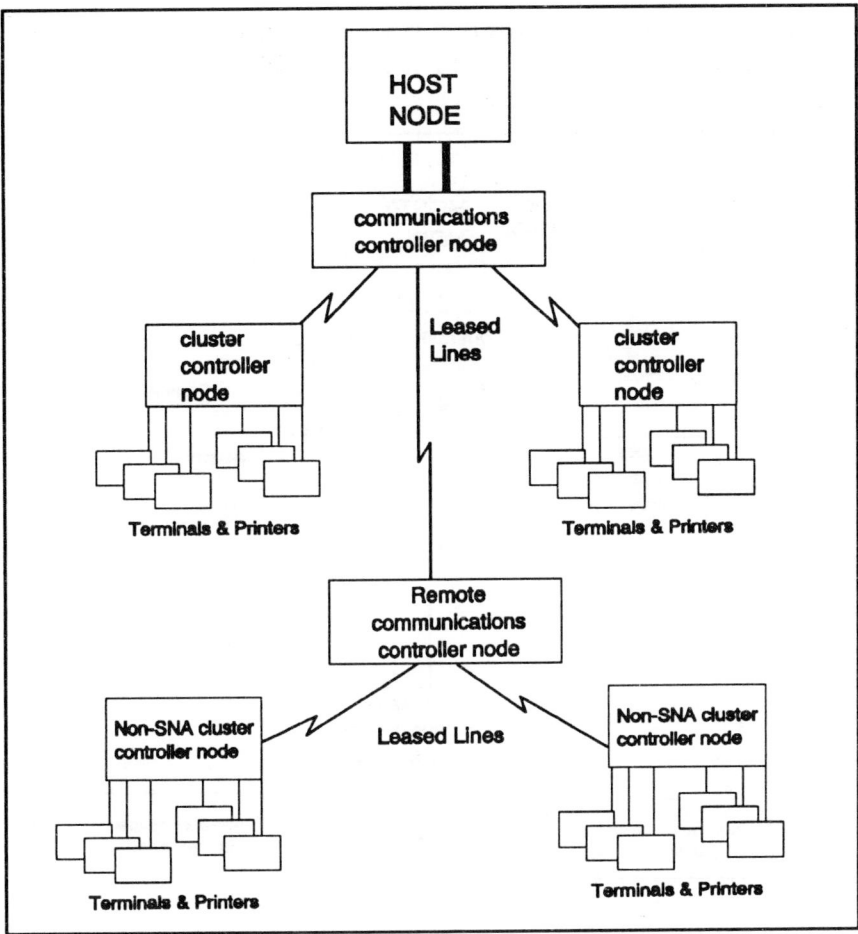

Figure 6.2

SNA's next iteration in late 1975 offered the following:

- Remote communication controller nodes supporting SNA as well as non-SNA devices
- Cluster controllers (to which terminals and printers attached) could now be channel attached to the host via bus and tag cables.
- Cluster controllers and terminals could be attached to communication controllers by way of leased or switched telephone lines.
- More than one communication controller node could be attached to the same host.

Chapter 6

- A remote communication controller could be attached to a locally attached communication controller node via a leased line. This has been referred to as cascading (specifically, one level).

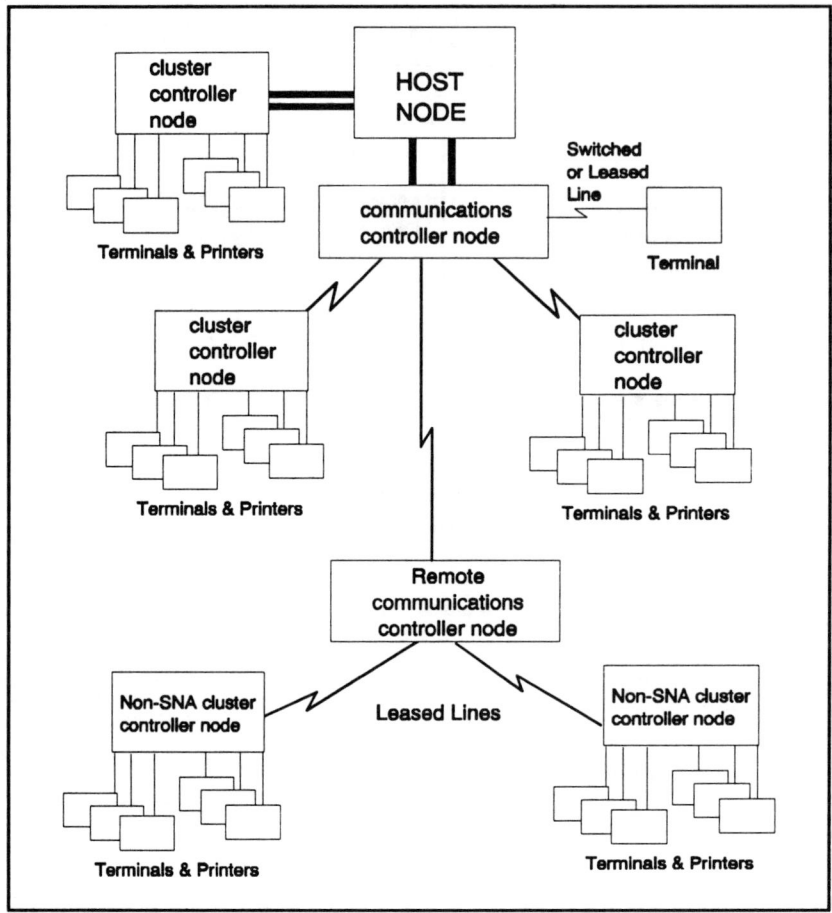

Figure 6.3

In 1977 IBM announced another release of SNA. It followed previous releases adding functionality in numerous areas. One breakthrough was the ability of an application in one host to communicate with an application in another host. This was probably the first "peer" implementation, and this release touted multiple host support via connection through communication controller nodes with leased lines or data channels as shown in figure 6.4.

SNA Fundamentals: Part 2

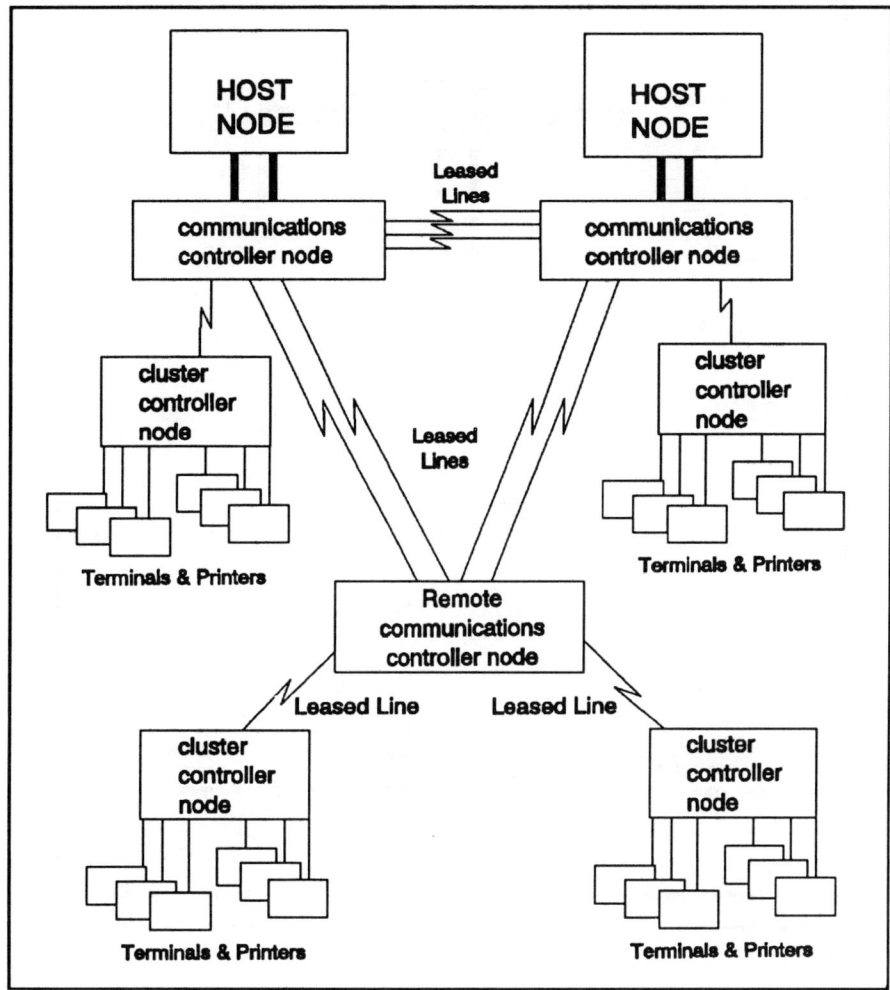

Figure 6.4

A break with SNA of the past occurred with the 1978 announcement. A big feature was that communication controllers cascaded beyond one level. This was significant. See figure 6.5.

Chapter 6

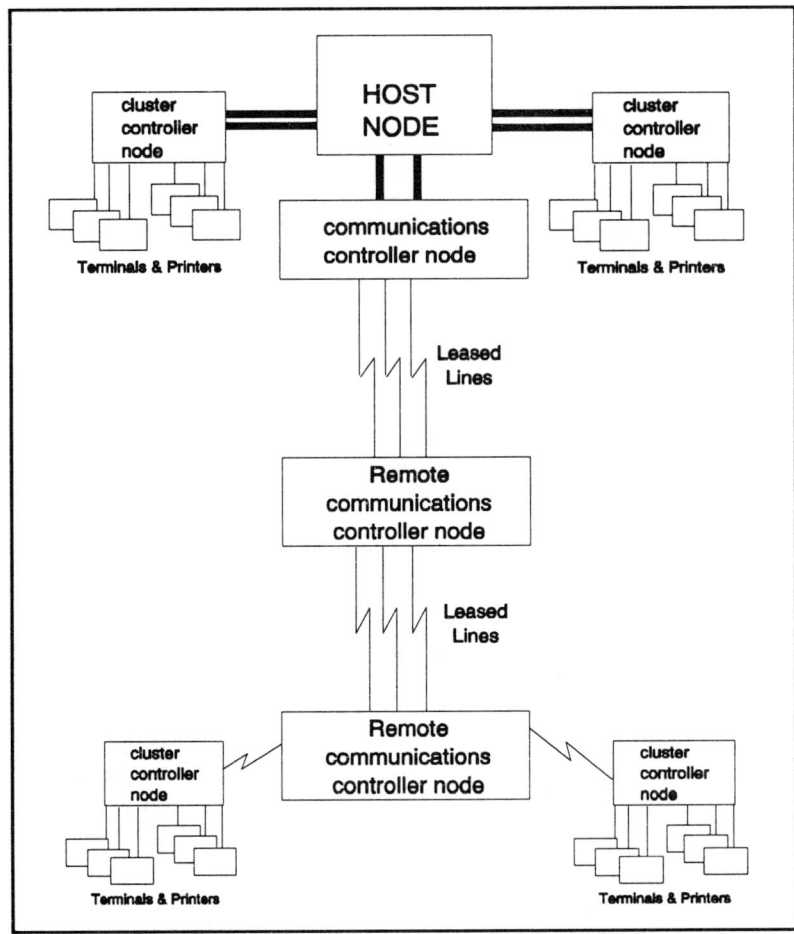

Figure 6.5

In 1978 the Communications Network Management (CNM) facility was added to the SNA network program offerings. These offerings focused on providing a centralized control within an SNA network for management facilities. The CNM announcement included a base function provided through the Network Communications Control Facility (NCCF). This was a valued addition because it supported execution of VTAM commands. Another application contributed additional abilities through which a network operator could identify, isolate, and monitor problems throughout the SNA network. This application, called Network Problem Determination Application (NPDA), made a step towards managing large networks spanning multiple physical locations. Examine figure 6.6 to understand conceptually NCCF and NPDA.

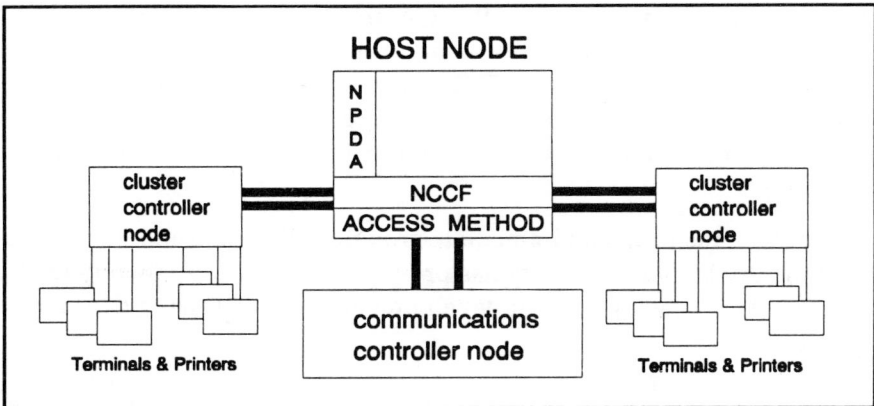

Figure 6.6

The 1979 announcement brought additional contributions to SNA; they included parallel links and multiple routes that were supported between communication controller nodes and hosts. This enhancement was a great contribution because of implications it had on routing and throughput. Consider figure 6.7 as it depicts this.

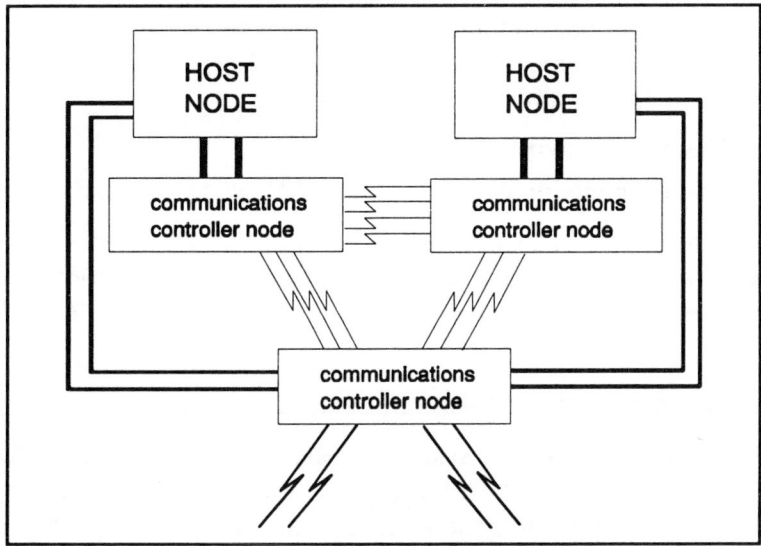

Figure 6.7

In addition to the example in figure 6.7, other contributions were made to SNA in the 1979 time period. For example, the capability to perform session cryptography (session level security), network terminal option (NTO) (a program supporting certain non-SNA devices), and parallel sessions. Parallel sessions are two or more simultaneously active logical connections (sessions) between two logical units (LUs) achieved via different network addresses.

The 1970s witnessed the birth and immediate growth of SNA in supporting products and acceptance in the marketplace. History has proven the 1970s were merely the beginning for SNA compared to the whirlwind of development in the following decade.

SNA in the 1980s

Due to the amount of enhancements and contributions in the 1980s, the following list of products, features, and functions are simply correlated to the basic time frame when they were introduced to the marketplace.

- 1980   X.21 protocol support, System Services Control Point (SSCP) takeover in cross-domain environments (two subareas with VTAM), transmission priorities, parallel links, and multirouting capability
- 1982   Advanced Program-to-Program Communication (APPC)
- 1983   Type 2.1 node architecture, Document Interchange Architecture (DIA), Peer Communications, and Non-SNA Interconnection (SNI)
- 1984   SNA Distribution Services
- 1985   Extended network addressing
- 1986   The introduction of Token Ring LAN support in an SNA environment

Other products, features, and enhancements were made from the early 1980s to the 1987 time frame are too numerous to list here. The purpose here is to get oriented to when some major products, features, and enhancements were introduced affecting SNA during the 1980s.

Systems Application Architecture Announcement

In March 1987 IBM introduced its System Application Architecture (SAA). It is very broad, encompassing products, architectures, and general development direction. It created a flurry of questions and general uncertainty in the marketplace because SNA users did not (and still do not) know how to respond to such sweeping announcements. SAA is a software based architecture designed to operate with certain operating systems; they include:

- OS/2
- OS/400
- MVS
- VM

The basic components of SAA include:

- Common User Interface (CUA)
- Common Programming Interface (CPI)
- Common Communications Support (CCS)

In essence SAA is a collection of protocols, with user, programming, and communication interfaces defining how an information system is built. The basic components of SAA previously listed are three interfaces. With these interfaces, SAA can be achieved. This provides a common approach to user interface, programming, and communications.

Basically, CUA defines standards focusing on ergonomics. It provides consistency and some level of intuition built into the standard. This means a user interacting with OS/400 will have fundamentally the same look and feel interface as a user interacting with an MVS operating system. This common interface is the goal behind CUA.

CUA is achieved by using common terminology across different platforms and interaction techniques. CUA is based on windows, title bars, action menus, and scroll bars. The interface was designed with clerical users, service representatives, management, and development personnel in mind.

CPI is the programming interface. It supports software development languages such as C, COBOL, or FORTRAN; the most common being the C language. This interface specification is focused with the Information System (IS) professional in mind. This interface can be used by programmers to develop applications in any of the aforementioned languages. The CPI goal is akin to CUA; that is, to provide a common interface between the user (programmer in this case) and the system.

CCS is the communications interface, and it defines formats and protocols thus allowing standardization across any SAA supported platforms. CCS includes data link level protocols that are defined in SNA, ISO, CCITT, and the IEEE. This provides broad options for the developer. The CCS part of SAA is critical because it is the foundation for communication between any SAA based systems.

SNA and Products From 1990 Through 1992

In 1990 IBM introduced products affecting the very heart of SNA. The following is a brief list of products announced and/or released from 1990 through 1992.

- The networking blueprint
- S/390
- ES/9000 processors
- ESCON fiber I/O
- 3172 Interconnect Controller (LAN support)
- NetView enhancements
- VTAM Version 3 Release 4 supporting:
  - multitail function
  - dynamic configuration of channel attached devices
  - dynamic network configuration
  - Type 2.1 boundary node function for MVS
  - dynamic network identification
  - varying support for independent Logical Units (LUs)
- VTAM Version 4 Release 1 supporting:
  - Advanced Peer-to-Peer Networking support
  - a VTAM node functioning as an APPN node
  - a VTAM node as a central directory server
  - problem diagnosis via a VTAM Internal Trace (VIT)
  - Command Tree/2 support for building commands
  - and other enhancements

From 1990 to 1992 IBM began breaking with the traditional hierarchical nature of SNA, where VTAM was the center of practically all activity, to a peer-to-peer type environment where VTAM is just another piece in the SNA network.

6.2 TRADITIONAL SNA LAYERS

Until the IBM announcement in 1992, the structure of SNA could be examined from a layered perspective similar to the OSI model presented in chapter 1 of this book. Because of the different variations of SNA in the marketplace, it is beneficial to understand the basics of a layered SNA model. Figure 6.8 presents SNA layers, and the following explanation makes the layered concept less abstract.

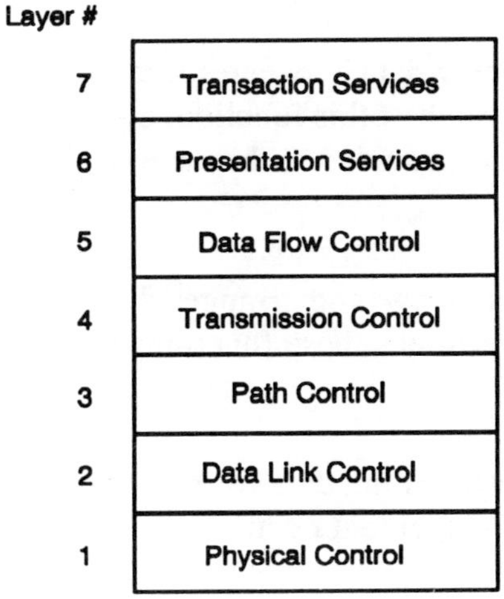

SNA Fundamentals: Part 2

Layer #	
7	Transaction Services
6	Presentation Services
5	Data Flow Control
4	Transmission Control
3	Path Control
2	Data Link Control
1	Physical Control

Figure 6.8

SNA layer names, functions, and related components are explained below.

Physical Control

This is the lowest layer defined in SNA. It consists of interface cards or ports where media attaches physically, making connections to other entities within the SNA network. This SNA layer generates the electrical or photonic pulses necessary for transmission.

Data Link Control

The path control layer is responsible for transmitting data between nodes. This layer is responsible for determining format data and passing it to the physical layer en route to the target host or conversely assimilated back into the required format and passed upward from the physical layer. Data flow control occurs at this level, along with establishing, maintaining, and terminating logical links at this level.

Path Control

This layer is responsible for routing data between source and destination nodes. Software plays a major role here; specifically, the Virtual Telecommunications Access Method (VTAM) and the Network Control Program (NCP). This layer is responsible for regulating data traffic in the network. For example, selecting transmission groups, virtual routes, and explicit routes.

Transmission Control

This layer is responsible for pacing data between source and destination nodes within the network. Software determines much of this function. Specifically, VTAM and NCP work here. In addition, data security is provided at this layer if desired.

Data Flow Control

This layer synchronizes data exchange and arranges data into units defined according to the rules of SNA. Software determines these functions also.

Presentation Services

This layer is responsible for determining data format. Syntax of data is determined here. This layer is where resource management occurs.

Transaction Services

This layer provides application services for application subsystems to operate. It also provides services supporting distributed databases and data interchange between nodes.

SNA architecture is achieved through hardware and software. Examples of hardware components to achieve this include:

- Processors
- Distributed Processors
- Communication Controller Nodes
- Enterprise Controllers
- Interconnect Controllers
- Workstations
- Printers

Software components used to achieve SNA implementation include:

- Operating Systems
- VTAM
- NCP
- Application Subsystems

6.3 IBM'S NETWORKING BLUEPRINT

IBM announced its networking blueprint in 1992. It is a clear break from IBM's historical networking approach because it embraces more than traditional ways of SNA networking. For example, it states support for the following upper layer protocols:

- SNA/APPN
- TCP/IP
- OSI
- NetBIOS, IPX, and others.

Figure 6.9 is IBM's networking blueprint.

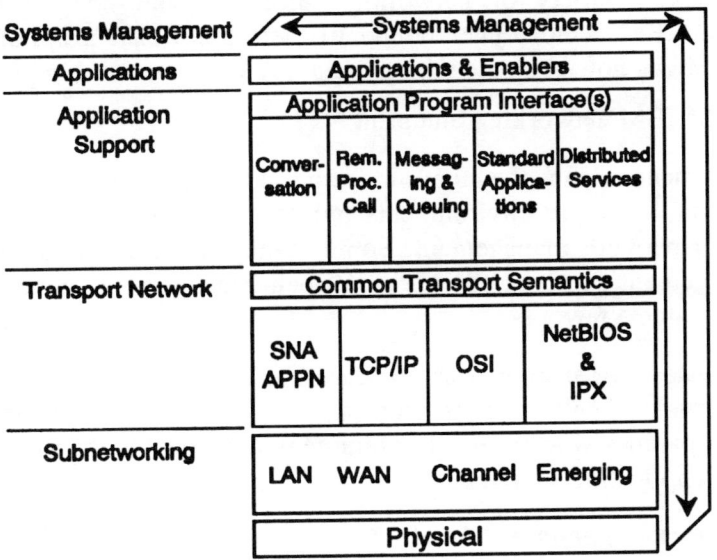

Figure 6.9

If nothing but the upper layer protocol support changed, this indicates a radical break from IBM's past, but this is only the beginning. The networking blueprint transforms how IBM approaches networking.

If the new IBM blueprint is contrasted with the traditional layered model, interesting observations can be made. First, the networking blueprint supports SNA. Second, it embraces TCP/IP, OSI, and other upper layer protocols. Ironically, it does not propose to solve existing dilemmas between disparate protocols, it merely states support for them. In all fairness, IBM does have the technical wherewithal to solve the technical problems thus resolving disparate protocol problems. But, in essence, IBM is saying, "Here's what we'll do. We'll offer, and support, popular industry protocols, providing a cafeteria style approach to networking." IBM appears to have proposed a networking blueprint capable of accommodating popular networking technologies, at all network layers, and marketing them in a new fashion.

In a very real sense IBM has bought an insurance policy by embracing this blueprint. Since it includes a variety of networking protocols and nonproprietary network services/support, IBM is no longer bound to their traditional proprietary method of networking. IBM can now compete with popular industry networking protocols.

A synopsis of the IBM networking blueprint is:

Systems Management Spans the blueprint from top to bottom, thus supporting different protocols and multivendor environments while providing a cohesive method of performing total network management. Some management protocols include: Simple Network Management Protocol (SNMP), X/Open Management Protocol (XMP), and SystemView to name a few.

Application Services Also known as standard applications, this part of the blueprint includes multivendor application service support. The thrust here is provision for application transparency whether local or remote with respect to the user, thus providing true distributed application support.

Application Program Interface (APIs) These provide necessary hooks bridging applications to the Application Support Layer.

Application Support Layer Applications operating higher in the blueprint require support. Basic application support includes three defined areas according to the blueprint. They include:

- Message Queue—This manages queues of messages.
- Conversational support—This deals with handling streams of related interactions.
- Remote Procedure Call—Its function is passing parameters to subroutines.

For clarification sake, TCP/IP's TELNET, FTP, and SMTP reside at the application layer. Additionally, distributed services are located at this layer.

Common Transport Semantics Herein lie functions linking applications to transport layer protocols. Actually, common transport semantics and transport network services fall into the same category. These are separated, isolating transport layer mechanisms to maximize the needs of application requirements. Because of this, multiprotocol routing is easily supported.

Subnetwork Layer This encompasses data link protocols and physical layer standards. Figure 6.9 shows multiple data link level protocols are supported, providing flexibility to choose existing data links while preserving room for growth and accommodating emerging technologies at this layer. Physical layer support is broad. Support includes many variations of hard media as well as soft media such as satellite and microwave.

6.4 SNA AND APPN IN BRIEF

SNA began as a hierarchical type network, meaning practically everything was managed in some way by a component in the telecommunications access method. For example, in order for a terminal user to establish a session (logical connection) with an application, a telecommunications access method was required to supply necessary parameters for these two entities to engage in a session. Figure 6.10 conceptually depicts this.

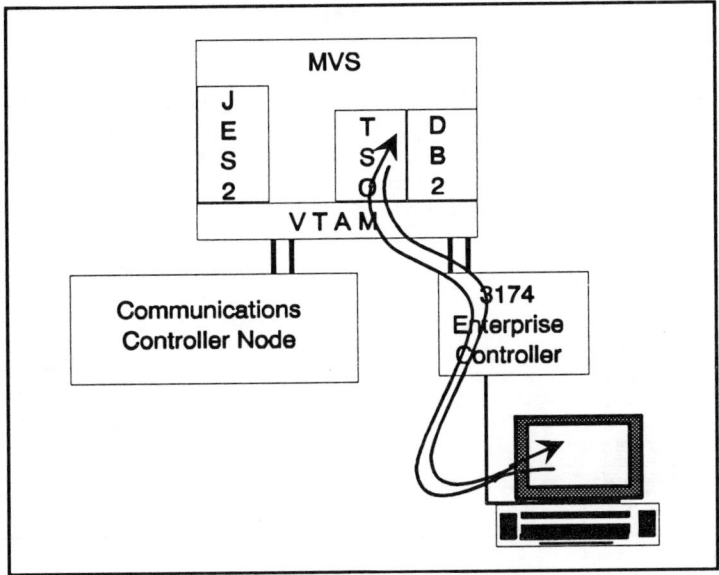

Figure 6.10

Hence, there was no peer concept. As SNA evolved, PU2.1 architecture and Advanced Program-to-Program Communication (APPC) were designed. The advent of these technologies began to change the way SNA operated.

Strictly speaking, SNA is an upper layer protocol. An SNA format and protocol manual is available from IBM. Specific formats, commands, and data streams are defined along with concepts, terms, and other aspects that make SNA a networking technology.

Advanced Peer-to-Peer Networking (APPN) has a lot to do with routing. Since APPN can interoperate within SNA, different capabilities are possible with APPN and SNA. SNA is evolving to embrace different ways of accomplishing advanced tasks. For example, APPN nodes (in the generic sense) support peer-to-peer communication, meaning that VTAM or other telecommunication subsystems are not required for session establishment. This changes SNA from a hierarchical based network to a peer-to-peer oriented network. Consider figure 6.11.

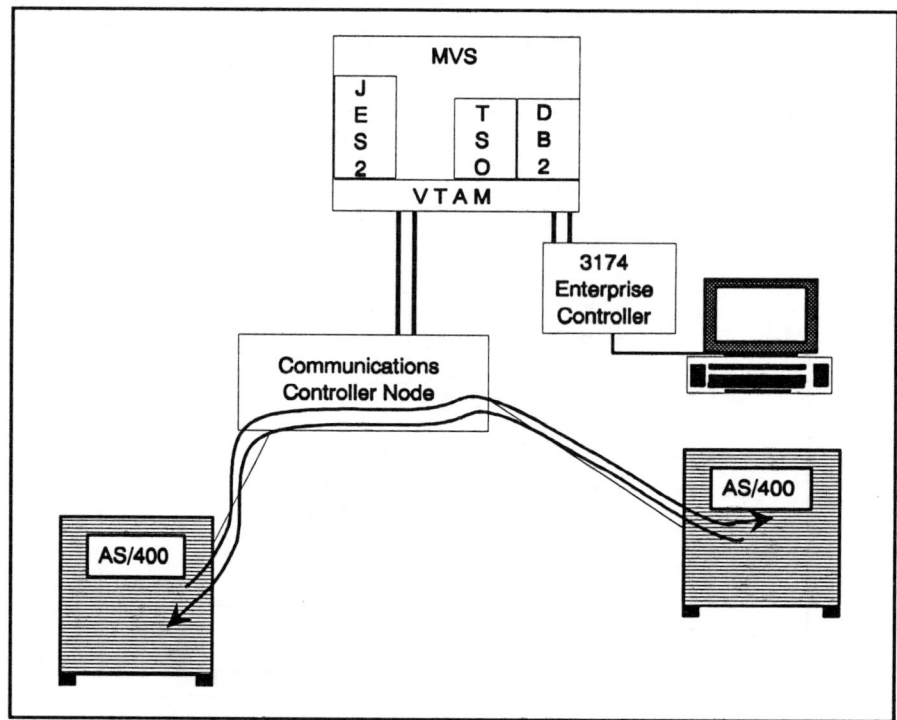

Figure 6.11

The thrust behind APPN is routing, how it is accomplished, and that true peer communications are possible. The impact of APPN on SNA is due to the number of devices for which IBM is providing APPN support. This alone is transforming the way SNA networking is accomplished.

6.5 SNA BUILDING BLOCKS

Within SNA are concepts and terms that need to be understood by those focusing on integrating TCP/IP into SNA. An easy way to break through the mountain of concepts and terminology is to examine prevalent topics encountered in practically all integration scenarios. Approaching SNA concepts and terminology in this manner provides a cohesive approach to integration requirements. Consider the remainder of this section a topical approach to SNA.

Types of SNA Nodes

Two categories of nodes exist: those which can be defined and explained from a traditional hierarchical perspective and those from an APPN (peer) perspective. A node generally consists of hardware and software performing specific functions.

Traditional nodes include:

- Subarea host node—This type node includes an SSCP. By definition this means it is a processor. It has a PU type 5 (PUs are explained in greater detail further in this section). It also provides control for network resources, support transaction programs, and end user services to name a few functions it performs.
- Communication Controller Subarea node—This is a communication controller node. It has a PU type 4. It manages links, data flow control, routing, and other communication functions.
- Peripheral Node—This can be a 3174 with a PU2.0 for example.

Consider figure 6.12 depicting the aforementioned nodes.

Chapter 6

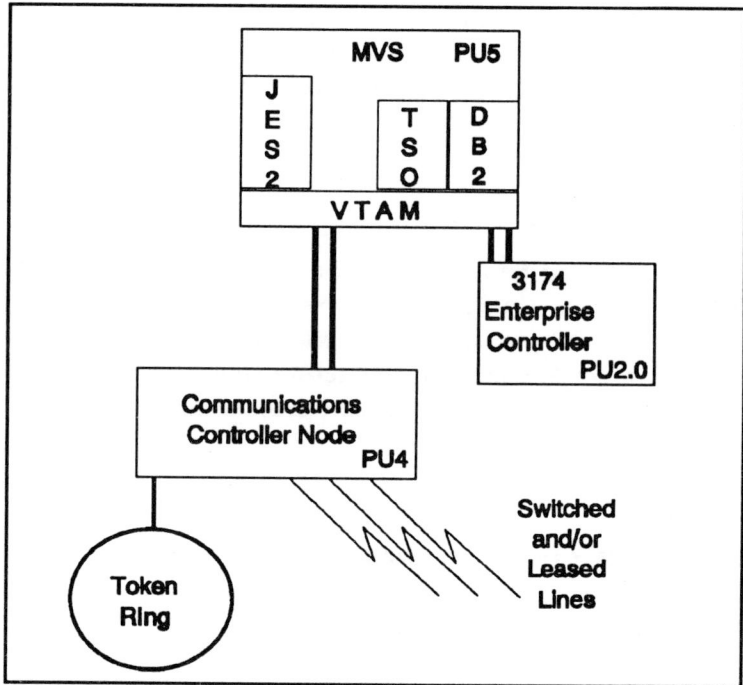

Figure 6.12

APPN nodes include:

- Network Node—This type node provides intermediate routing services. It can also function in a subarea network as a peripheral node. It maintains routing tables, keeping track of nodes attached directly or indirectly. This type node supports CP to CP sessions. (This type session is explained further in this section.)
- Low Entry Networking LEN Node—This type node supports independent LUs, but it does not have the ability to support CP to CP sessions as the networking node.
- End Node—This type node is viewed by the APPN network as an end point in the network. Is does not support CP to CP sessions, neither can it support routing in any form. It does, however, offer what is called end user services.

With traditional support for hierarchical SNA still existing, the evolution of APPN is affecting implementations of existing SNA networks. Now, the hierarchical arrangement exists (traditional SNA), and peer communication (APPN) is possible, breaking the hierarchical environment. Customers win having the best of both worlds, whichever meets the need.

Network Accessible Units

In the world of SNA, a concept of network accessible units (NAU) exists. They are addressable entities. NAUs consist of:

- System Services Control Point (SSCP)—The SSCP is in every host node (processor) with VTAM. It is implemented in software, and it manages and controls resources in an SNA network. In traditional hierarchical networks the SSCP is responsible for establishing logical connections between users and application subsystems.

- Control Point (CP)—This is the focal point that manages resources in APPN nodes. Commonly found in PU2.1 nodes (more explanation is forthcoming explaining PU2.1 nodes). In some ways a CP is similar to an SSCP.

- Physical Unit (PU)—Physical Units are not *physical units*! A PU is implemented in software in most cases. A PU is software that controls physical devices, operation of data links, control of these links, and activation and deactivation of physical devices. In PU type 4 and 2 nodes, the physical unit control point (PUCP) is the name for the control point (CP). In SNA large systems can be characterized by how a PU is architecturally defined.

- Logical Unit (LU)—This is an addressable end point. An LU is also considered an entry point into an SNA network. Application subsystems have LUs defined so they may be used by another program, terminal, or other devices. These devices (printers, terminals, etc.) are known to the SNA network as LUs.

Types of Physical Units

As described previously, PUs are defined and implemented in software and provide capabilities to perform controlling functions in actual physical devices. PUs manage links, link stations, virtual and explicit routes in PU type 5 and 4 nodes, and the PU is the recipient of requests from SSCPs and CPs. The following lists PU types and nodes that they are implemented within:

- PU Type 5—Host nodes (Processors)
- PU Type 4—Communication Controller nodes
- PU Type 2.0—3174 Establishment Controller nodes
- PU Type 2.1—ES/9000 Processors, APPN nodes, AS/400, and others

PUs can be explained according to their characteristics. Consider the following:

- PU 5—Is capable of supporting all types of Logical Units. It will have an SSCP located in it. PU type 5 nodes are considered host nodes.

Chapter 6

- PU 4—A PU type 4 node is primarily responsible for routing and flow control. It is a communications controller node.
- PU 2—This type PU supports dependent logical units. This means an SSCP is required to aid in session establishment.
- PU 2.1—This type PU supports independent logical units (LU6.2). This means an SSCP is not required for session establishment. Certain PU 2.1 nodes have a control point (CP) located in them.

Types of Logical Units (LU)

SNA has defined different types of logical units (LUs) that perform different functions. An LU is an addressable end point in an SNA network. Consider the following LUs and their basic characteristics:

- LU0—This uses non-SNA protocols. Custom applications can be written using LU0 protocol.
- LU1—This supports SNA Character String and Document Content Architecture. Some applications use LU type 1 for printing.
- LU2—This is used by applications and workstations in an interactive environment using the 3270 data stream protocols.
- LU3—This is a 3270 data stream used by printers.
- LU4—The SNA Character String uses this type LU. Peripheral nodes communicating with each other and certain distributed processing environments use this LU.
- LU6.1—This type LU is used between application subsystems communicating with others in a distributed processing environment.
- LU6.2—This LU supports user defined data streams or the SNA General Data Stream. It supports sessions between two or more applications in a distributed environment. This type LU supports multiple, concurrent sessions. This LU is defined and used with peer program communication.
- LU7—This type LU supports a 5250 data stream used in the AS/400 environment.

In addition to the explanation of LUs, two categories of LUs exist, they include:

- Dependent LUs
- Independent LUs

Dependent Logical Units (DLUs) require an SSCP to aid in session establishment. This is a hierarchical type session where the application subsystem is the Primary Logical Unit (PLU) and the terminal user is considered the Secondary Logical Unit (SLU).

Independent Logical Units (ILUs) do not require an SSCP for session establishment. Hence, these type LUs are considered peer-to-peer. These type LUs are LU6.2 and supported by PU2.1, PU5, and PU 4 nodes.

Types of Sessions

In SNA, a session is a logical connection between two end points. Different types of sessions have been defined and perform different functions. The following is a list of session types defined in SNA and their basic function.

- SSCP-to-SSCP—This is used by PU 5 nodes to communicate with one another for purposes of establishing cross domain sessions.
- CP-to-CP—This is used between two control points exchanging information necessary prior to LU-LU sessions. This type session is characteristic of APPN networking nodes; in essence the CP is the controlling point in network nodes.
- SSCP-to-PU—This session is used initially to send the SNA Activate PU (ACTPU) from the SSCP. This command causes a particular PU to become active.
- SSCP-to-LU—This session is used to send the SNA command activate logical units (ACTLU) to the LUs in a given device. This command causes particular LUs to become active.
- LU-to-LU—This is a user to user session. An example of this type session is a user logging on to an application; once the user is logged in, an LU-to-LU session exists.

Types of Links

SNA supports different types of data links. Termed link in SNA nomenclature, the meaning behind the word is, "to connect two nodes." The following list provides types of links supported in SNA and the new IBM networking blueprint.

- Parallel Channel—This is a type of processor. The connection is made via two copper stranded cables called BUS & TAG. The parallel channel is IBM's new name for what was called channel. The name changed with the announcement of Enterprise System Connection Architecture (ESCON). The parallel channel is also known as the S/370 data channel. The parallel channel can accommodate high data rate transfers. It transmits data in parallel from source to destination. Typically, these channels can operate up to 200 feet maximum, when daisy-chained.
- ESCON—The acronym for Enterprise System Connection architecture. This is IBM's fiber optic based subsystem comprising the media, physical, and data link portion of the network. ESCON is used with ESA/390 (S/390) architecture, can transmit up to 17 million bytes per second, span over 14 miles (over 26 miles with additional control units and over 37 miles with chained ESCON directors to another channel), consist of 2 conductors per interface, and support up to 1,024 device

addresses per path. An ESCON environment consists of an ESCON I/O interface, ESCON Manager, ESCON directors, fiber optic cable, ESCON channel, and an ESCON director console.

- Token Ring—Physically implemented via a Media Access Unit (MAU), the actual ring is inside the MAU. Token Ring technology is available in 4 or 16 megabit offerings. Token ring technology is connection oriented at the data link level. Token ring technology is ideal in large environments where it can be used in flow control and routing. See figure 6.13.

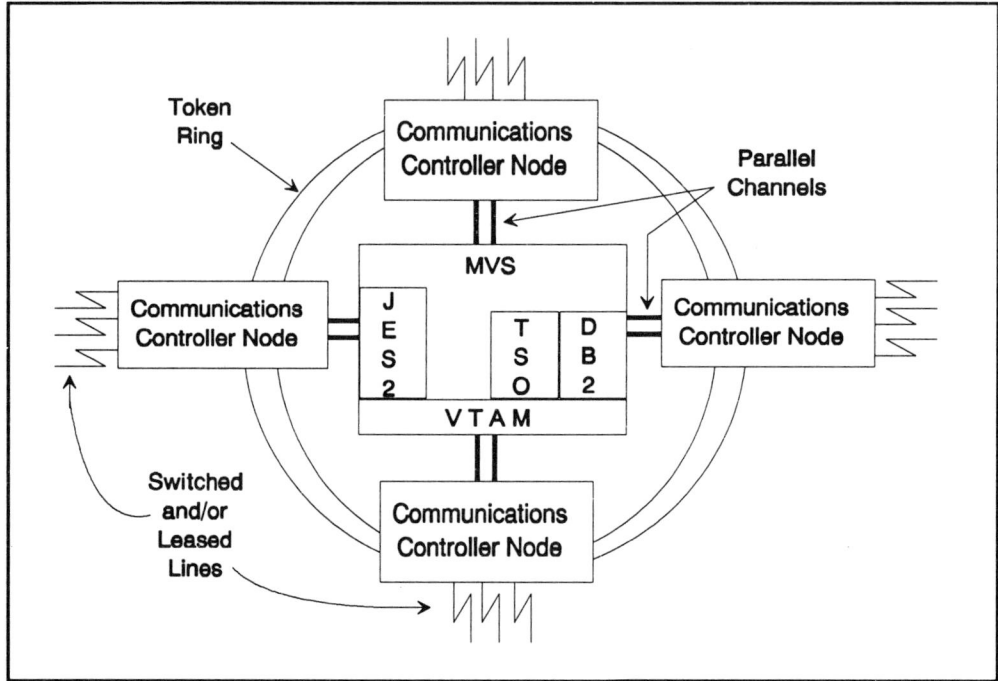

Figure 6.13

It is also an ideal LAN technology because it is relatively inexpensive and very reliable. It is fault tolerant, meaning nodes can be inserted and removed from the MAU at will without disrupting data transfer. It is considered a self-healing technology.

- SDLC—The acronym for Synchronous Data Link Control. It is a method for connecting nodes via telecommunication lines. SDLC is a bit oriented protocol providing robust data transfer. It is mature and prevalent in the marketplace.
- FDDI—The acronym for Fiber Distributed Data Interface. This is a high speed data link level protocol; typical data rates are 100 megabits per second. It is an industry

standard and is accepted throughout the world. Some specific IBM products now support this protocol.
- ETHERNET—Some specific IBM devices now support ETHERNET as a link connection. ETHERNET as described earlier in the book is a broadcast technology, capable of using thick or thinnet coaxial cable or copper twisted pair cabling. Technically, ETHERNET is a data link level protocol implemented in firmware (microcode) on network interface boards.
- X.25—A packet switching technology. IBM has supported this for a number of years now. X.25 is prevalent in many parts of the world. Certain software packages are required to support this technology in SNA.

IBM has broadened its link support with its networking blueprint announced in 1992. Traditional link support is still provided, but support has broadened.

6.6 SNA DEFINITIONS: A PRACTICAL APPROACH

SNA has a definite structure based on the terms, concepts, and components defined by IBM. Some topics need discussion for those new to an SNA environment. This section provides a basic starting point for those working with SNA and who need some point of reference to get acclimated to the way things operate in SNA.

Defining Nodes

Within the operation of SNA is the concept of definition. For example, a 3174 Enterprise Controller may be physically installed and connected appropriately, but that is only half of the job required to make that device functional. All nodes (devices of any kind, be they a 3174, 3172, 3745, terminal, printer, third party gateway, et. al.) must be appropriately defined to VTAM, NCP, and /or the I/O subsystem.

For example, if a 3174 is physically installed and appropriately connected, then a VTAM Generation (GEN) is required for it to be operational. Assuming it is channel attached to a host processor, three statements must be included in the VTAM GEN: An appropriate VBUILD statement, a PU statement, and LU definitions. This must be done because of how SNA operates. VTAM requires a VBUILD statement for operational purposes. It also requires a PU definition statement with appropriate parameters to define devices containing PUs. This includes defining things like buffer size, logon defaults, and special parameters. LU definitions are required for each end point that will access the network. This means if five 3270 type terminals are attached to the 3174, then five LUs must be defined reflecting the 3270 terminal characteristics for them to function. Characteristics about the terminals such as how many columns and rows supported are defined, whether or not the terminal supports color or graphics, and other related characteristics are included. VTAM is like an intelligent door keeper. All resources outside the processor must be defined as well as all resources inside the processor and throughout the network. In the SNA world, only LUs, PUs, SSCPs, and CPs exist with certain defined characteristics. Consequently, when VTAM receives a request to make a session possible, it looks for session parameters that define the LUs desiring LU-LU session status.

The concept of definition is true for all attached devices. A VTAM and or NCP GEN may be required; in some instances an I/O GEN is required. An I/O GEN is a device definition to the I/O subsystem so the subsystem will be aware of its presence. And, in some cases, depending upon the version and release of VTAM and other controlling entities, *no* definition is required.

The Logon Mode Table

A member in the VTAM partitioned data set (PDS) called the Logon Mode Table (LOGMODE) is where LU characteristics are defined. These definitions reflect characteristics about the terminals, printers, specific LUs, or other defined entities.

This LOGMODE table consists of entries, one per requirements of the LU being defined. The contents of each entry is called a BIND image. This BIND image is used by the SSCP and desired application to create a "BIND" (logical connection) between the requesting LU and application. A scenario where the SSCP uses the BIND image to aid in creating a logical connection between a requesting "party" and an application depicts the traditional hierarchical SNA network. For this reason they are called dependent logical units (DLUs). Independent logical units (ILUs) do not require SSCP assistance for a BIND to occur between two defined end points within an SNA network; consequently, the term peer is used to describe this environment.

Defining Applications to VTAM

Just as devices attached to the processor directly or indirectly must be defined to the I/O subsystem, VTAM and/or NCP, so must host applications be defined to VTAM.

Applications differ, and so does how they are defined to VTAM, but commonalities exist. For example, each application has to be defined to VTAM via application id statements (better known as APPLIDs [pronounced apple ids]). Also, an estimated number of concurrent active sessions must also be defined. Other parameters may need to be added to an application definition, and this requires understanding the application, users, and having access to the appropriate VTAM manuals which explain in detail what must be done to define applications to VTAM.

Activation and Deactivation

The concept of "states" exists with PUs and LUs. Hence, the concept of active and inactive states exists. Once a device, a 3174 for example, has been physically installed, connected, and defined to the I/O subsystem, VTAM, and/or the NCP, it must be activated before it will become operational. This means the PU must be varied online.

Activation (and/or deactivation) is a VTAM function performed by a systems operator at the operating system console or via an IBM product offering called NetView. NetView provides the ability for an authorized operator to issue VTAM and other commands from a remote terminal, thus having "remote control" over the SNA network.

An example of a VTAM command to vary online a device such as a 3174 appears like figure 6.14.

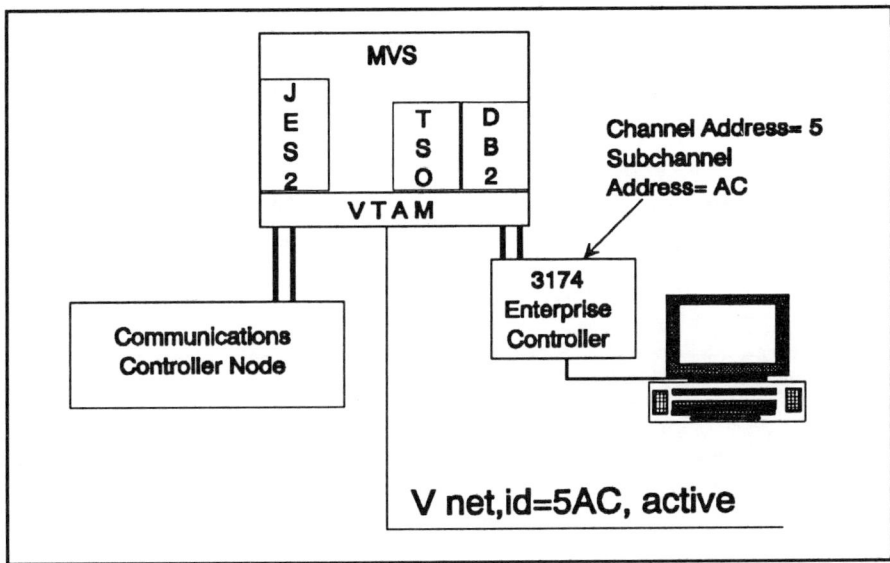

Figure 6.14

In SNA, devices must be installed, connected appropriately, and activated before they are physically and logically operational.

VTAM commands entered to activate or deactivate a PU or LU are interpreted, then the SSCP sends an SNA command ACTPU or ACTLU to the destined PU/LU to bring that PU/LU active. Once the ACTPU/ACTLU command is received, the receiving PU/LU sends a positive acknowledgement back to the SSCP which sent the ACTPU/ACTLU command, then the activation process is complete. This is true when deactivating devices, except a different command is entered, specifically the appropriate command to deactivate a device. Also this is true for activating/deactivating links, lines, and other entities that are identified by a state of active or inactive.

Other knowledge is required to define devices and applications appropriately. It is not the purpose of this section, chapter, or book to explain how to perform VTAM definitions because of the sheer size of that task. IBM has numerous I/O, VTAM, and NCP reference manuals, and this author suggests these be available to those integrating TCP/IP into SNA, because for integration to be successful, correct definitions must be made.

CHAPTER 7
When is a TCP/IP LAN Needed?

This chapter begins in section 7.1 with a brief look at recent computing history and culminates with typical questions being asked today. Section 7.2 explores the details of when a LAN is needed. Section 7.3 concentrates on how to determine which LAN is best in different situations. Section 7.4 addresses the topic of need assessment. Section 7.5 focuses upon synthesizing results obtained from the need evaluation. Section 7.6 examines the concept of selecting a network protocol. Section 7.7 lists required components to build an example TCP/IP network. Section 7.8 discusses component purchases. Section 7.9 provides a high-level checklist as a guide when creating a LAN. Section 7.10 concludes by assimilating each section into a concise perspective of what is entailed when determining if a LAN is needed and which type LAN might be best.

7.1 A HISTORICAL SNAPSHOT

Barely a decade ago IBM introduced its first PC. Unknown was the magnitude it would have on business in less than a decade. In a few years the PC penetrated the corporate world transforming how business is conducted. From a technical standpoint, the decade of the '80s was a whirlwind. Every kind of computing device appeared on the horizon. Personal computers went from infancy to early adulthood, printers went from noisy and barely above a typewriter in quality to silent and typeset quality, and PC memory went from a standard 64 kilobytes to a typical installment of 2 megabytes.

This same decade shed new meaning on the term networking—once known as what one did when looking for another job, to being the dominant technology in the technical community. Networking itself added significant impetus to the technological engine. Not many years ago it seemed as if mankind was driving technological development, now it seems technology is driving technological development significantly. One only needs to look at the networking industry to see direct results. Networking (and specifically internetworking) spawned a synergy making the sum of technology greater than the parts.

Questions are asked today: "How do I know when my department, or company, needs a LAN?" Subsequently: "Is TCP/IP right for me? What components do I need and how do I create a TCP/IP LAN anyway?" If you think you are the only one asking these questions, relax.

7.2 WHEN A LAN IS NEEDED

A typical indicator that a LAN is needed is when the answer is obvious! Proliferation of technology can cause sudden realization that acquiring equipment from different vendors has created a nightmare. Even if much of the computing equipment is from the same vendor, or compatible, this does not necessarily mean interoperability is easily attainable. However, if you are fortunate to plan your computing destiny, all the better. This means you are asking these questions before taking the "leap."

Whatever the case, the usual conclusion is a network of some type is needed.

An increasingly common scenario found in Fortune 500 companies worldwide is where a company acquires one or more smaller corporations in geographically different locations. When this happens, incompatibility between computer equipment is almost a foregone conclusion and demographic considerations must be addressed to achieve a true enterprise network. For years SNA, and increasingly APPN, has become entrenched with many Fortune 500 companies as a networking solution; this is not necessarily so with smaller companies. Smaller companies typically have non-SNA based networks, or in some cases no network(s) at all. This is not unusual because company size has traditionally dictated technical decisions.

Assume a corporate acquisition occurred, the acquired company has approximately 500 employees, a number of departments exist, and the company has *no* networks. The acquired company's documentation department will be our focus.

The documentation department has multiple writers working on different documents needing to share glossaries, diagrams, references, etc. They need a departmental LAN, but future plans are to integrate the documentation LAN with other departmental LANs as they are designed and implemented. Documentation wants independence from the UNIX host they share with other departments throughout the company but the ability to interoperate with other departments as LANs are deployed. Since no network exists, all users of the UNIX system, including documentation, are directly attached. The system is not stable because software engineers develop programs and impact system performance by testing their programs. Thus, documentation department performance is hindered. Writers compete for printer time and rely on a different department for data backup. They realize a LAN is needed and understand their choice for a LAN must be capable of future interoperability with other departmental LANs. They assume interoperability with the company which acquired them will be required at some point. Since they know the now parent company is SNA/APPN based, this factors into consideration of the LAN which is selected.

The documentation department needs EMAIL, file transfer, and remote logon capability to the UNIX host and some of these services among only the writers. They decide to research possible networking solutions and now have an advantage because of this initiative and time devoted to researching possible LAN solutions. The group has writers with technical backgrounds and nontechnical backgrounds. Since this department is starting with no LAN they must address a fundamental question: Which LAN is needed?

7.3 DETERMINING WHICH LAN IS BEST

LAN technology has arrived and can be purchased from many computer vendors. Large computer stores sell LAN hardware and software over the counter. But, the decision is still the customer's, and many find themselves asking: "Which LAN technology is right for me?"

LANs and sports seem to be approached in similar ways; many people have a favorite. Problem is, a favorite sports team may win or lose a game; but in LAN technology a "favorite" technology, if not appropriately matched with the need, could cause significant financial losses. Understanding LAN technology is a must to make an educated decision.

Different terms are used to describe LANs. Sometimes, terms used to describe a LAN refer to an operating system, network topology, lower or upper level protocol, or a proprietary vendor term. Popular terms used with LANs include the following descriptions:

First, are references reflecting an operating system; but these terms do not describe a LAN. For example, UNIX is sometimes used to refer to a LAN; it is an operating system not a LAN. Likewise, references are made to an OS/2 LAN. OS/2 is the operating system, not a LAN.

Second, references reflecting network topology such as BUS, ring, or star are used; but these refer to the physical and/or logical implementation of the medium. They are LAN characteristics.

Third, references reflecting lower level protocols such as ETHERNET, token ring, and FDDI are used, but these describe how data is manipulated at lower levels in a network. These protocols alone do not make a LAN.

Fourth, references reflecting upper layer protocols such as SNA, TCP/IP, IPX, NetBIOS, and DECNET are used; but they reflect software and services provided. These alone do not constitute a LAN.

Fifth, references reflecting a specific vendor can be used; but this does not communicate pertinent information about a LAN. It merely denotes the provider.

LANs consist of computers and related devices. Computers require operating systems. Topologies are implementations of a medium. Lower level protocols provide the method of data link connection. Upper level protocols prescribe user capabilities such as remote logons, file transfers, EMAIL, windowing support, etc. Vendors typically combine one or more of these, thus offering a LAN.

Determining which LAN is right for you means understanding and evaluating existing equipment, operating system(s), physical environment, current user needs, potential user needs, and financial resources.

7.4 NEED EVALUATION

Some need a starting point when considering purchasing a LAN. An appropriate way to begin is to know how many computers, printers, and other devices currently exist. Start by documenting the type operating system(s) in use. Be specific, include the version and release if applicable. Examine the physical environment for the proposed LAN. Where will cabling be placed? What type electrical and/or other wiring is present? Must LAN cabling be contiguous to wiring of any type? If so, can this be avoided? What operational disruption will occur when a LAN is installed? If additional devices may be added to the LAN, where will they be located?

How many users need to be networked? What daily operations do they perform? Does each user need file transfer capabilities with other users on the LAN? Do all users require EMAIL? Identify any users (if any) needing remote logon to a mini or small multiuser system. Assuming maximum utilization, estimate how many users will use the LAN simultaneously. Does the network need to be operational 24 hours a day? What would be the worse case scenario if the network became totally dysfunctional?

Calculate reasonable user growth anticipated for the department/company in the next twelve to twenty-four months; double it.

Document projected plans for procurement of supplementary equipment in the foreseeable future. For example, if adding a processor is a consideration, identify the type operating system. Include details of peripheral equipment; estimate the type, size, and maximum number of users the new processor accommodates. Obtain processor support specifications for upper and lower layer network protocols.

Lastly, speculate possible connectivity scenarios that could occur once the LAN is operational. Could the need arise for a remote LAN connection? If this is possible, identify the other network by upper and lower layer protocol.

Seems like homework; it is prudent. Many potential buyers address these questions without realizing it until after a decision is made. The latter usually results in constantly reverse engineering the LAN.

7.5 SYNTHESIZING EVALUATION RESULTS

After accumulating information reflect on what equipment is present and anticipated. For our purposes, an artificial scenario can provide grounds to learn the basics without spending money! Consider the following hypothetical situation.

Six PCs using DOS, two PCs using OS/2, and one minicomputer using UNIX exist. The UNIX host has one terminal attached. Three laser printers exist, one dedicated to the minicomputer, the other two shared by PC users through an intelligent switch. A database exists on the UNIX host which requires updating at the end of each business day. Information stored in this database is used by all office personnel. They currently obtain a printout, but if additional terminals could provide host access, printouts could be eliminated. The PC DOS users create files that need archiving for a minimum of five years. One PC DOS user creates diagrams, artistic work, and requires data files created by DOS, OS/2, and UNIX users. All users need EMAIL. Six month growth projection anticipates three additional PC DOS users, one OS/2 user, and possibly an additional UNIX host, or at least an upgrade to the current host. Additional information indicates at least one PS/2 host will need connectivity on a peer basis with an SNA/APPN network within fifteen months. Plans indicate APPC programming will commence on a PS/2 host (using OS/2) within six months after the LAN is operational. Consider figure 7.1.

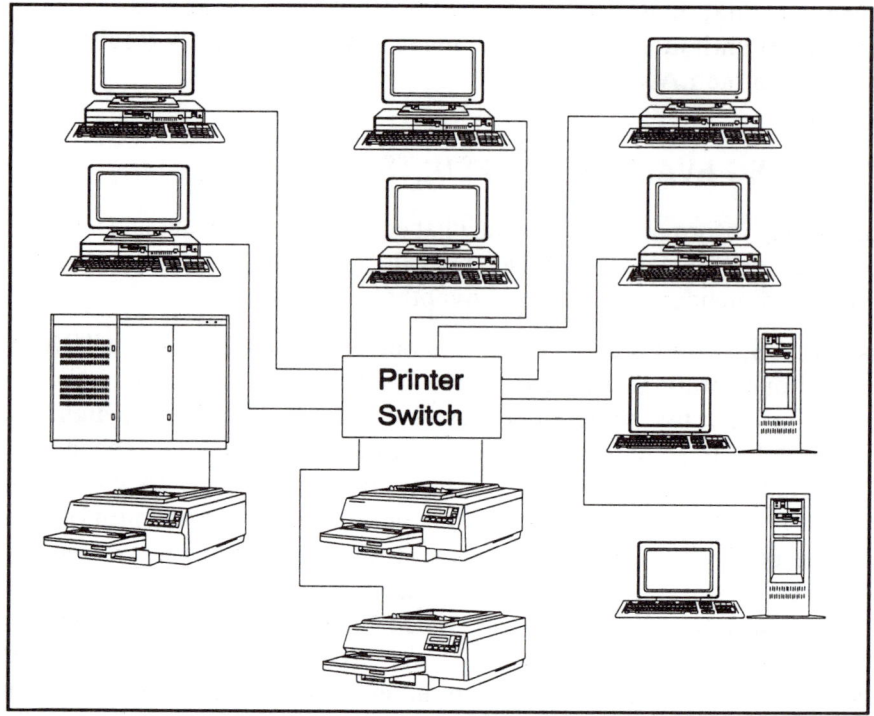

Figure 7.1

7.6 SELECTING A PROTOCOL

After synthesizing data from the LAN requirement evaluation focus upon which type LAN meets identified requirements. The evaluation revealed users need EMAIL, file transfer and remote logon capability, a windowing environment, and integration capabilities to an SNA/APPN network with minimal impact in daily operation and costs.

More than one upper layer network protocol could meet some needs of our hypothetical environment, but the diverse requirements identified eliminate possible contenders for an upper layer protocol. The breadth of identified requirements include: File transfers between different operating systems with different file structures, APPC programming support in a UNIX environment and connectivity with an SNA/APPN network, EMAIL across all platforms, terminal server support, maximum flexibility for future growth, and nominal costs. These needs indicate TCP/IP is best for an upper layer network protocol.

TCP/IP, by default, provides EMAIL, file transfer, and remote logon facilities regardless of the host operating system. It can operate with minor modifications on diverse operating system such as DOS, OS/2, and UNIX. If used, integration with other networks is easily achieved. TCP/IP also supports a distributed windowing system that can operate with different hardware and software platforms. TCP/IP can also be integrated into an SNA/APPN environment through a variety of vendor offerings. It is not proprietary and does not force utilization of proprietary vendor equipment. APPC can be integrated into a TCP/IP environment thus making APPC possible between TCP/IP and SNA/APPN. Terminal servers and dumb terminals can operate easily with a TCP/IP network. This combination inhibits the need for multiple terminals directly wired connected to a host. Dumb terminals connected to a terminal server have dynamic connectivity to any valid host on the LAN. From a user perspective, these terminals appear to be directly attached to any host a user has logged onto, but in fact a dynamic (logical) connection exists. TCP/IP operates well with few hosts and is capable of supporting a couple hundred or more as well. TCP/IP is inexpensive, proven effective in the marketplace, and it is a mature protocol.

Because of the number of vendors who support TCP/IP, it is an attractive solution. In addition, a large number of people in the technical community understand it and know how to implement it. Products already exist for TCP/IP to SNA/APPN integration, and these components are almost plug-n-play.

TCP/IP is the upper layer protocol of choice, but a lower layer protocol must be selected. To a significant degree this will determine the topology and even the cable used. TCP/IP's flexibility is exemplified by its support for more than one lower layer protocol, but in this case ETHERNET is the best choice.

ETHERNET is best because it is easily installed, reliable, and inexpensive, and it is also prevalent in the marketplace. It is implemented on a Network Interface Card (NIC) and supports different media types. If implemented via a hub, ETHERNET literally becomes plug-n-play. This type implementation makes adding hosts easy. It works well with TCP/IP and, like TCP/IP, a significant number of individuals in the technical community understand it. ETHERNET is popular among vendors who make LAN devices, thus connectivity to other LANs (of like, or unlike, kind) is easily accomplished.

7.7 COMPONENTS REQUIRED TO BUILD TCP/IP NETWORK

To create a TCP/IP based ETHERNET LAN requires nominal expenditure and components. For example, to implement ETHERNET on eight PCs costs less than $200.00 per interface card. Deploying hubs to connect the PCs and UNIX host would be approximately $1,000.00. Wiring, less than $100.00. TCP/IP software for the PCs would be less than $400.00, and probably less than $1,500.00 for the UNIX host. ETHERNET adapters for the laser printers would be less than $400.00 each. A terminal server costs approximately $900.00 and approximately $300.00 per dumb terminal.

What is the total cost? Based on our example environment and figures, approximately $9,400.00. This cost reflects the following benefits/capabilities:

- File transfer among all users
- Remote logon to the UNIX host for all users
- EMAIL for all users
- All printers available to all users
- Printers can be logically assigned and maximum utilization can be achieved.
- PC DOS users can transfer files across the network and archive them on the UNIX based host.
- All current and future users have access to the database *on-line* rather than sharing one terminal or obtaining a printout.
- A program could be written to automate database updates each day, eliminating manual updates.
- Files on the UNIX host would be usable on the PCs and files on the PCs would be usable on the UNIX host.
- Data required to accompany diagrams and drawings can be transferred across the network without having to manually perform this function by diskette.
- Required installation space is virtually insignificant.
- No professional installer is required.
- Physical cabling can be changed easily if office modifications are made.
- Integration to an SNA/APPN network is easily attainable.
- Connectivity to other networks is easily achieved.
- A distributed windowing environment is provided.

The terminal server and dumb terminals eliminate the need for printouts and provide interactive access with any applications on the UNIX based host. A benefit of terminal servers and "dumb" terminals include connectivity with any valid host, even SNA/APPN network hosts, once a link is established and terminal emulation is provided. These terminals by default have remote logon capabilities because the terminal server is based on TCP/IP. Once the LAN is in place data transfer, EMAIL, and operations are enhanced because individual pieces of equipment are working together maximizing resources. Consider figure 7.2.

When is a TCP/IP LAN Needed?

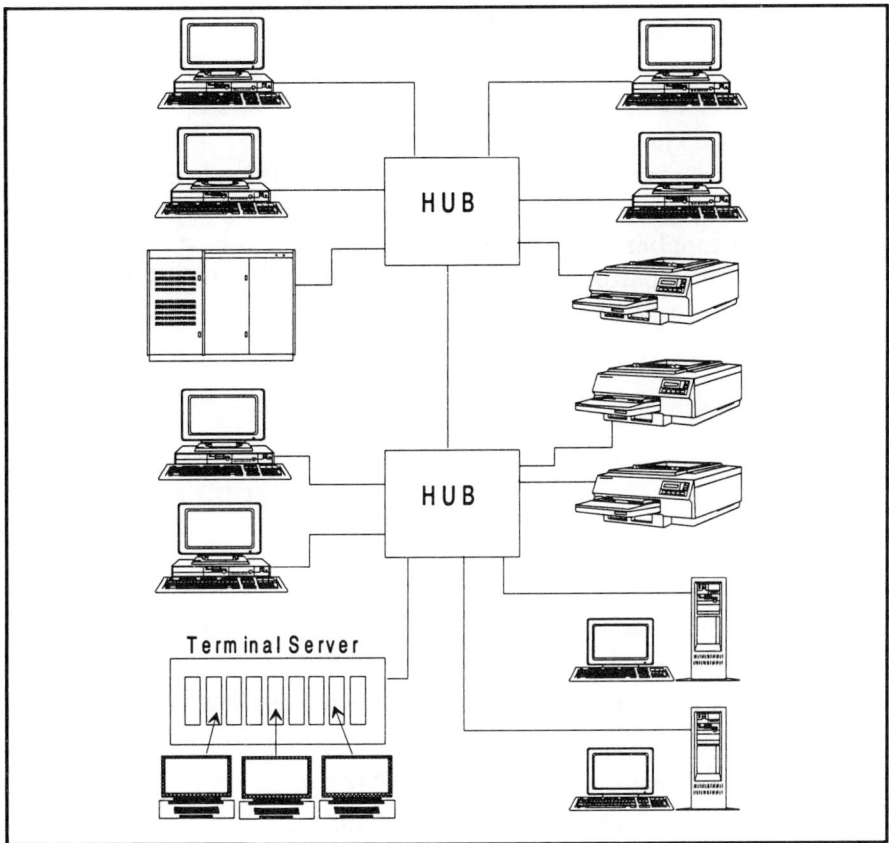

Figure 7.2

7.8 COMPONENT PURCHASES

Almost all previously listed components can be purchased through a computer store. In some instances LAN software and hardware purchases may be recommended from a specific vendor. When purchasing software for minicomputers or larger, it is best to check with the original manufacturer before purchasing LAN software or hardware from a different source. Software versions and releases require certain specifications from LAN components for operability. In most cases, more than two or three suppliers of a particular LAN component (be it software or hardware) exist.

A technical difference does exist between PCs and PS/2s. Operationally, they may appear the same, but from a hardware architecture perspective they differ. Much PC hardware cannot be interchanged with PS/2s and vice versa. No guarantee exists that software operating under DOS will operate under OS/2. Again, they have been architected differently.

Because the purpose is to combine components so they interoperate thus forming a network, it is prudent to know model and specification numbers. It is also important to know software version and release numbers. This level of detail is required to achieve component level integration, making a LAN possible, with the least amount of pain. When searching for a supplier of a particular component, it is best to shop around. Talk to more than one supplier before purchase; a delayed informed decision usually pays greater dividends than a rushed and possibly biased decision.

7.9 CREATING A LAN

Assuming required components are present and everything needed is accessible, installation can begin. The following order is more of a check list than a particular order of installation.

- Make a system backup of each PC, PS/2, and UNIX host (a cheap insurance policy).
- Make time to familiarize yourself with the installation manual from each component to be installed.
- Determine the location of the ETHERNET hub and begin wiring from this location to each device requiring a connection.
- Install ETHERNET boards in the PCs and PS/2s.
- Install the ETHERNET adapters on the printers.
- Connect the wiring from the hub to all the interface cards.
- Place the terminal server in an easily accessible location and connect it to the hub.
- Place the terminals in their destined places and connect them to the terminal server.
- Install the TCP/IP software on the UNIX host.
- Install a copy of the TCP/IP software on a PC.
- Configure the aforementioned software appropriately.
- Attempt a remote logon from the terminal server and from the PC to the UNIX host; if successful, continue. If not, determine the problem at this point before proceeding.
- Continue installing TCP/IP software on the PCs and PS/2s.
- After installation is complete, verify remote logons, file transfers, and EMAIL is possible.
- Determine a place and save original documentation for all hardware and software components.

7.10 CONCLUSION

Determining when a LAN is needed is site dependent. Some realize after acquiring different equipment over time that computer gridlock exists and a LAN is needed to resolve this predicament; others plan for a LAN making hardware, software, and other related purchases based on the services the LAN is designed to provide. LANs provide maximum utilization of hardware, software, and personnel resources. The net effect of a LAN is its synergy.

Determining which LAN technology is best depends on a number of factors: user's application needs, physical location of the LAN, possible future interconnections with other LANs or WANs, maximum number of users utilizing the LAN at a given time, the dominant function for the LAN (for example to provide file transfer capabilities, remote logons, EMAIL, distributed windowing, etc.), security issues if pertinent, potential growth capabilities and ease of adding additional equipment, and implementation, support, and costs.

Evaluating needs indicative of your needs should be approached from an objective perspective. Make a list of user needs, expectations upon implementation, major applications to be used, estimated increase in users over a reasonable period of time, marketplace reputation of the type network being considered, technical support personnel generally available, hardware and software vendors that support the proposed LAN, and then evaluate its technical strengths and weaknesses.

Once evaluation results are compiled, some types of networks will be discounted by default. Appropriately interpreting and understanding results is critical. Numbers from surveys and evaluations can be misleading, so attention to the details is important here.

Selecting a LAN protocol should be after collecting and analyzing your site requirements. Many times, more than one network protocol appears to be plausible to meet your needs. When this occurs, probe into a comparison and contrast between the competing protocols. This will usually indicate which is the better choice.

An important task is identifying necessary LAN components. This should be performed from a technical and a financial perspective. Differences exist in the quality of technical components that purport to perform identical functions. Likewise, shop around for the best price. Networking has come of age, and many LAN components are generally available in local computer stores.

How a LAN is created depends on which LAN technology has been selected. Some types of LAN technologies can be installed and configured by varying levels of computer literate individuals. Some LAN technology is more specialized and requires select individuals who have previously worked with this technology. This, along with time factors for implementation, should be considered before embarking on LAN installation.

Also consideration should be given to the impact installing a LAN will have on the working environment.

Selecting a LAN is more involved than selecting a PC. A LAN is technology which has the purpose of connecting various computing devices. By definition this is more complex than simply purchasing and installing a PC. Unlike PCs, LAN technology differs because of the original design intent. PCs and compatibles for the most part are designed with similar guidelines making them fairly "compatible." Remembering this when beginning to purchase a network can save time, money, frustration, and hopefully help you obtain your goal(s).

CHAPTER 8
Integrating Remote TCP/IP LANs into SNA

Increasingly, SNA oriented businesses are finding themselves surrounded by islands of TCP/IP based LANs. In many cases, computing needs are growing exponentially. In such cases user patience is short and waiting for traditional solutions is being circumvented. Users are impacting corporate planning by purchasing technology piece meal.

This chapter investigates considerations for integrating remote TCP/IP LANs into SNA. Section 8.1 begins with a typical scenario faced by many individuals with the task of integration. Section 8.2 states those issues that factor into integration but go beyond technology. Section 8.3 poses technical considerations of integration and typical pitfalls encountered. Section 8.4 solves the integration problem posed earlier in the chapter; and, section 8.5 concludes by reminding the reader that more factors into the integration equation than merely technology.

8.1 A PERSPECTIVE ON REMOTE TCP/IP LANS

Compounding this problem are issues many corporations face increasingly; that is, integrating newly acquired, geographically dispersed companies into an existing SNA environment. Figure 8.1 depicts this scenario.

Chapter 8

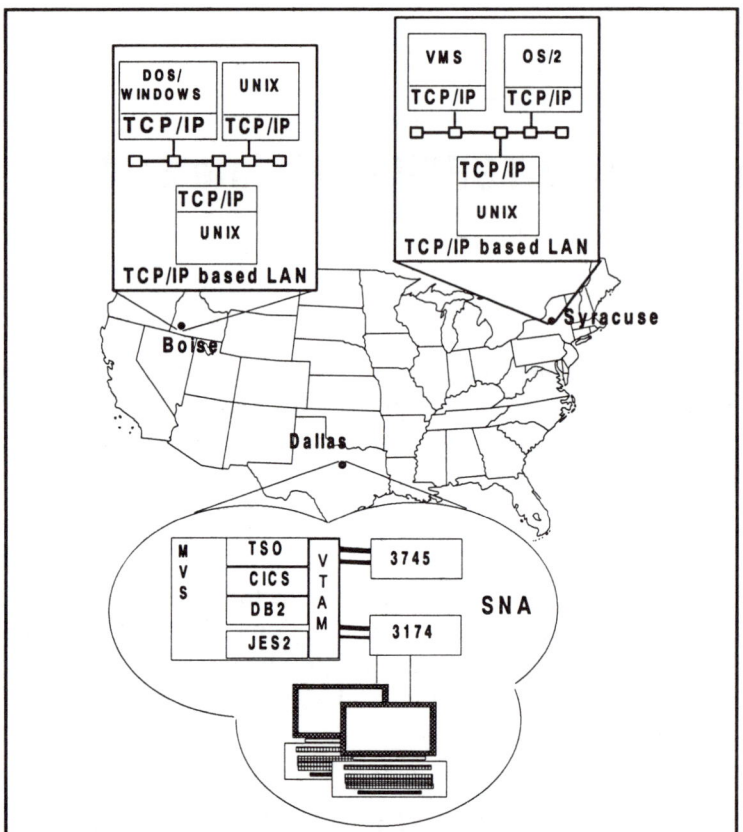

Figure 8.1

Assume in figure 8.1 the Dallas office is the corporate location and is SNA based. Assume also offices in Boise and Syracuse must be integrated into the Dallas environment. Because of geography technical incompatibilities between Boise, Syracuse, and Dallas exist by default; and these issues must be resolved to achieve integration.

Also, assume the corporate location has approximately 2000 users utilizing system resources daily; the processor is a large IBM ES/9000 processor and has a significant communications capabilities and other supporting devices. Assume Boise and Syracuse have multiple TCP/IP based hosts and approximately 100 - 200 users. Assume Boise and Syracuse users require daily interaction with Dallas's corporate data center. Specifically, Boise and Syracuse users need logon and file transfer capabilities. Assume these problems should have been solved yesterday, finances are limited, and top performance from all equipment is expected. Sound realistic? Let us examine what is involved in integrating these newly acquired TCP/IP LANs into SNA.

8.2 FACTORS BEYOND INTEGRATION

Before examining technical issues, consideration for factors beyond technology is in order. Often overlooked or added on at the last moment is the issue of adequately trained personnel. Without knowledgeable individuals to utilize technology, nominal benefit is derived and typically much frustration is generated.

Basic deductions can be made from figure 8.1. For example, corporate personnel have probably been using SNA based equipment since each individual's employment date. Inferential is that these individuals are proficient (albeit to varying levels) in the SNA environment. They are accustomed to daily tasks required for corporate operations sustaining business. The element of the unknown has been foregone because of experience. Hence, productivity is reasonably predictable. From a corporate standpoint training can be focused on refining personnel skills thereby making employees more productive.

Considering the Boise and Syracuse sites, it is reasonable to assume integrating these offices under the corporate umbrella means addressing different training needs. Typical training topics include acclimating the LAN users to SNA based operations, file structures, security, basic operating system commands for navigating the system, and other pertinent topics. In addition, it is reasonable to assume users will need to know procedures for resolving technical problems when they arise.

Assuming users in the LAN sites have no prior exposure to SNA based operations is normal. My experience supports this, and acknowledging this merits concerted effort from management and technical support personnel as well. Since employees's productivity are proportional to their understanding how to perform required tasks, it is reasonable to assume that the initial learning curve for those new to SNA based applications may be steep. Unfortunately, this aspect of integration can go unnoticed until questions begin surfacing regarding why tasks are not performed in a timely manner. Integrating TCP/IP into SNA is not solely a technical matter.

Assuming prior to integration, internal technical support was provided locally, this may no longer be the case. Clear delineation of whom to call with problems is in order. Besides users facing this dilemma, so do technical personnel. When remote TCP/IP based LANs are integrated into SNA clarification of who supports what can solve a lot of questions before they arise.

Integrating TCP/IP into SNA, regardless of physical location, poses questions from both users and technical support alike. Successfully integrated sites typically share commonalities also. They tend to have adequately trained users and technical personnel who understand component functions used in integration. Their personnel can be characterized as workers who share knowledge from their respective backgrounds aiding in the merging of the two networks.

8.3 FACTORS OF INTEGRATION

Using figure 8.1 as our integration example, the question of how to achieve integration arises. Integrating TCP/IP into SNA implies merging TCP/IP services into an SNA environment and likewise the converse. Typically, this means providing TCP/IP based LAN users with logon, file transfer, and EMAIL capabilities with the SNA host(s). With this as a starting point, integration limitations immediately arise when different attempts are made at integration.

First, attempting to integrate TCP/IP based LANs into SNA might include establishing an asynchronous link between remote LANs and the SNA environment. That is, connecting a modem (or modem bank) to the LAN and providing user access to the SNA environment. This is not true TCP/IP to SNA integration; it merely provides an asynchronous link between the two.

Beyond establishing a link between remote TCP/IP LANs and the SNA environment, terminal emulation must be provided. LAN based hosts use ASCII data representation and transmit data asynchronously. In SNA, hosts use EBCDIC data representation and connections are usually synchronous. Hence, if an asynchronous link is established between LANs and the SNA environment, the issue of data translation must be addressed on the communications controller node where the remote link is made. This means additional software must be loaded onto the FEP to accomplish this.

If this method of connecting LANs to SNA is implemented, significant expense is incurred because multiple telephone lines, modems, communication packages, and other resources are required. The number of users and frequency of SNA resource utilization dictate the component requirements to solve link connections between TCP/IP and SNA. But, integration (merging TCP/IP services into SNA and vice versa) is *still not* achieved; only a terminal emulation is provided. Hence, this is not integrating TCP/IP into SNA.

Secondly, attempting to integrate TCP/IP based LANs into SNA can be achieved by installing an SNA host and peripheral equipment on each LAN, implementing TCP/IP on the SNA hosts, and connecting the SNA hosts together via a distributed SNA network. Figure 8.2 depicts probably the most costly way to achieve integration.

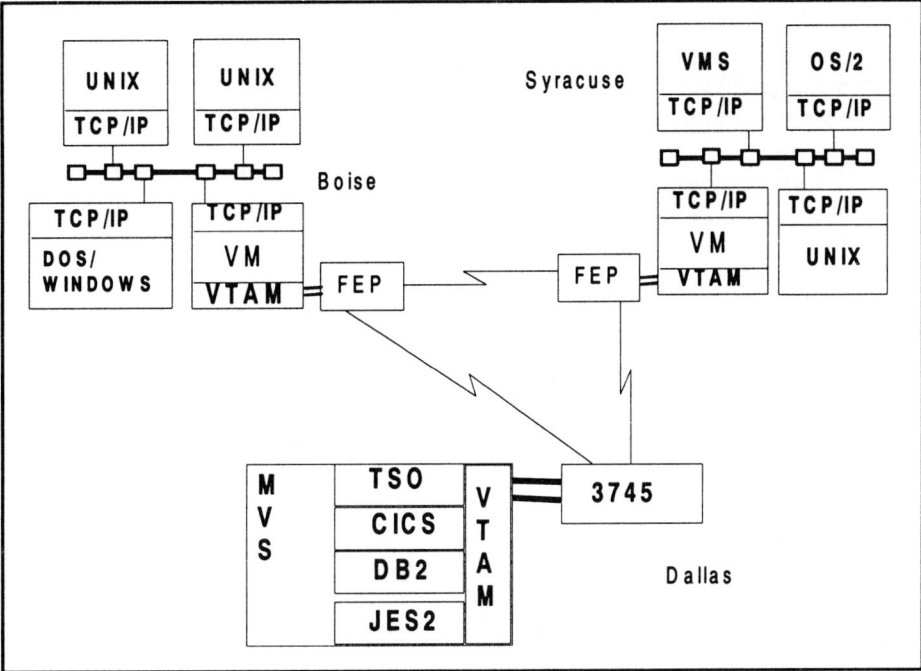

Figure 8.2

It will work, but this attempt increases overhead, expense, and basically defeats the intent to integrate TCP/IP into SNA, this intent being to maximize resource utilization and minimize expenditure. Thus, integration can be achieved, but at significant costs.

Third, bringing different environments together can be achieved through a specific network device called a gateway. Gateways designed to integrate TCP/IP into SNA will suffice for our example integrating TCP/IP LANs in Boise and Syracuse into the SNA headquarters in Dallas. This solution achieves the best of both worlds at the lowest possible price.

8.4 INTEGRATION BY GATEWAY

To solve the needs in this scenario, a TCP/IP to SNA gateway is the best choice for integrating TCP/IP into SNA. In cases such as presented here, solutions are fairly straightforward. Upper layer protocol conversion must be achieved, and most gateways will offer options for link connections from the LAN to the SNA environment, and by default lower layer protocol conversion is achieved.

The best gateway implementation here will convert ETHERNET to SDLC and the physical link between Boise, Syracuse, and Dallas is achieved over switched or leased lines. Figure 8.3 depicts this type of solution.

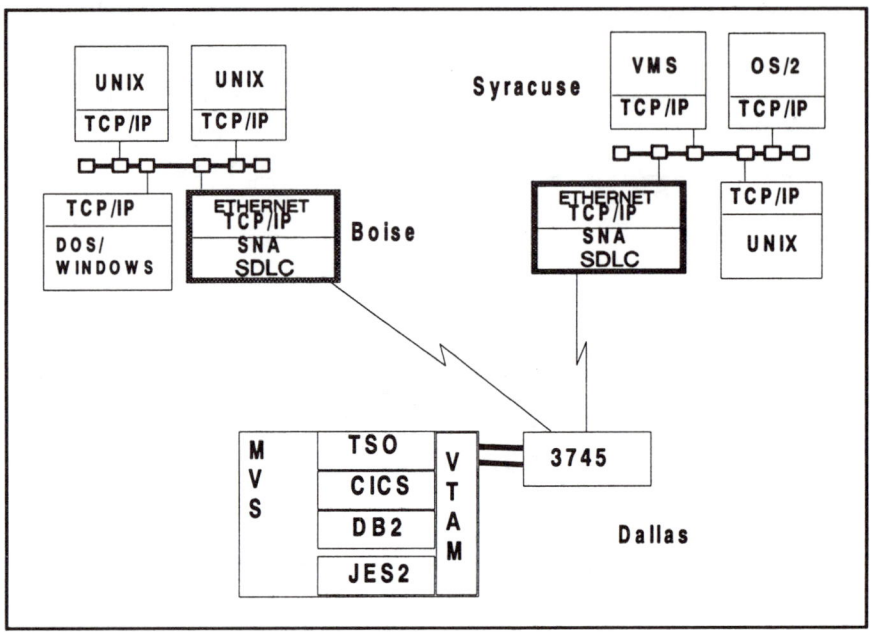

Figure 8.3

This solution shows TCP/IP to SNA protocol conversion taking place on the gateway (a hardware gateway as this picture shows) in the physical location of the LAN. It also shows ETHERNET to SDLC protocol conversion occurring on the gateway as well. As a result the data stream leaving the LAN is SNA and SDLC—quite acceptable for the FEP.

Figure 8.3 assumes remote logon capability from the LAN is achieved via software on each LAN host and/or some mechanism in the gateway. A specific way of performing file transfers to or from the SNA host is not identified because multiple ways exist to accomplish this. Likewise, no particular EMAIL implementation is presented. Requirements to achieve logons, file transfers, and EMAIL vary depending upon the gateway vendor. For example, logons can be achieved by a TN3270 client application, file transfers can be achieved with IBM's IND$FILE program or via unbundled TCP/IP software located on the IBM host, and achieving bidirectional EMAIL can be achieved different ways as well.

LAN TIMES Buyer's Directory (July 1992) has a section listing gateway vendors. Not all vendors in this section provide TCP/IP to SNA gateway products, but many do. A hair-split remains in terminology; that is, ambiguity remains concerning the term gateway. For example, some vendors in this section are listed as "gateway vendors" when in fact their main product is terminal emulation. A chasm exists between terminal emulation and protocol conversion. Granted, terminal emulation is required to integrate the LANs into SNA, but fundamental to TCP/IP to SNA gateways is TCP/IP to SNA protocol conversion. The former without the latter is merely terminal emulation, and the latter without the former is only protocol conversion. One without the other does not achieve integration.

Granted, protocol conversion and data translation do have to occur on the same device (gateway). But, these two issues have to be resolved for integration to occur. The question remains, where is each function being performed? And, practically speaking, are these functions being performed in the most expedient way possible?

8.5 CONCLUSION

When TCP/IP based LANs are geographically removed from SNA environments, evaluating the LAN and SNA environment should occur in the earliest stages of considerations. This evaluation will normally yield what type data link is best suited to connect the two. Generally, answering this question answers where lower layer protocol conversion must occur. In the recommended solution here it meant implementing a TCP/IP to SNA gateway on each LAN site. By default converting TCP/IP to SNA and ETHERNET to SDLC protocol was performed on the gateway.

Complete TCP/IP to SNA integration provides, at a minimum, capabilities for bidirectional logons, file transfers, and EMAIL which are commonly used services in both environments. Providing all these services is not necessary to achieve integration, but selecting a vendor should include considering one that has these common services available. Beyond these, other services are available from different vendors. Some of these include: APPC support from LANs to SNA, Distributed Data Base support, Remote Job Entry (RJE), and other special services.

Integration can be achieved technically, but productivity can be lacking if users are not adequately trained. Integration encompasses more than physical and logical connections. Some of the original forces driving TCP/IP to SNA integration was providing a vehicle to maximize resources. However, overlooking those users performing day-to-day tasks who perform core functions of many organizations is short-sighted. Maximizing resources also includes human resources. Both users and technical support staff may need training to help leverage the investment and maximize resources, and to overlook this is to miss a fundamental ingredient in integration.

CHAPTER 9
Integrating Local TCP/IP LANs into SNA

Achieving TCP/IP to SNA integration means factoring more than technical issues such as protocol conversion into the solution equation. It means awareness of the physical location of all equipment to be integrated. The previous chapter concentrated on integrating remote TCP/IP LANs into SNA. This chapter focuses upon integrating local TCP/IP LANs in an SNA environment. Section 9.1 presents typical computing problems faced by departments in many companies. Section 9.2 is an account of a real experience of a department's struggle, throughout the past decade, with its needs and the company's large SNA data center. Section 9.3 explores one solution for the department's problem. Section 9.4 shows still another way to solve the department's computing problems. Section 9.5 concludes succinctly stating that more than one solution exists to solve the problem put forth in this chapter, and that clearly defining expectations beforehand typically yields satisfactory results in the end.

9.1 TYPICAL DEPARTMENTAL PROBLEMS

An increasingly common scenario is where an SNA/APPN oriented company discovers departmental LANs have crept into the organization. Many companies have found it difficult to provide all services required by various departments. For example, one department's needs might include: having file transfer capabilities among departmental employees, having a dedicated printer, being isolated (production-wise) from other departments so corporate data center downtime does not impact their department, having the ability to produce reports on demand, but maintaining interoperability with the company as a whole. Meeting needs such as these takes time to plan into the corporate computing scheme. But, in the past decade many departments have circumvented the corporate data center structure and embarked upon solving their own problems.

Solving departmental needs such as mentioned here could take more time than some companies can tolerate. Traditionally, when a need arose it was commonplace to go by company policy requesting desired resources. An evaluation was normally in order to validate the request, bids would be taken on proposed equipment, the order would go through approval channels, and then the order would be placed. Some time after navigating this procedural hoop the order would arrive.

This method of solving departmental computer needs, the proliferation of computer equipment over the past decade, company *disorganization* that has occurred throughout the marketplace, and user impatience provide necessary ingredients to create chaos. Reality is that computer technology of all varieties has found its way into corporate world, and only in the past few years have many companies begun to realize the impact of this technology upon the corporation as a whole. A typical scenario is where multiple vendor equipment exists alongside the corporate standard (whatever that may be).

9.2 A REAL DEPARTMENT COMPUTING PROBLEM

Though unaware at the time in the early 1980s, I witnessed a company begin down a technical road which would end in diversity requiring large amounts of resources to solve the problem. After working with network integration for some time now, maintaining close friends at this company, and being aware of their decisions regarding technology over the past decade, I understand some of what happened.

To maintain confidentiality, I will refer to the company as XYZ. I had (and still have) many friends at XYZ. In the early 1980s their computing needs were met by SNA based equipment. They had an SNA based data center dedicated to meeting day-to-day computing needs, and as in most real world situations they experienced technical glitches resulting in downtime. XYZ was not small then, and now it is much larger. It occupied a multistory building in the downtown district of a large city. During the 1980s it acquired other entities throughout the state where it conducts business.

XYZ comes to mind because it depicts the focal point of this chapter; that is integrating local TCP/IP LANs into SNA. One day in the early 1980s I visited XYZ department T (named T here to maintain its anonymity) and witnessed the beginning of a technical revolution that over time would change the company. While visiting, I noticed boxes being unpacked and equipment being removed, and in short order a PC was set up. I remember wondering why they had bought a PC anyway. I remember thinking to myself, "What are they going to do with this thing?"

Weeks later I visited department T again. The PC was in place, and I saw a person gazing at the display and attempting to read some kind of instruction manual. I remember mentally dismissing the PC as something that XYZ bought which did not seem to have any importance (at least on the surface) at the time.

Sometime later I visited department T again. The PC was still there, and this time the printer was printing. I continued down the hall to the person I came to see. I asked, "Why does this department have a PC?" As memory serves, the answer was something like,

"Well, so-and-so decided to get a PC so we (department T) could complete our daily reports without having to rely on the computer people (data center) upstairs." The person continued, "We cannot afford not to complete our daily reports, and we cannot be tied to another department for our survival. Mr. so-and-so had an idea to get a PC, do our own reports, and print them ourselves." It made sense to me; I went about my business.

Now, I am some decade removed from that encounter at XYZ, and looking back I can see the impact one PC had on the XYZ company. I think it was the beginning of the technical revolution that company experienced over the past decade. It was the first PC XYZ had purchased, but now XYZ has PCs everywhere. They are on every floor and in almost every office. Ironically, they still have the data center with a significant amount of mission critical data in their SNA environment. The acquisition of the PC was unplanned from a formal company perspective. It seems this one purchase fueled a technological revolution in that company, and over time their environment became so diverse that they have PCs, an SNA environment, and multiple TCP/IP LANs.

An individual at XYZ realized the benefits of a PC and printer to solve one department's problems encountered by relying upon another department. Shortly, that same idea spread throughout other departments. From a company perspective, XYZ did not take into consideration the technical revolution occurring in the marketplace and attempt to parallel their computing environment with it, rather they allowed a response imposed upon themselves. XYZ had no departmental computing continuity and diversity planned into their environment and, consequently, they realized an unraveling so to speak of the corporate data center. They were in a paradox: on the one hand most departments needed daily access to the SNA based host, but on the other hand each department needed independence and flexibility to perform operations on an as-needed basis. In retrospect, the technical revolution happened and XYZ got caught offguard.

Only recently (within the past year or so) did XYZ examine their computing environment as a whole. When they did, they realized the only computing continuity existing was the lack of continuity. They realized data, critical to most departments, existed in the SNA data center and at the same time each department was accumulating large amounts of data which was becoming more important company wide.

XYZ is not alone. This response to computing needs in the marketplace has been the norm for years. As with most technology, where there is growth without a plan there is an inevitable price to be paid. In this case solving XYZ's problem will require money, additional equipment, retraining personnel, and time. Shortcuts to fix problems like XYZ's do not exist as far as I know.

9.3 SOLUTION A TO THE PROBLEM

Using XYZ's problems we will explore how these problems can be solved. XYZ has an SNA host used by practically every department. They have 3270 type equipment in most departments requiring SNA host access. Most departments have now migrated to TCP/IP LANs. These LAN hosts include DOS, UNIX, and OS/2 operating systems. This approach provides users access to the SNA host, and they have interdepartmental computing abilities provided by the LANs. Consider figure 9.1 depicting XYZ's data center and multiple departmental LANs.

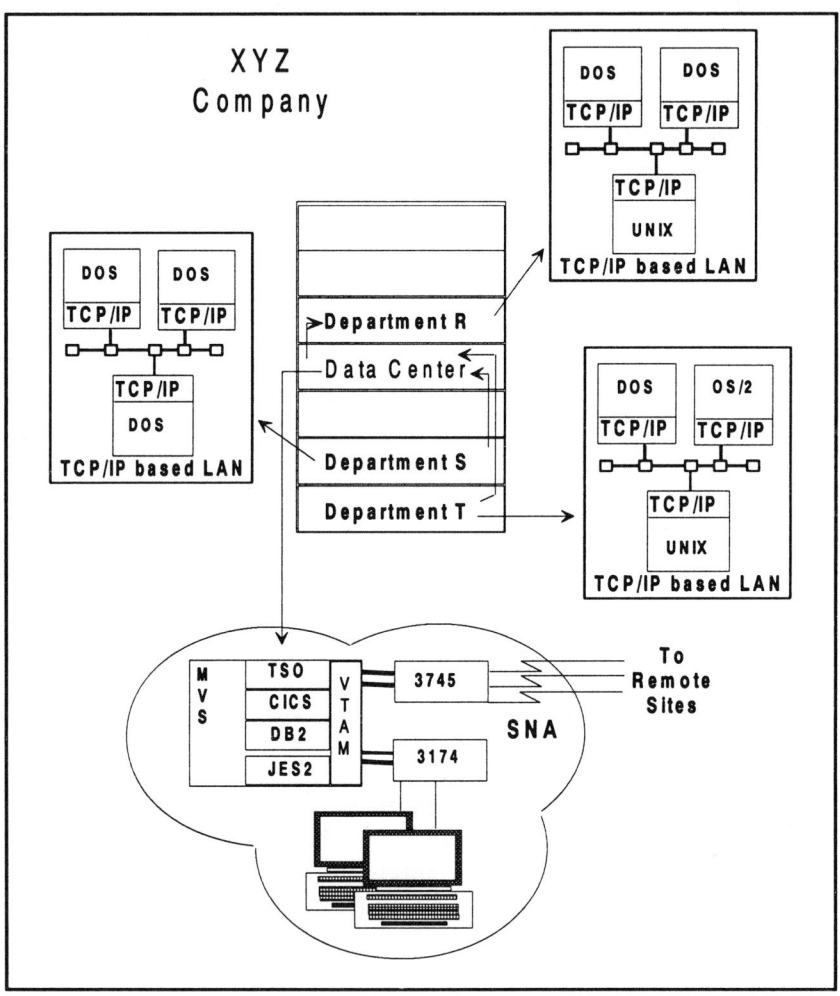

Figure 9.1

Figure 9.1 shows two distinct computing worlds. TCP/IP networks and a large SNA environment. Everything is physically under one roof, and the goal is to maximize all resources and minimize expenditure. The question is how to integrate different environments and leverage all resources.

Assume the goals are interoperability between all TCP/IP LANs, meaning users on different LANs need interoperability with other users in different departments on an as-needed basis. All departmental LAN users need logon, file transfer, and EMAIL capability with the SNA host, but the amount of interaction from departmental LANs with the SNA host varies. All departmental LANs want to remain independent, capable of sustaining operation should problems occur on another LAN or the SNA host.

Figure 9.2 depicts a solution to meet the aforementioned needs.

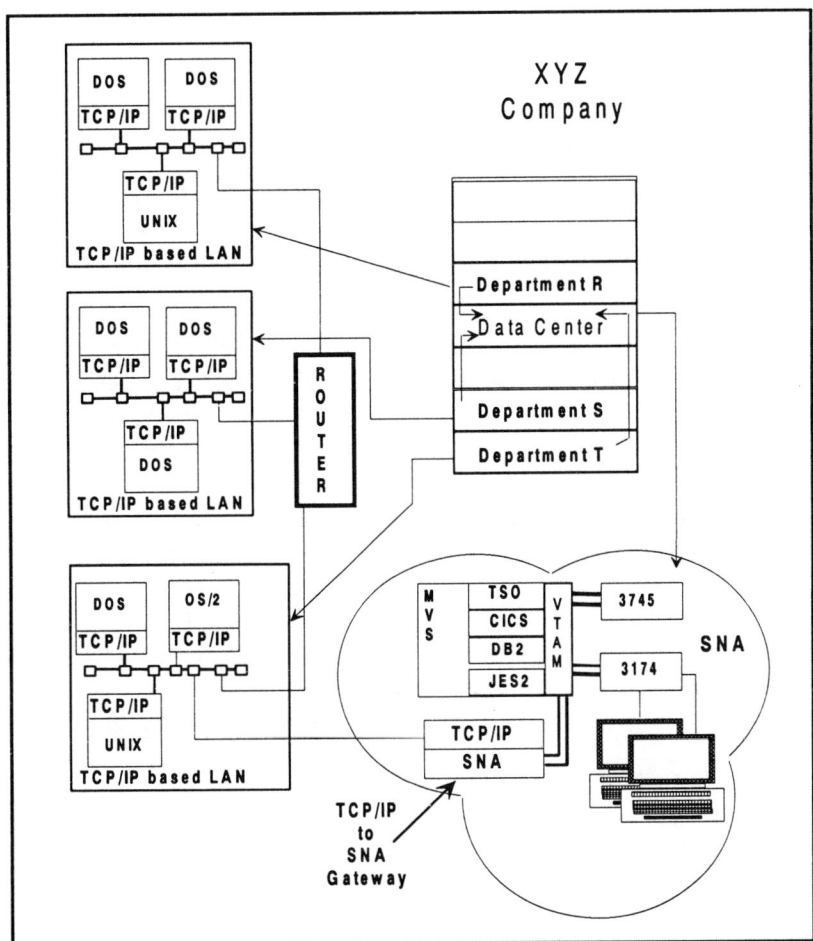

Figure 9.2

Figure 9.2 shows departmental LANs connected to a router. This achieves interoperability between departmental LANs. Notice a TCP/IP to SNA gateway is connected to department T's LAN and to the SNA host. This provides connectivity between not only department T's LAN, but also department S and R's LAN because they can access the SNA via the router connecting the LANs.

The vendor supplying the router and gateway determines what software services are provided with the router and gateway, respectively. This example of a solution provides the greatest flexibility with nominal expenditure. Actual details of what software pieces are needed for this solution are contingent upon user needs and the vendor; consequently, it is difficult to be precise and define specifics for solving connectivity problems in this case.

9.4 SOLUTION B TO THE PROBLEM

The previous approach solving integration and interoperability issues is one example. Others exist.

Since the LANs are in the same physical environment with the SNA host, a different solution is equally viable. This solution includes adding a 3172 interconnect controller model 003 and TCP/IP in an offload feature to the existing SNA host. Figure 9.3 reflects this arrangement.

This solution provides routing between departmental LANs via the 3172 interconnect controller. In addition, it provides necessary TCP/IP to SNA protocol conversion, thus permitting SNA host access for all TCP/IP based users. The 3172 offload feature functions so that no protocol conversion is performed on the SNA host. In summary, one piece of hardware is added to this solution, whereas in figure 9.2 a router and a gateway is required. The author is not attempting to endorse one solution or the other, merely pointing out the differences of the available solutions to achieved desired goals.

Integrating Local TCP/IP LANs into SNA

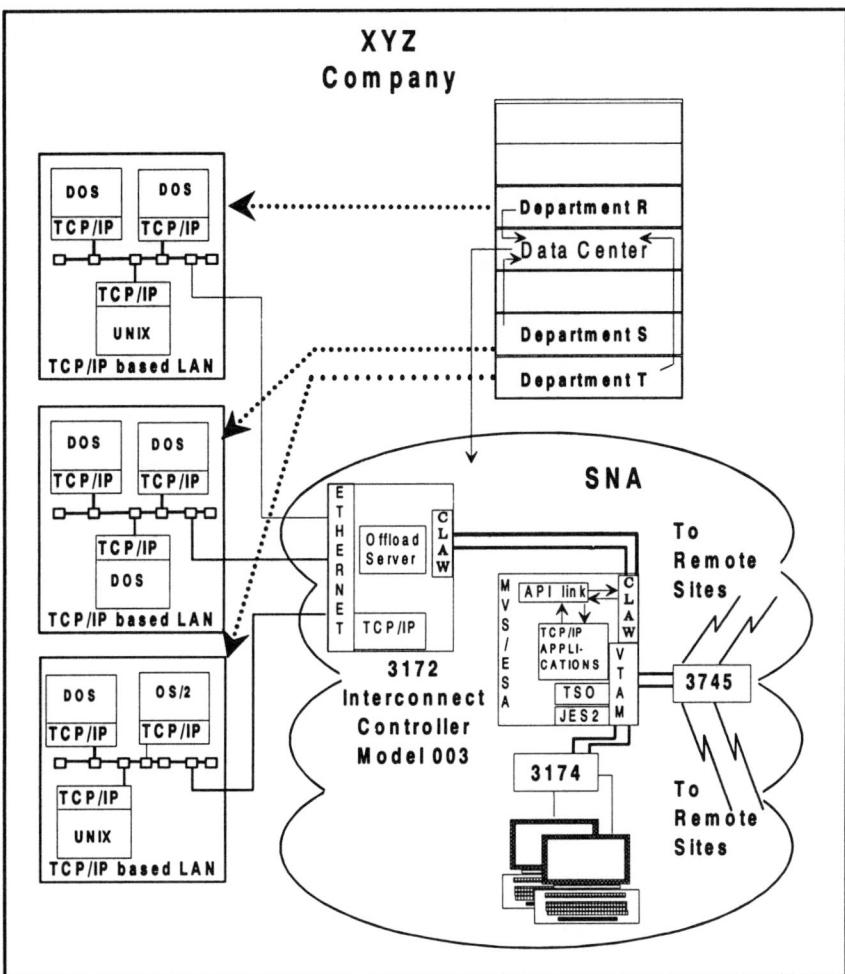

Figure 9.3

9.5 CONCLUSION

Solving TCP/IP and SNA integration problems are different when all equipment to be integrated is located in the same physical facility. More options are available. In this chapter two options were presented. Further clarification of a particular site would dictate which solution would be best. Solving problems like the scenario presented in this chapter can be accomplished. Usually, best results culminate from clearly defining expectations prior to the integration process.

CHAPTER 10
How to Achieve Integration

This chapter explores how TCP/IP and SNA integration is achieved. It begins in section 10.1 by exploring what integration is in greater depth. Section 10.2 examines network devices in greater detail. First, network layers are examined in light of where network devices operate. Media type is also discussed. Gateways, routers, bridges, and repeaters are discussed from a point of functionality. A brief listing of vendors providing these devices is provided. Section 10.3 presents viable methods of integration. Section 10.4 discusses TCP/IP integration on an SNA (particularly MVS) based host. A brief list of hardware and software requirements is presented. Customization is discussed and a user perspective is presented. An option with TCP/IP in SNA (SNALINK) is presented. Section 10.5 explains the TCP/IP offload feature. Section 10.6 explores integration via workstation gateway software. Data link protocol support is discussed along with information provided by vendors supplying this type solution. Section 10.7 examines integration via hardware gateway. Different vendors have provided information reflecting offerings they have with these network devices.

10.1 WHAT IS INTEGRATION ANYWAY?

Genuine TCP/IP integration into SNA means interoperability between the two or more disparate network protocols, and if integrated properly, the appearance of seamless operation between them exists. If achieved, it means having the best of both worlds! Integrating TCP/IP into SNA requires upper layer protocol conversion, at a minimum. At a maximum, it means all layers from a TCP/IP host (or network) must be converted into SNA. In addition to protocol conversion, data translation must be performed. The location of protocol conversion and/or data translation is always the pivotal question.

Protocol problems are inherent when TCP/IP is integrated into SNA because they were not originally designed to interoperate. Resolving these protocol discrepancies and data translation problems means true integration. Depending upon who is asking, integration means different things; and despite the answer, a network device is typically mentioned as part of the solution equation for integration.

Chapter 10

Additionally, routers and or bridges may play an integral role in TCP/IP to SNA integration depending upon the site and its requirements. If so, a variety of network devices may be required to achieve TCP/IP to SNA integration.

10.2 INTEGRATION AND NETWORK DEVICES

If ambiguity exists, it is typified in the meaning of network devices. Network devices were previously discussed and include: gateways, routers, bridges, and repeaters. For clarification, they are explored in greater depth here. Figure 10.1 depicts network devices correlated to the network layers in which they operate.

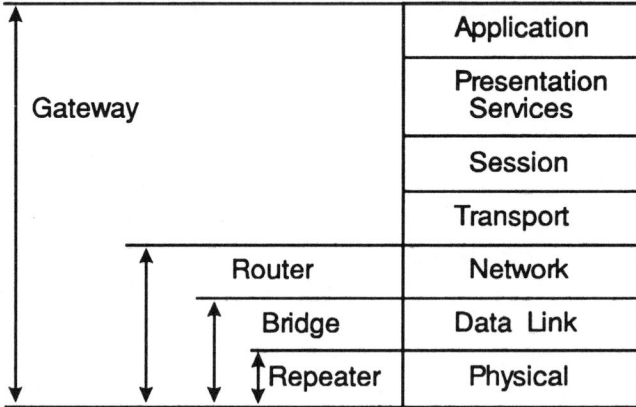

Figure 10.1

Notice in figure 10.1 the repeater works at the physical layer. A bridge works at the data link layer, but it also operates at the physical layer. A router operates at the network layer, but it works at the data link and physical layer as well. Notice the gateway operates at all layers in a network. Figure 10.1 represents the layers as the OSI model represents them; however, eight layers actually exist in any network. Consider figure 10.2.

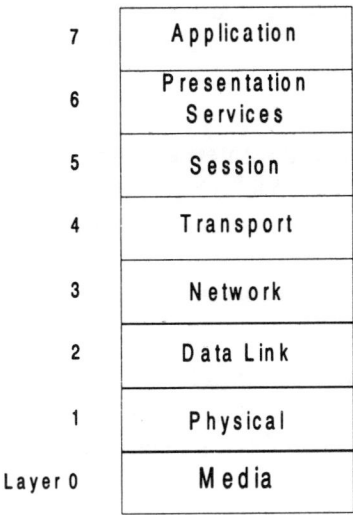

Figure 10.2

Layer zero (0) is the media. Though not defined by most network models, it exists. This layer is the medium that carries the data from one point to another. Media can be divided into two categories, and in these categories are the following media types:

- Hard Media
    - cable
    - Copper stranded cable
    - Fiber optic cable
- Soft Media
    - Microwave
    - Satellite
    - Radio Frequency (RF)

One or more of these media types will be present connecting networks or hosts together. Some network protocols specify a particular media, and some do not. The media layer is normally left out of the network model, but it does exist and should not be confused with the physical layer. The physical layer is actually the interface between the media and a device.

Chapter 10

Closer examination of network devices clarifies their function(s) and provides a foundation for understanding specific vendor devices.

Gateways

The term gateway has its roots in the Internet community dating back to the '70s. Then the Internet (commonly known as ARPANET) consisted of networks dispersed around the country. These networks were connected together thus forming a large *virtual network*. Devices connecting these physically separated networks were called gateways. If we were to define gateway functions of that time based upon today's definitions of network devices, it would be called a router.

However, many everyday terms were used to describe a function or thing in the computer community even though a new technical vocabulary was already in the making. The term gateway was coined identifying devices connecting networks to other networks, typically in different locations.

Consider the definition of gateway in the third edition of the *American Heritage Dictionary*. It defines a gateway as: "An opening or a structure framing an opening, such as an arch, that may be closed by a gate. Something that serves as an entrance or a means of access." The latter explains precisely what a gateway does as a networking device. However there is a consideration in order; that is, time.

In the '70s few, if any, individuals were thinking of integrating TCP/IP into SNA, if for no other reason than SNA was not introduced until 1974, and TCP/IP did not begin market momentum until the late '70s, and did not have widespread momentum until 1983 via the DOD endorsement. So, the idea of integration (as accepted today) was practically nonexistent in the 1970s. During that time delineation of network devices did not exist as it does today. For example, today network devices include: gateways, servers (communication, terminal, file, print, etc.) brouters, routers, bridges, repeaters, and other devices. In the '70s these devices may have existed in some form but did not have marketplace acceptance as today. Evolution of the technical vocabulary has imposed a plethora of terms still being digested by users and specialists alike.

Terms seem to connote different meanings in the technological arena, normally proceeding from a general to a particular meaning. For example, years ago a gateway was considered an entryway, used to refer to a device connecting networks in different locations. Today, it has evolved to a more specialized meaning; that is, performing protocol conversion from one type network to another.

IBM has eight gateway related terms in their *Dictionary of Computing* (SC20-1699-8). This dictionary has seven defined meanings under the term *gateway*. IBM defines a gateway as: "A functional unit that interconnects two computer networks with different network architectures. A gateway connects networks or systems of different architectures. A bridge interconnects networks or systems with the same or similar architectures." Because IBM created SNA and SNA's evolution, the term *gateway* has had a special meaning within SNA. But, according to IBM's latest version of their dictionary, they acknowledge its meaning outside of the context of SNA.

Because of the constant technological flux, agreement is lacking on the meaning of terms, thus ambiguity results. This is part of the reason obfuscation shrouds the networking community today. Users and specialists alike are mystified more by the terminology than by the technology itself.

A number of companies make gateways in some form or another. For example, gateway offerings may be hardware, software, or a combination of both. Some companies providing TCP/IP to SNA (or vice versa) gateways include: 3COM Corporation, OpenConnect Systems Inc., Harris Adacom Networking Services, Inc., McDATA, and Brixton Systems, to name a few. This is a cross section of vendors providing gateways; others exists, and a brief list is included in the appendices.

An example of how a gateway connects an ETHERNET based TCP/IP LAN to an SNA environment would appear as figure 10.3. Three examples are shown here depicting the different lower level protocols accommodated by the SNA environment.

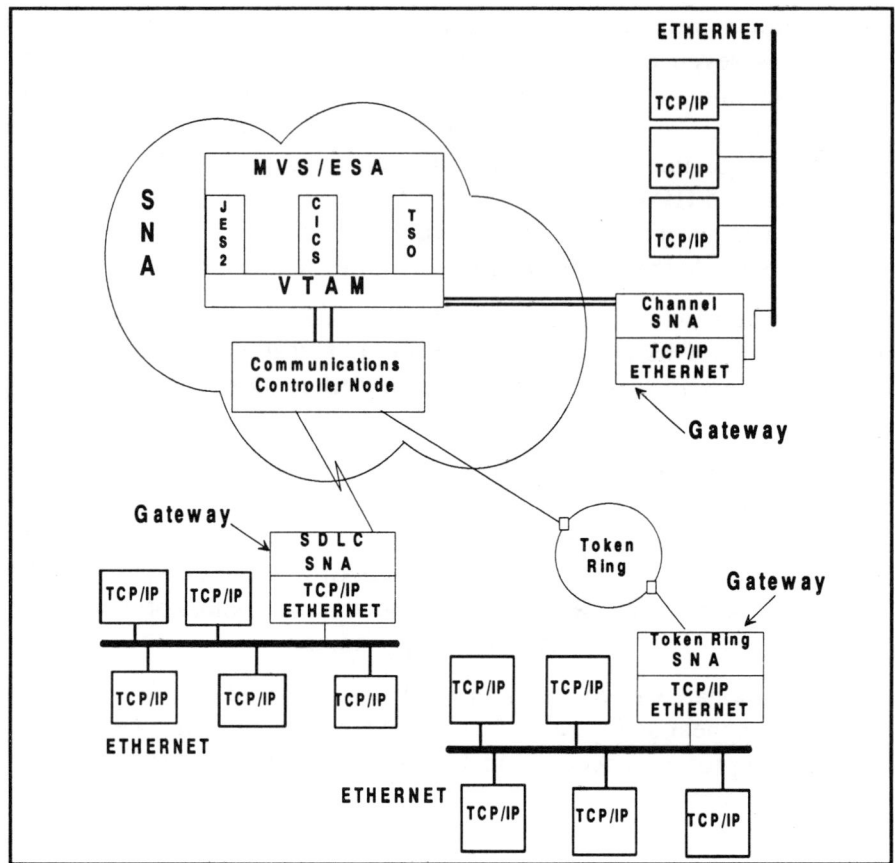

Figure 10.3

Figure 10.3 gateway implementations include: Channel, SDLC, and Token Ring. Different vendors offer varying gateway solutions. For example, some gateway vendors specialize in channel, SDLC, or token ring, while others offer FDDI, or X.25 support. It is a vendor specific issue.

Routers

Some consider TCP/IP and SNA integration a matter totally solved by routers. It is not. Routers are, in many cases, part of the integration equation; but at this point in time they (generally) do not resolve upper layer protocol conflicts. As figure 10.1 has shown, routers operate at the network layer. They also operate at the data link and physical layer by default, but their emphasis is at the network layer. Routers merely route what has been passed to them; they do not convert data in the sense of upper layer protocol conversion.

How to Achieve Integration

Routers are an integral part of integration in many cases, but once data is routed, it is of no use if its associated upper layer protocols are incompatible with the destination point.

A number of companies offer routers, some include: Cisco Systems, Wellfleet, Interlink, Vitalink Communications Corporation, Synoptics Communications Inc., RETIX, IBM Corporation, Eicon Technology, Fibronics International Inc., and many others. Other vendors may offer routers as well; and a good source of vendor products can be found in the LAN Times Buyers Guide, a supplement to subscribers to LAN Magazine. Figure 10.4 shows a basic implementation, containing three routers; one in Dallas, San Francisco, and Chicago.

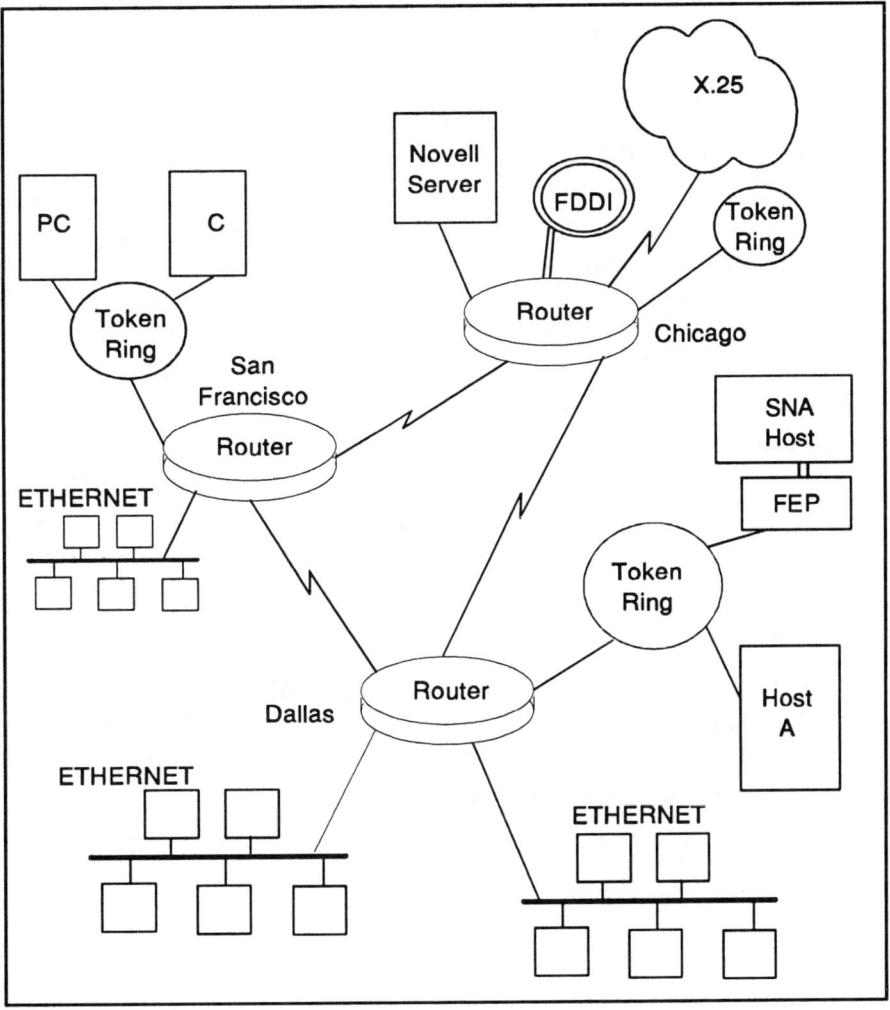

Figure 10.4

Figure 10.4 depicts the ability to route data from one type LAN or host, in one location, to another type LAN or host, in another location.

The act of routing, whether one or multiple protocols, means getting data from a source to a target destination. When routing is performed and a protocol is encapsulated, then passed through a network of unlike protocol, this is called tunneling. This has nothing to do with protocol conversion and/or data translation.

Different types of routers exists. In their most basic form, routers determine which path to route data throughout multiple networks. Different algorithms exist providing different ways to perform routing. Some of these and their basic functions include:

- EGP—Exterior Gateway Protocol. This is an Internet protocol used to exchange routing information *between* autonomous networks.
- IGP—Interior Gateway Protocol. This is an Internet protocol used to exchange routing information *within* autonomous networks.
- IGRP—Interior Gateway Routing Protocol. This protocol was developed by Cisco systems. It was designed to address problems associated with large, heterogeneous networks. The name is somewhat of a misnomer; the term gateway should be router, because this is the function of IGRP. Cisco has a family of routers to meet various needs in the emerging heterogeneous networks today.
- GGP—Gateway-to-Gateway Protocol. This is a MILNET network protocol used to specify how gateways (should be named routers) exchange routing information and how they can be reached.
- OSPF—Open Shortest Path First. This is a proposed successor to RIP. Its features include determining the least costly method of routing, multipath routing, and load balancing.

The previously mentioned routing algorithms are different mechanisms used to achieve routing. Different vendors support different methods.

Devices supporting multiprotocol routing exist today. IBM introduced its 6611 network processor in 1992. According to the IBM manual, *The IBM 6611 Network Processor*, September 1992, IBM part number GG24-3870, it supports multiprotocol routing for network layer protocols used by the following protocol suites:

- TCP/IP
- NetWare
- XNS
- DECnet Phase IV
- Apple Talk Phase 2 (Some restriction apply on the initial offering.)

Specific network layer protocol names and their correlating protocol suites include:

- IP. Internet Protocol. Part of TCP/IP.
- IPX. Internet Packet Exchange. Part of NetWare.
- IDP. Internetworking Datagram Protocol. Part of XNS.
- DDP. Datagram Delivery Protocol. Part of Apple Talk.
- CLNP. Connectionless Network Protocol. Part of OSI.

SNA and DECnet have similar network layer protocols, but not a naming convention as the aforementioned.

Bridges

Bridges can serve a purpose in the integration equation, but from a protocol perspective, they operate with lower level protocols. Basically, two types of bridges exist: those which connect networks of like lower level protocols, and those which connect networks of unlike lower level protocols. Bridges can achieve a certain degree of integration by resolving lower level protocol conflicts. It is faulty to think bridges can convert TCP/IP into SNA and vice versa, because these are upper layer protocols. Bridges can perform routing functions to a certain degree, but their forte is connecting like or unlike lower layer network protocols. Figure 10.5 shows a bridge between two ETHERNETs and a bridge between a Token Ring and ETHERNET LAN.

Chapter 10

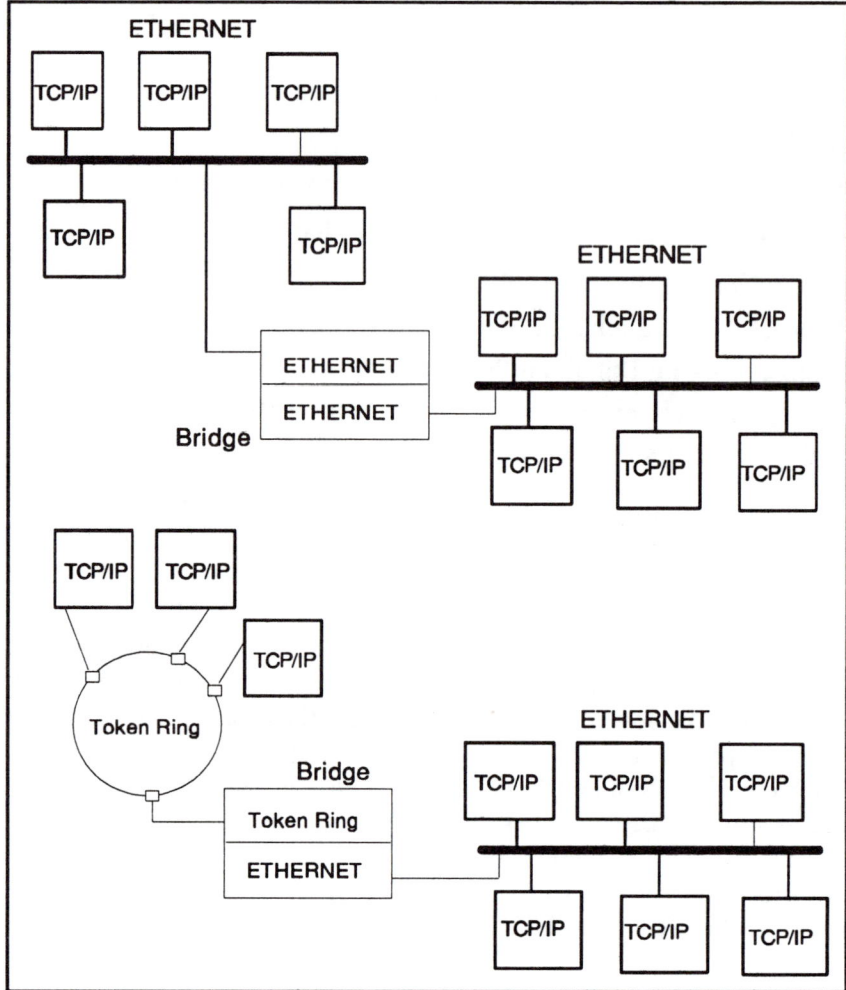

Figure 10.5

Repeaters

Repeaters can factor into the integration equation also, but repeaters boost either electronic or photonic signals. They are used to extend the distance of a network. They operate at OSI layer one.

10.3 VIABLE METHODS FOR INTEGRATION

Four identifiable solutions exist to achieve integration of TCP/IP into SNA. These solutions indicate *where* upper layer protocol conversion and/or data translation occur:

- On an SNA host
- On an Offload feature with a 3172 interconnect controller model 003
- On a TCP/IP host (a workstation with gateway software)
- On a hardware gateway between a TCP/IP and SNA network

10.4 INTEGRATION BY SNA HOST

IBM introduced TCP/IP for SNA hosts in the mid to late '80s. Since then IBM has refined, and continues to refine, TCP/IP for MVS, VM, and other operating systems. This section uses MVS as an example for discussing TCP/IP and SNA integration. This section does not attempt to take the place of IBM manuals that explain how to load, customize, and use TCP/IP on an MVS host. It does, however, explain how TCP/IP appears when implemented on an MVS host and clarifies common misconceptions regarding TCP/IP on an SNA host. It also points out customization considerations and includes an explanation of a specific function IBM offers with TCP/IP in SNA called SNALINK. Operational aspects from a user perspective are also presented. The thrust behind this section highlights how TCP/IP is integrated into SNA, specifically on a MVS host. This section does not attempt to recreate the wheel and explain step-by-step details of how to integrate TCP/IP into MVS.

Considerations of TCP/IP on an MVS Host

When TCP/IP is loaded onto an MVS host it is defined as a VTAM application using LU0 sessions. Figure 10.6 depicts how this appears.

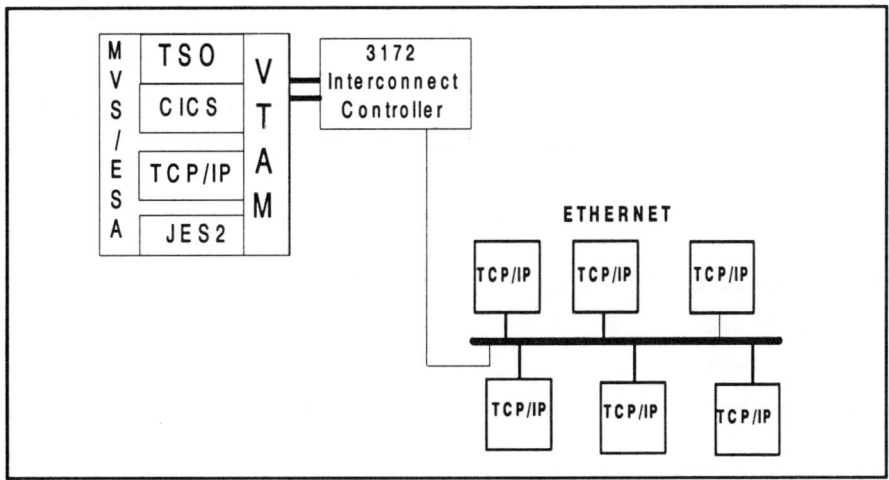

Figure 10.6

Because TCP/IP operates on the MVS host, data translation (ASCII-to-EBCDIC and vice versa) and TCP to SNA protocol conversion take place on the MVS host. IBM designed it to function in this manner when loaded and used on MVS hosts. IBM has effectively implemented TCP/IP as closly as possible as it appears and operates in its native environment; that is ASCII based, asynchronous, character oriented. Just because it appears to function as in a non-SNA environment does not remove differences between TCP/IP and SNA that must be resolved from a technical standpoint and understood from a user standpoint.

When TCP/IP is installed and running on an MVS host, it still has fundamental characteristics inherent in its architecture. TCP/IP protocols are still different than SNA. For example, the TCP header is still in stark contrast to its SNA equivalent at that layer. TCP/IP still utilizes a 32-bit addressing scheme at the IP layer. This does not fit into any native SNA addressing scheme. It is still a client/server architecture at the application layer, whereas SNA applications are predominantly menu (panel) oriented. Just because TCP/IP is loaded and operates on an MVS host does not mean the fundamental differences between TCP/IP and SNA have disappeared. The correct conclusion is: these differences are resolved on the MVS host.

Hardware and Software Requirements

IBM has defined and explained hardware and software requirements to install and operate TCP/IP on an MVS host in the manual: *Transmission Control Protocol/Internet Protocol TCP/IP Version 2 Release 2.1 for MVS: Planning and Customization*, IBM order # SC31-6085. In this manual, chapter 2 explains hardware and software requirements in detail. The author recommends acquiring a copy of this manual during the discussion/decision making phase, before deciding how to integrate TCP/IP into SNA. Doing homework is still prudent, even if not in school.

For insight here, some hardware and software requirements to install TCP/IP on an MVS host are listed below. This list is not exhaustive, but it provides enough information for enlightenment of some requirements.

Hardware Requirements:

- 500 MB of direct access storage to hold the libraries and data:
  - base = 165 MB
  - source = 335 MB
- 200 KB of main storage to be permanently used while TCP/IP Version 2 for MVS is running. (The amount of storage required by TCP/IP V2R2.1 for MVS is dependent on the TCP/IP configuration options.)
- Sufficient paging space to hold at least 10 MB of virtual storage

- A tape/cartridge drive for installing IBM TCP/IP V2R2.1 for MVS
- An S/370 channel for attachment of one or more of the following:
  - 8232 LAN Channel Station
  - 3172 Interconnect Controller (model 001, 002, or 003)
  - The family of IBM 37XX Communication Controllers for X.25 support and SNA backbone support or IBM 3745 ETHERNET LAN adaptor
  - High Performance Parallel Interface (HIPPI)
  - NSC IBM channel adapter for NSC HYPERchannel
  - A network attachment device
  - One or more terminals using IBM 3270 protocols for maintenance functions

Software Requirements:

The following list does not include all necessary requirements to install and operate TCP/IP under MVS. Consult the previously mentioned IBM manual for complete details. Specific requirements vary depending upon the TCP/IP options selected.

- IBM VS Pascal Runtime Library
- TSO/E Release 1.3 or later
- VTAM Version 3.3 or later for MVS/XA and MVS/ESA
- DB2 V2R2
- NetView V1R3 for MVS or later
- GDDM/MVS V2R2 or later
- RACF (5740-XXH) or equivalent
- CICS V2.1 or later

This information is a partial excerpt from the following IBM manual: *Transmission Control Protocol/Internet Protocol TCP/IP Version 2 Release 2.1 for MVS: Planning and Customization*, IBM order # SC31-6085.

Customization Considerations

Some procedures involved in customizing TCP/IP under MVS include defining TCP/IP as a VTAM application to VTAM. Once installed, and defined to VTAM, the MVS system requires a re-IPL, specifying the Common Link Pack Area (CLPA). Also, customizing appropriate TCP/IP supplied data sets to reflect specific site requirements and copying them as the default data set requires predefining site requirements.

During TCP/IP installation under MVS, data sets are created. The names of these data sets and a brief description include:

Data Set	Description
tcpip.hosts.local	A sample internet name table
tcpip.sezainst	Installation related members
tcpip.standard.tcpxlbin	Translate table
tcpip.telnetse.tcpxlbin	Translate table
tcpip.telnet.tcpxlbin	Translate table
tcpip.etc.services	Well-known port numbers

Customization includes configuring a TCP/IP address space. This means updating the TCP/IP procedure tcpip.sezainst (TCPIPROC) and specifying configuration statements in the tcpip.profile.tcpip data set. Site requirements dictate required modifications. DEVICE and LINK statements are required because devices are not automatically initialized, and a network interface link is not automatically associated with a device. Precise server functions (such as TELNET, FTP, or SMTP Server) are normally controlled as tasks that must be started and stopped appropriately; this is done during the customization of TCP/IP. These server tasks operate in a TCP/IP address space. Customization also includes physical and data link level definitions to the I/O subsystem (if applicable), VTAM, and/or NCP. Specific definition statements are required, and most are driven by site requirements. For example, a GATEWAY statement is required to route datagrams to a specified network or host. A TRANSLATE statement is needed to define the relationship between an internet address and the correlating network address (reflecting the link name) on a specific link.

Depending upon what TCP/IP applications/services are desired dictates customization to some degree. The importance of appropriate IBM manuals cannot be overstated. Anyone anticipating purchase, or even debating the purchase of TCP/IP under MVS, should acquire the appropriate manual.

User Perspective

From a user perspective, TCP/IP client commands are used to invoke specific applications and are user initiated. Thus, if MVS users are not familiar with TCP/IP or how it operates within an SNA environment, then some training and/or familiarization is in order. Users need to understand what common TCP/IP applications provide, how to invoke these applications, and how to interact with target hosts, since odds are these hosts will not be SNA (or MVS) based. Users will need time to get acclimated to TCP/IP application operation, messages, and file structures in other systems they may interact with.

Normally, users have TELNET, FTP, and SMTP applications available for use. Users who program may have the API programming support. This support is a TCP/IP Socket Interface for CICS. This CICS Socket interface is a front-end program (API). It serves a special purpose making programmatic interaction possible between TCP/IP and CICS. Programmers use this socket interface as the vehicle to exchange data between CICS and TCP/IP based hosts.

Users may also have access to SNMP. It is supported under MVS via NetView. This part of the TCP/IP offering provides network management operators with the capability to monitor TCP/IP based nodes and permits NetView to be the focal point in a heterogeneous environment.

Users may also have access to the X windowing system. X is a protocol, part of the TCP/IP protocol suite and supported under MVS. It supports the Graphical Data Display Manager (GDDM) interface and permits GDDM displays on workstations supporting the X window system. From a user perspective, the windowing environment has the OSF Motif look and feel interface to it.

Another aspect a user will encounter is keyboard mapping issues if the TCP/IP product is used to communicate with TCP/IP hosts outside the SNA environment. This includes two considerations for users: First, understanding the difference in block and character mode operation. And, second, understanding keyboard mapping from a 3270 terminal to an ASCII terminal. Additionally, if a user interacts with a TCP/IP host and transfers files to or from that host, then file structures on the target host need to be understood.

A Perspective on SNALINK

IBM has a program called SNALINK that permits TCP/IP on one SNA host to connect to TCP/IP loaded onto another SNA host, thus achieving IP routing (tunneling) through an SNA environment. Consider figure 10.7.

Chapter 10

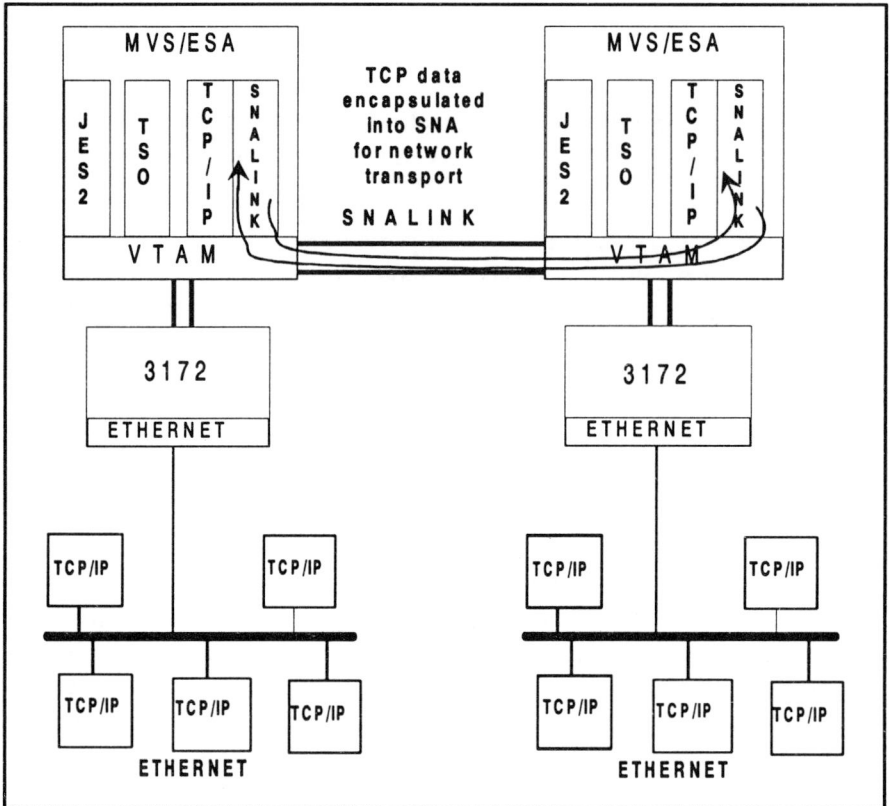

Figure 10.7

SNALINK provides IP datagram routing through an SNA network by encapsulating IP datagrams into SNA and routing them to the target TCP/IP LAN destination.

10.5 TCP/IP OFFLOAD FEATURE

The TCP/IP Offload feature was introduced by IBM in 1992. It involves downloading TCP/IP from an SNA host to a 3172 model 003 Interconnect Controller where upper level protocol conversion is performed. Examine figure 10.8

How to Achieve Integration

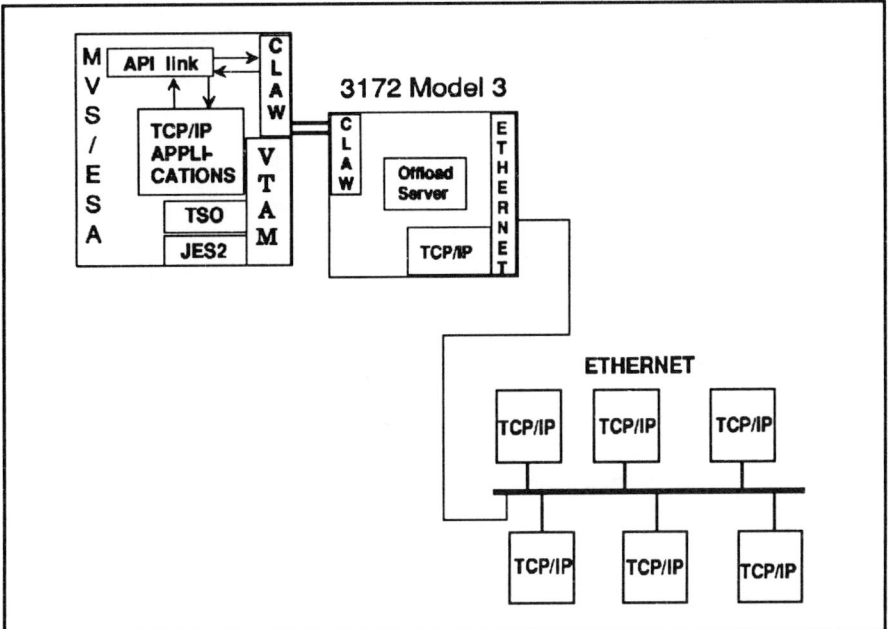

Figure 10.8

Figure 10.8 shows an IBM 3172 Model 003 Interconnect Controller with TCP/IP running in an address space. After processing TCP/IP protocols, the Offload Server program sends the data to an Application Program Interface (API) running in the SNA host via the Common Link Access to Workstation (CLAW) driver.

CLAW is used to maximize subchannel bandwidth, keeping the subchannels *busy* (available for data transfer of processed TCP/IP data) while data exists to be transferred to the SNA host. By exercising the subchannels in this fashion, any interrupts generated are inhibited; and maximum subchannel utilization is realized. Additionally, applicable TCP/IP routing tables can be downloaded to, and stored in, a 3172 Model 003. This means that routing can occur through the 3172 without impacting CPU processing. With this offload processing utilized by the API and CLAW driver, no protocol processing is performed on an SNA host, only passing data from a TCP/IP application and the CLAW driver.

10.6 INTEGRATION BY WORKSTATION GATEWAY SOFTWARE

Integrating TCP/IP into SNA can be achieved by resolving protocol conversion and/or data translation on a TCP/IP host, such as an RISC/6000, SUN, or DEC workstation. Figure 10.9 depicts this gateway software solution as it is called.

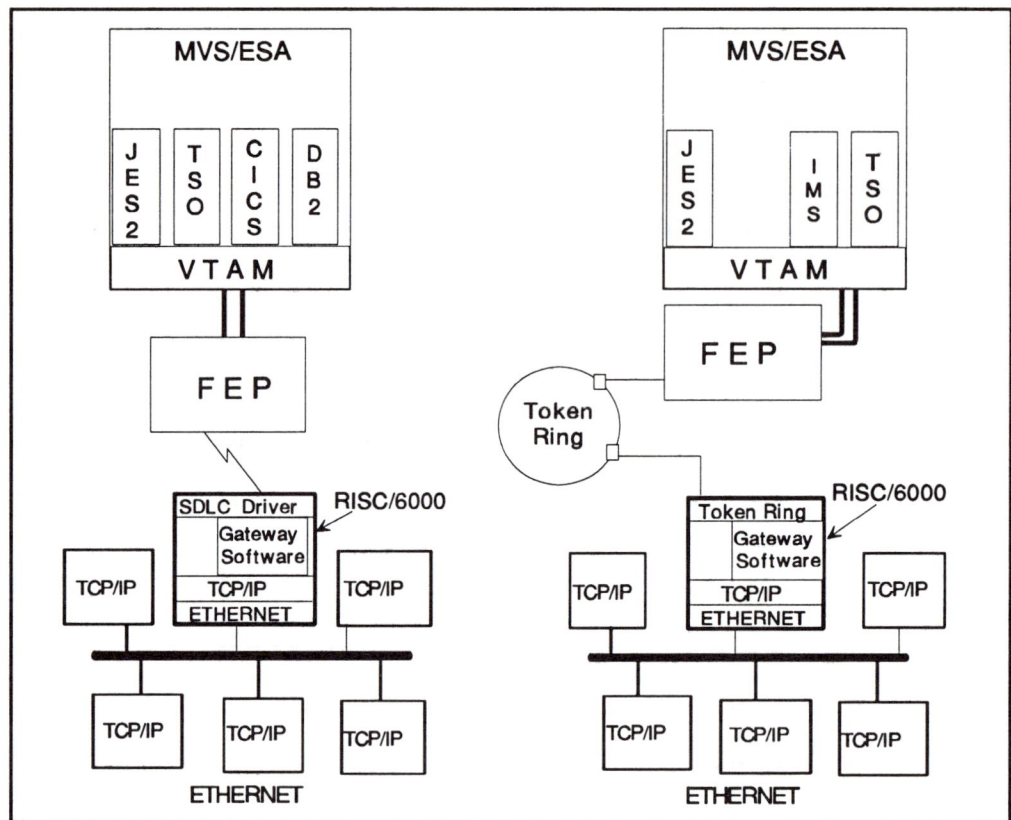

Figure 10.9

Figure 10.9 shows the TCP/IP host converting TCP/IP to SNA and vice versa. The LAN host with gateway software does not have to be dedicated. It can function as any other workstation supporting user applications and other processes. In figure 10.9 the workstation with the gateway software can be dedicated (meaning serving a gateway purpose only) or nondedicated, which is normal (where the gateway function is just another process operating on the workstation).

Figure 10.9 depicts the capability for data link protocol conversion from ETHERNET to SDLC or Token Ring, depending upon the workstation. Data link conversion is a function provided by the vendor, hence it is vendor specific. For example, based upon accessible information, IBM's RISC/6000 supports Synchronous Data Link Control (SDLC) and Token Ring data link protocols as well as ETHERNET; and it is capable of converting these data link protocols. Additionally, based upon information provided to this author, SUN Microsystems has workstations capable of supporting SDLC and ETHERNET data link protocols. But they also have workstations that support other data link protocols as well.

OpenConnect Systems, Inc. provided information stating it has gateway software for workstations such as the RISC/6000, SUN, and others as depicted in figure 10.9. Their information also indicated a hardware gateway product line, supporting channel, SDLC, and token ring protocols.

According to OpenConnect, the software gateway called OCSII was designed to operate on workstations. It operates as any other UNIX process, hence processing impact is nominal; it simply operates as any other UNIX (or AIX) process. It does not require a dedicated workstation to provide gateway functionality, but if desired it can operate on a dedicated workstation and perform gateway functionality for TCP/IP LANs and SNA.

OpenConnect Systems's OCSII product supports a variety of features, and others can be purchased providing additional functionality. Some features available include: 3270 and/or 5250 terminal emulation for TELNET clients on LAN hosts, APPC support for APPC programs on LAN hosts interacting with SNA, TN3270 and TN5250 Server capabilities, 3770 RJE support, and others.

OpenConnect Systems also indicated further product offerings addressing the issue of integrating TCP/IP into SNA. Some included products for SNA based hosts. These offerings are unbundled; this means you purchase only desired products to achieve a specific purpose. Examples they provided were two products: TELNET Client Full Screen and FTP Client. Figure 10.10 depicts OpenConnect's FTP Server software.

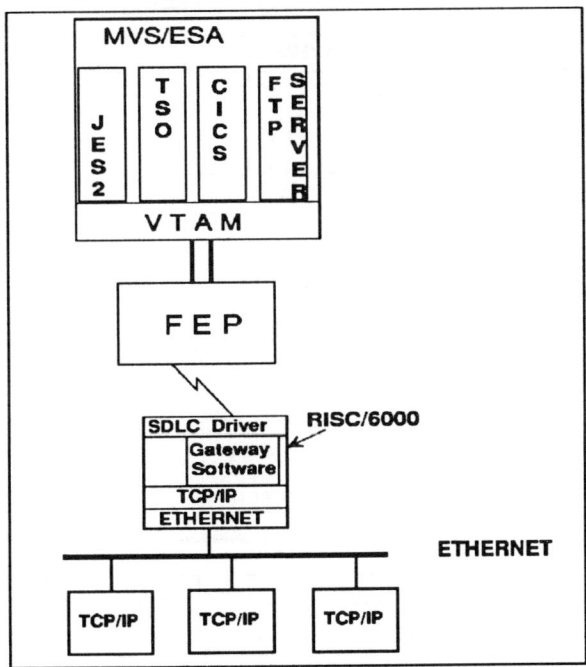

Figure 10.10

Chapter 10

OpenConnect's FTP Server software on the MVS host provides service for requesting FTP clients on TCP/IP hosts. FTP Server, used by FTP clients on LAN hosts, provides bidirectional file transfer capabilities, according to OpenConnect.

Brixton Systems, Inc. provided literature about their software gateway solution for workstations. Their approach to gateway software on a workstation is different architecturally than OpenConnect Systems. One piece of information provided by Brixton explained that SNA users accessing TCP/IP host applications did so by menus; this contrasts with the client/server approach from an application standpoint. Brixton's literature indicated 3270 terminal emulation software as well as 5250 terminal emulation.

Brixton's product line is broad in scope encompassing topics outside the purpose of this book, but frame relay and X.25 support was indicated. Their literature seemed to indicate a variety of software based solutions.

10.7 INTEGRATION BY A HARDWARE GATEWAY

A hardware gateway is normally located on the site of the TCP/IP LAN. Depending upon the vendor, the hardware gateway may provide multiple data link protocol and physical interface support for the LAN. Likewise, depending upon the gateway, it can provide multiple data link protocol support for SNA. Figure 10.11 shows an SDLC hardware gateway.

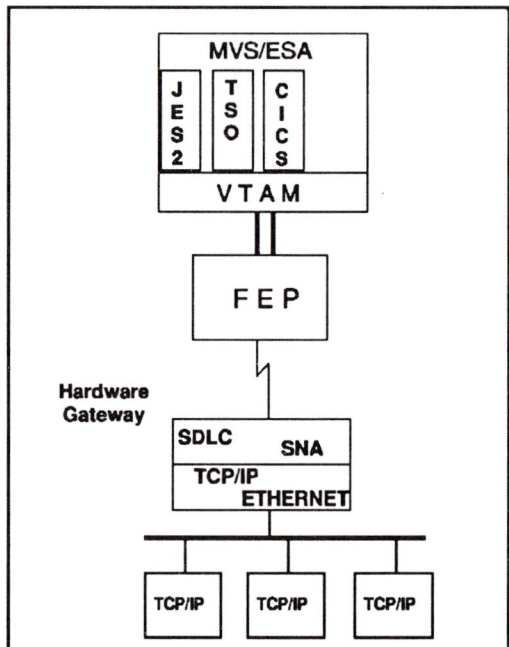

Figure 10.11

Here, the gateway takes an ASCII, asynchronous, TCP/IP data stream from the LAN and translates it into EBCDIC (particularly a 3270 data stream), synchronous, SDLC, and SNA protocol; then sends it to the communication controller node.

Multiple vendors supply gateways such as this. One such vendor is the 3COM Corporation. According to information supplied by them, their hardware gateway, such as figure 10.11 depicts, is capable of providing 3270 terminal emulation on the gateway. 3COM states their product line supports a variety of terminals, TCP/IP and XNS protocols, and other integration services. 3COM's network interface options for the gateway used as an example here supports IEEE 802.3 (and compatible) interfaces, coaxial, or fiber-optic cable.

3COM also provides networking devices such as repeaters, bridges, routers, and terminal servers. 3COM listed other products/services in their literature providing a comprehensive solution to integration from the perspective of network devices.

McDATA Corporation provided literature explaining their product offerings for connectivity solutions between TCP/IP and SNA networks. They too have a TCP/IP to SNA gateway, thus solving interoperability problems between these two environments. McDATA's Link Master 6100 series is similar to the example shown in figure 10.11. But the 6100 series has broader capabilities than shown in figure 10.11.

McDATA Corporation has other products besides those addressing the TCP/IP and SNA integration issue. However, these are not the focus here. They do have multiple ways of solving the TCP/IP to SNA integration issues, and they utilize devices besides gateways to solve integration problems. One product worth noting is the LinkMaster 7100 network controller; it supports multiple language keyboard support. For example, Scandinavian, Eastern European, Western European, United Kingdom, North American, Oriental, and South American language keyboards and code sets are supported.

Harris Adacom Networking Solutions provided literature explaining their product offerings to achieve TCP/IP and SNA integration. They provide multiple hardware gateways supporting SDLC, Channel, and Token Ring protocols. Figure 10.11 would be an example of their SDLC gateway solution. In addition, Harris offers a software gateway solution similar to OpenConnect Systems's OCSII product (based on the information provided). According to their literature, their software gateway operates on most SUN platforms except for IPC/IPX platforms.

Harris also offers software services such as 3270 and 5250 terminal emulation products. Their literature states 3179G (IBM graphic emulation) support as well. Harris has other solutions, one called, "SuperNet Communication System." This goes beyond the scope of the purpose here, but it supports a variety of networking data links and operating environments.

10.8 CONCLUSION

Integration connotes different meanings to different individuals. Essentially, it means true interoperability between different protocols. Many networks employ different types of media, some dictated by lower layer protocols. Network devices include gateways, routers, bridges, and repeaters to name a few. Normally, a combination of these devices are employed to meet integration requirements. A brief list of vendors who provided information about their devices aiding in the integration process was presented when this information contributed to understanding concept(s) being explained. Vendors presented in this section were used as examples; others providing specific network devices exist.

TCP/IP and SNA integration is achieved by loading TCP/IP on an SNA host, offload processing, gateway software on workstations, and hardware gateways.

Sites integrating TCP/IP into SNA should not assume users or systems personnel will quickly adapt to this new environment. TCP/IP and SNA are two distinct network protocols and one could devote a lifetime to mastering either. Integrating the two requires time and understanding of each environment's fundamental characteristics, and it demands patience on behalf of users. Regardless how integration is achieved, they are still two distinct ways of networking.

Some factors to consider when planning integration include:

- A list of expectations for what integrating TCP/IP into SNA will provide
- The amount and size of resources needed to integrate the two environments
- The reasons for integration (remote logon, file transfer, EMAIL, etc.)
- The physical location of networks to be integrated
- An estimation of costs, upper limitation
- The performance expected during maximum utilization after integration
- An adequate understanding of protocols involved
- An understanding of network devices to be used in the integration process
- How and where data translation will be achieved (converting ASCII to EBCDIC and vice versa)
- A realistic expectations of future growth after integration

Achieving integration between TCP/IP and SNA presupposes one knows the requirements that make these two heterogeneous networks interoperate. This dictates understanding what protocol conversion and/or data translation is necessary, being able to identify specific layer functions within a network, and being cognizant of precisely what operations certain network devices perform. In essence, accomplishing true interoperability between TCP/IP and SNA networks is proportional to the ability to grasp different network architectures, discern necessary obstacles that must be overcome, and comprehend the services networking devices propose, then being able to assimilate the components to achieve integration.

CHAPTER 11
Concluding Thoughts on Integration

Integrating TCP/IP into SNA is no trivial task. It requires understanding both environments. It also requires understanding vendor products to the extent of knowing what function(s) a given device perform(s). For example, if a bridge is used in the integration process, then the importance of understanding the bridge abilities and limitations should not be underestimated. Vendors implement different features and functions. Therefore, it is erroneous to conclude that *all* bridges, for example, perform the same functions.

Some vendors agree on functions different networking devices perform, but there is not necessarily a consensus or governing body stating *thou shalt* do this in order for a network device to fit into certain category. Because of the lack of standardization in terminology, many network devices are misnamed based upon their technical function. Consequently, it is more prudent to understand what a network device does than it is to know how it is categorized.

11.1 DISPARITIES

Even when TCP/IP is integrated into SNA, disparities still exist. They are merely compensated for. These two networking protocols are not plug-n-play (at this point in time) from a standpoint of interchangeability. The point here is these protocols were designed with different design intents. The fundamental theme behind TCP/IP was, and is, implementation with multivendor hardware and software. Conversely, SNA was designed for IBM's hardware and software architecture. In effect, SNA was designed to be a *closed* network environment, not having interoperability with multivendor equipment.

Understanding these concepts and the fact that TCP/IP has world-wide acceptance are two fundamental reasons why IBM is changing SNA. The radical evolution that SNA is presently undergoing acknowledges the presence of more than one way of networking. Seven to ten years ago this concept was unheard of in IBM circles. Suffice it to say, IBM's networking blueprint supports traditional SNA, SNA as it is evolving today, and

Chapter 11

embraces TCP/IP, and other upper layer networking protocols. Figure 11.1 clarifies the IBM networking blueprint.

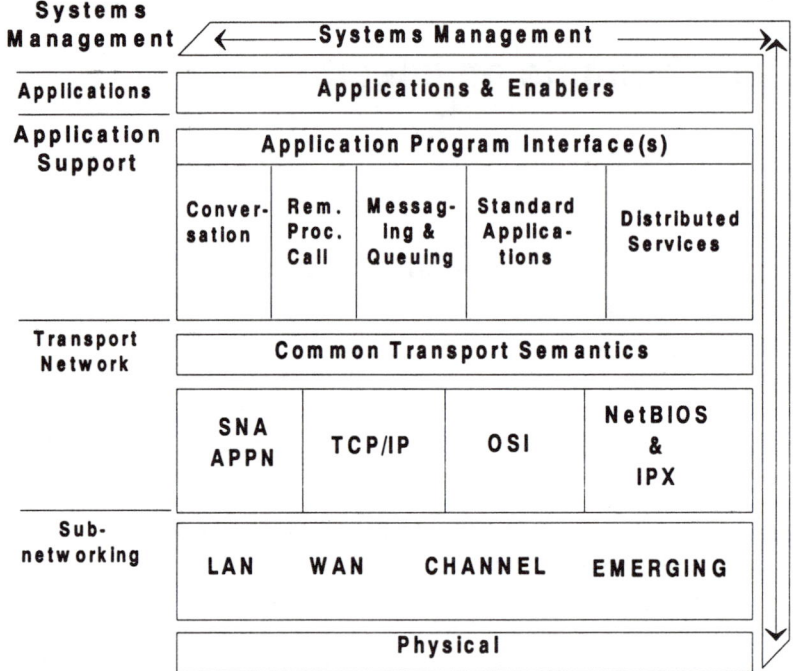

Figure 11.1

11.2 BASIC INTEGRATION REQUIREMENTS

Integrating TCP/IP into SNA can be achieved by a variety of methods. The method of integration is more of a preference than a requirement. The requirement for integration is resolving two fundamental issues: protocol conversion and data translation.

The method used to integrate TCP/IP into SNA dictates what protocol conversion is necessary, and to a certain degree where this must take place. For example, at a minimum TCP/IP protocol must be converted to SNA and vice versa. This is known as upper layer protocol conversion. This type protocol conversion can be performed on an SNA host, or in other places.

Where it is done is optional; that it is done is imperative. Integration cannot occur without upper layer protocol conversion. This is why the term *integration* exists.

Data translation (ASCII-EBCDIC and vice versa) must also occur. It is not optional. Where it occurs is a matter of how the integration process is accomplished. It can occur in a number of places. For example, this may be accomplished on an SNA host, or it can be done on a TCP/IP host. It must be done because of the architectures of the two protocols and the underlying hardware supporting them.

Beyond performing protocol conversion and data translation, other requirements may exist also. For example, connecting multiple remote sites may be necessary. Whether this is a job for a bridge or router will be driven by the need to a degree, but more so by the lower level protocol implemented in the various sites.

Pure integration of TCP/IP into SNA can be achieved by a gateway designed to offer such services. Sometimes integration can be this straightforward, but other times it may not. For total interoperability multiple network devices may be needed.

For example, a remote bridge may be needed to connect physically disconnected LANs. A router may be needed if many LANs exist and communication among all of them is a requirement. A router may be needed in other instances to provide bridge functions and routing capabilities for specific LANs.

Integrating TCP/IP into SNA is not achieved unless these protocols are resolved (converted) and data translation takes place. Beyond this the question becomes one of interoperability between all equipment, possibly in different physical locations.

11.3 BLOCK MODE AND CHARACTER MODE

A topic seldom discussed when integrating TCP/IP into SNA is block mode and character mode operation. Some vendors point out the benefits of integration but not some issues that are a natural consequence of integration.

For example, take the simplest integration scenario. A TCP/IP based LAN is integrated into an SNA environment. Assume protocol conversion and data translation is resolved. What are the implications of such environment?

Let us assume a UNIX and VMS based host is located on the LAN. Now they have access to both MVS and VM based hosts, and vice versa. These UNIX and VMS users have remote logon and file transfer capability between the MVS and VM hosts.

No plausible reason exists to assume UNIX users will know how to navigate the MVS operating system. Likewise, it would be presumptuous to think these users understand MVS file structure. Conversely, MVS users probably have little or no prior exposure to a UNIX or VMS environment. This may seem trivial, but from a production standpoint, it is not. Let us explore this in greater depth.

Chapter 11

Editors in UNIX systems such as Vi and Ez are totally unlike the ISPF editor supported by IBM's TSO. Users who know Vi will have a learning curve for ISPF; and the converse is true. The time involved in the learning curve can only be measured on an individual basis. Natural considerations follow.

Two known facts exist: First, UNIX users logging into MVS will use some type of ASCII to 3270 terminal emulation package. On the other hand, users of the MVS host will use reverse terminal emulation; that is, 3270 to ASCII (with normally some variation of a VT100 keyboard). This is done via a TELNET client on the MVS host.

If we examine an MVS user logging into a LAN based UNIX host, some observations can be made. Once a user logs into the UNIX host, the second hurdle is at hand. The user has to get accustomed to the character oriented nature of TCP/IP based LAN hosts. Character mode operation (the nature of UNIX based hosts) is sometimes difficult for MVS users to understand. This is because MVS users have a different operating environment. MVS users work in block mode operation, which is sometimes difficult for UNIX users to understand. Both sets of users have to make adjustments in their learning when integration is implemented.

Character mode operation is best described by example. Consider a user pressing a key. The output of the key is sent to the processor (application). With SNA based hosts (MVS, VM, and VSE), when an SNA based user presses a key, the output generated does not go anywhere until an Attention Identifier (AID) key is pressed. This is normal because this type environment was architected as such. Now, interject the integration of TCP/IP into SNA and ramifications abound.

If you are new to system integration, this may take some time to grasp. A practical understanding sometimes requires working in the system environment. SNA based users have probably never encountered this. The same is true for TCP/IP LAN based users. Either way the dilemma exists. Consider the following example.

Assume that a TELNET client resides on an MVS host. See figure 11.2. This means any valid MVS user can execute the TELNET client and initiate an outbound session to a UNIX host. Assume a user has done this. The user now will encounter nuances as a result of the architectural difference between the UNIX based host and the MVS host. Specifically, the user will encounter this character mode and block mode phenomenon.

Concluding Thoughts on Integration

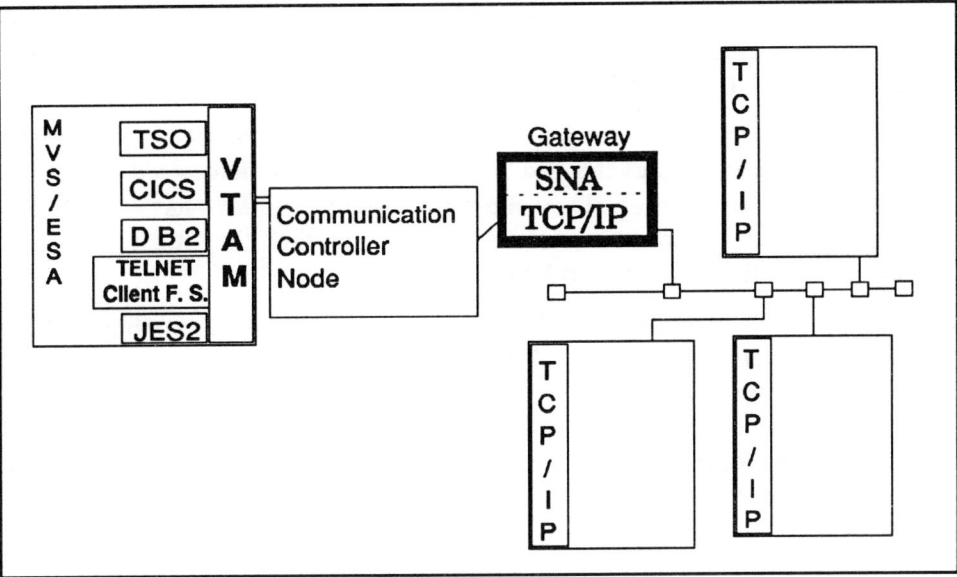

Figure 11.2

Before examining how an MVS user would use the Vi editor in UNIX, let us examine the nature of Vi in its native environment. To use the Vi editor, a native UNIX user would enter a vi filename, then press Enter and that file would be opened or created.

The Vi editor has two modes of operation. The first is "Escape" mode. This mode is used to enter commands required to save a file, delete lines of text, or cut and paste a block of text.

The second mode is "Input." This mode is required to accept alphanumeric characters to create text such as a letter. Escape mode is the default mode when a file is opened. Once a file is opened, one must press the [i] key to enter input mode. Notice no Enter key was pressed to get into input mode. The input mode was invoked because Vi (from an application standpoint) is character oriented. It interprets characters without the need of pressing an Enter key.

Now, if an MVS user invokes Vi after establishing a connection between the MVS and UNIX host, different operating procedures exist. For example, once an MVS user (using a 3270 type terminal) invokes Vi, then to enter input mode the user must enter an [i] and press the Enter key on the 3270 terminal. The reason for this is that the TELNET client application on the MVS host captures the [i] and keeps it until an Enter key is pressed. Why? Because the MVS environment is block mode oriented. Applications normally do not do anything until the Enter key or some other AID key is pressed. The Enter key or other AID keys simply tell the application (or system) interpret this block of data. In the case of trying to get an [i] from the 3270 terminal to the Vi application on the UNIX host the Enter key is required to cause the TELNET client application to pass this onto Vi. Once this is passed to the UNIX host Vi goes into input mode.

To exit input mode from a 3270 terminal is a different matter. A UNIX user attached to the UNIX host normally presses the Esc key and then enters the desired command. Not true for the 3270 terminal user. They must press whatever key has been defined to generate the output equivalent of the UNIX Esc key, and then they must press a defined AID key to pass this Esc key value to Vi on the UNIX host.

Seem cumbersome? It is. It requires time to get accustomed to operating with reverse terminal emulation. Now, you may ask, "Why does this problem not occur for those logging into MVS from a UNIX host?" Good question. The answer is data inbound to the MVS host application is going inbound in character oriented mode, filling up predefined fields the application accommodates. Consequently, nothing will happen until the user on the UNIX host enters the equivalent to an Enter or AID key; just like it would be on a native 3270 terminal user.

These concepts of block and character mode of operation are often overlooked during the integration process. It is also that part of integration that requires the most time for users to reach a knowledgeable level from a production standpoint. Based on what I have experienced, nothing about these two modes of operation is intuitive. Beyond that, the ease or difficulty in using an application on a UNIX host from an MVS host is application specific.

This means if three different applications reside on a UNIX host, and all three will be accessed from MVS, then odds are great that each application will seem to operate differently from the MVS user's perspective. This is because of terminal emulation and because of the block oriented nature of the MVS environment.

11.4 NAVIGATING OPERATING ENVIRONMENTS

Integration means bringing unlike environments together so they can interoperate. This does not change the respective environment, it merely means they can work together. An example of the differences is best exemplified by examining file structures on different operating environments.

MVS

Users who work with the MVS operating system are accustomed to what is called a data set. Different type data sets exist. For example, a partitioned data set is popular. For all practical purposes, it is like a directory with files similar to a DOS or UNIX environment. Differences do exist, however.

A partitioned data set is sometimes called a parmlib. A partitioned data set consists of three components:

- directory
- members
- records

Figure 11.3 is an example of a partitioned data set.

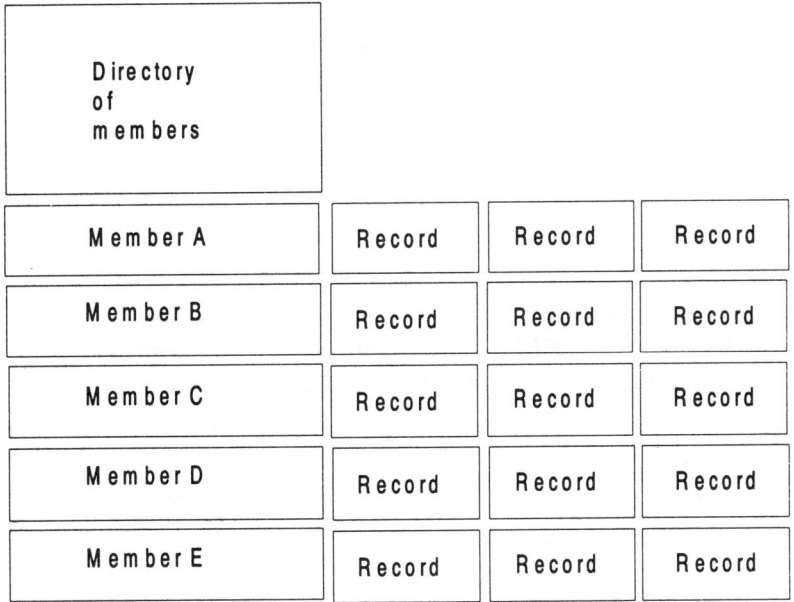

Figure 11.3

The directory is a listing of members. Members are basically equivalent to files. Members, in turn, are made up of records. Records are the data.

Records in the MVS world can take different forms. For example, three record types include:

- fixed length
- variable length
- unspecified length

Another popular data set is a sequential data set. It is similar to a file in DOS or UNIX. It has no members. It consists of records which are the data. Figure 11.4 is an example of a sequential data set.

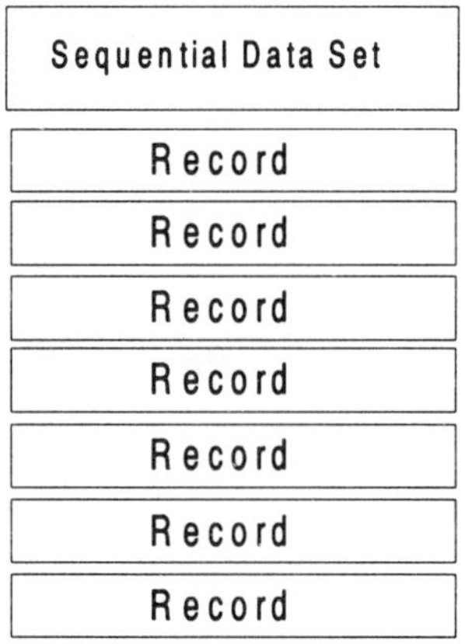

Chapter 11

Sequential Data Set
Record
Record
Record
Record
Record
Record
Record

Figure 11.4

The naming convention used with data sets is not necessarily obvious. Partitioned data sets can be created by users or they may be a "system" data set. The former type data set can be named virtually anything as long as the naming is syntactically correct. System data sets are used by the controlling components of MVS. These type data sets have a "SYS" or a "SYS1" prefix in their naming convention.

The naming of sequential data sets can be user defined. If not, the first part of the data set will match the logon id of the user. Thus an example might be: [DET.test1]. Here [DET] is the logon id, and test1 is the name given to the sequential data set.

More about records. In the world of MVS, record length is defined when a data set is created. Like directories in DOS or UNIX, a partitioned data set must be created before anything can be stored in it. During this creation process, a number of variables are defined. For example, the amount of disk space allocated for the data set to use, a number of other parameters relating to how data is stored, and the record type is specified. Users new to the MVS operating system and particularly to partitioned and sequential data sets may find it somewhat restraining. The nature of MVS, and how data is manipulated, is structured more so than say the UNIX operating environment. Finding a data set can be an arduous task the first time or two.

One way of locating a data set is by looking at the Volume Table of Contents (VTOC). Before explaining this, be aware that disks are considered volumes in the MVS world. Knowing this makes understanding the term VTOC easier. It is as its name implies, a table of contents.

In order to browse a VTOC it is assumed the user has certain information. For example, a user should know how to navigate the Interactive System Product Facility (ISPF) and find the menu for examining the VTOC. Once a user finds this menu, the name assigned to the volume must either be known or provided to the user. If it is known, then it is only a matter of entering the information and the VTOC can be displayed to a screen or printed.

This is totally unlike a UNIX environment. A UNIX environment has no VTOC. Neither does it have data sets. Granted a UNIX environment keeps track of data, but it does it differently than MVS.

The MVS environment is structured, but once the structure is learned it is easy to work with.

UNIX

UNIX is considered an "open" operating environment. It is offered by different vendors with different twists, but typically UNIX is UNIX. For example, data is stored in directories similar to that of PCs. Files can be created and exist in a directory somewhere. Creating a directory is straightforward. Directories can be created by entering a command and a desired name for the directory.

The concept of UNIX being an "open" environment is debatable. For example, different vendors have implementations of UNIX such as AT&T, SUN Microsystems, Hewlett Packard, IBM, and others. But, no guarantees exist that a program operating on one UNIX system will run *unmodified* on another UNIX system. Sometimes only nominal change is necessary, but change is nevertheless required.

The idea that UNIX is an "open" environment seems to pivot around the fact that nobody owns it. In contrast, IBM owns the MVS operating system.

11.5 REALITY 101

Integrating TCP/IP into SNA has customarily implied at least two possibilities. First, the probability is great that one or more individuals do not understand both TCP/IP and SNA. This is reasonable to assume because until recent years individuals in these networking environments traditionally concentrated their efforts in one or the other environment.

Second, odds are that not many, if any, individuals in the environments where these two networks are being integrated understand the components used in the integration process. This is neither good nor bad, right nor wrong; it is, in most cases, reality.

Thus, in most cases where integration of these two network protocols occur, training is a requirement, not an option. Traditional on-the-job training to bring personnel up to speed understanding these environments is naive at best. Integrating these two networking protocols creates a new heterogeneous environment whereby only brains win out.

The idea that personnel training is optional when integrating these two environments is basically an illusion. This type of integration is not comparable with learning a new word processor, spreadsheet, or even a new way of networking. The core issue at hand is to understand that two totally different networking protocols have been integrated. This means network integration.

Understanding PC, UNIX, or MVS operation is one matter. Understanding Local Area Networking is another. Understanding Wide Area Networking is still another. Beyond all this is network integration which presupposes a considerable amount of knowledge.

More individuals are in the marketplace now who understand and have had experience in network integration, but the number of truly qualified personnel who understand beyond buzzwords is still limited. This whole movement of integrating TCP/IP into SNA is evolving, and it is likely to take years before the marketplace produces a good crop of expert personnel. Until that time two camps of individuals will dominate. Those who have done integration and most likely have been involved in it since its early inception. And, those who are somewhere along the learning curve to competence.

Further delineation of personnel is clear. I see two groups of individuals in the arena of integration. Those who are programmers working at a hardware and/or software engineering level, and those who work at a systems level, understanding the concepts of how to make the components work together to achieve integration. It takes both types. And the latter is more difficult to master than the former. Working at a conceptual, architectural level is much more encompassing than writing a program (no discredit intended to programmers). For some reason it seems easier for those who work and understand the architectural level to concentrate upon a certain program than the reverse.

Regardless how the integration process is evaluated, training is a must. The only question is how much is required to bring a staff up to speed for production ability. This is site (personnel) dependent, and management should not neglect this nontechnical aspect of integration, because the potential losses in time spent on problem resolution can be much more costly.

When integrating TCP/IP into SNA, knowledge is power. And the most productive integrated environments can be characterized as *brain based*.

CHAPTER 12
Beyond Integration

Integrating TCP/IP into SNA is achieved! Now what? This question should not be asked after the fact, but many times it is. Practically speaking it should be as much a part of the requirement planning as any other criteria deemed necessary. And certainly the larger the environment the more critical it becomes.

This chapter presents network management in general, listing questions that should be addressed *prior to* the purchase of integration equipment, and certainly before integration is achieved. Next, IBM's SNA network management tools, then TCP/IP's network management tools are presented and briefly explained in light of integration devices.

12.1 THE CONCEPT OF NETWORK MANAGEMENT

What is network management anyway? The idea is similar to networking devices in the sense that little consensus surrounds the topic. Ask IBM oriented professionals, and they typically think of IBM's product offering called NetView. On the other hand, ask TCP/IP oriented professionals and they typically respond with comments about Simple Network Management Protocol (SNMP). Ask vendors supplying network components to achieve the integration process and they typically have a different response. Their response is normally focused upon their product offering and how it is managed in light of the two networking protocols. This may have nothing to do with NetView or SNMP.

Network management when integrating TCP/IP into SNA takes on a variety of considerations. Some of these considerations can be listed, pointing out areas that network management should address. The following list is more of a checklist of questions to consider when the topic of network management arises in the integration process. Consider:

- How will SNA network management work with existing (native) SNA equipment?
- Can SNA network management work with network devices used to integrate a TCP/IP network into the SNA?

Chapter 12

- How will SNA network management work with network device(s) used to integrate TCP/IP networks into the SNA? Is Network Management Vector Transport (NMVT) Protocol support used on behalf of the vendor supplying the network device(s) being used?
- What level of management detail will be available to SNA network management from network devices used to integrate TCP/IP into SNA?
- What amount of customization and/or limitations are involved from SNA network management in respect to network devices providing integration support for TCP/IP networks?
- If SNA network management is supported for network devices required in the integration process, then do these network devices provide "see through" capabilities to host on a TCP/IP network? If so, what degree of detail is available to the SNA network management service?
- What degree of depth, from an SNA network management standpoint, is available about TCP/IP based LAN hosts? Is the degree of depth provided only indicating a host is active or inactive?
- What network management tools (be it software or hardware) are available on network devices used in the integration process?
- Are these network management tools used on network devices accessible from a remote location? Can these network management tools be usable from a remote location via some type virtual connection to the network device?
- What information is provided by the network management tools on the network device? Is it possible to isolate problems such as a link failure, hardware and/or software problems, or whether a problem lies in the TCP/IP network or SNA network?
- Does the network management capability of the network device(s) have the capability for logging information about statistics that could be used to provide a tracking mechanism in a troubleshooting process?
- Does the network device(s) operate with TCP/IP network management, normally SNMP?
- What level of information does the network device provide to SNMP?
- Does the network device(s) support DDN specifications (normally in the form of RFCs) with regard to how it handles network management with TCP/IP networks?
- Can the network device(s) be configured to support remote network management operation from the TCP/IP network?

- How do TCP/IP based hosts appear to SNA network management? Do they appear as other SNA network devices? If so, how?
- If a link failure occurs, can a TCP/IP network based host store management information, then ship it up to the SNA host upon restoration of the link?

12.2 IBM'S NETVIEW

NetView has been the mainstay for SNA network management for some time now. It evolved, and is evolving, originally consisting of other IBM product offerings, and now these components work together comprising NetView as a program offering. Those new to NetView may wonder what capabilities it has. These will be considered first. Consider how NetView appears conceptually in figure 12.1.

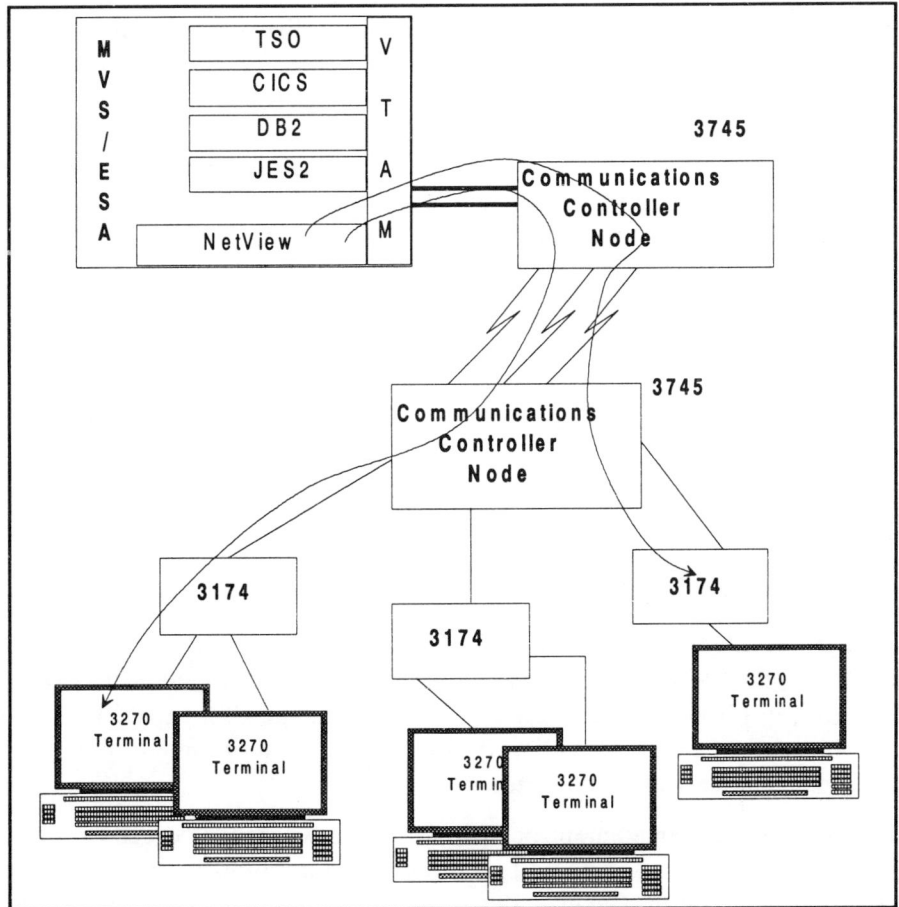

Figure 12.1

First, NetView has the Network Command Control Facility (NCCF). This is a command line where commands can be entered enabling acquisition of hardware and software status. For example, valid VTAM operator commands can be entered here to ascertain the status of resources defined to VTAM. The state of a PU can be determined by entering a command at the NetView NCCF prompt.

Second, NetView has the Network Logical Data Manager (NLDM). This component of NetView enables determining the status of sessions between logical units (LUs). It is beneficial when troubleshooting LUs and session status.

Third, NetView has the Network Problem Determination Application (NPDA). This is the hardware monitor component of NetView. Through its menus, hardware component status can be determined.

Combining NCCF, NLDM, NPDA, and other aspects of NetView make it robust from a network management perspective. NetView is capable of displaying the status of an entire SNA network from a single controlling point. Interestingly, this "single controlling point" does not mean a NetView operator must be in a specific physical location. As long as a virtual connection can be made to the host where NetView is operating, NetView can be executed from any place in the world. Thus the single point of management is somewhat moot. It is meaningful in that NetView is the central point of focus, but it does not mean that physical location restrictions apply. Beyond that, NetView can be used with dumb terminals, a PC, or any display capable of having a session with NetView. Hence, NetView does have distributed management support abilities as a result of VTAM, not NetView itself.

The implications of this support via NetView means a user on a TCP/IP based LAN can in fact log on to NetView from anywhere and "manage" the SNA network. It also means the TCP/IP network, if support is provided to NetView, can also be managed from NetView.

12.3 NETWORK DEVICE MANAGEMENT SUPPORT

Devices used in the integration process of TCP/IP and SNA should support both network management from the SNA perspective as well as from a TCP/IP perspective. And, if the networking device(s) is architected well, it will have management capabilities unto itself so it can be managed as a separate entity, thus making it an additional tool to manage the overall heterogeneous network environment.

From an SNA network management perspective, a network device used in integrating TCP/IP into SNA should perform two functions at a minimum. First, it should support alerts, notably generic alerts. Generic alerts can be user (vendor) customized to report alert conditions to NetView, specifically an alert receiver. This is important because these type alerts can report time and date stamps, identify the device sending the alert in terms that NetView will understand, and a number of other specific states that can be customized to pass along to the NetView receiver.

Another support that is extremely helpful for NetView operators is Response Time Monitor (RTM). This is beneficial to large shops who monitor response time. Response time is a measuring tool used to define how much time it takes for a response to be sent back to the terminal once a user presses an AID key.

Network devices should support SNMP also. Currently, this is the popular networking management in the TCP/IP network arena.

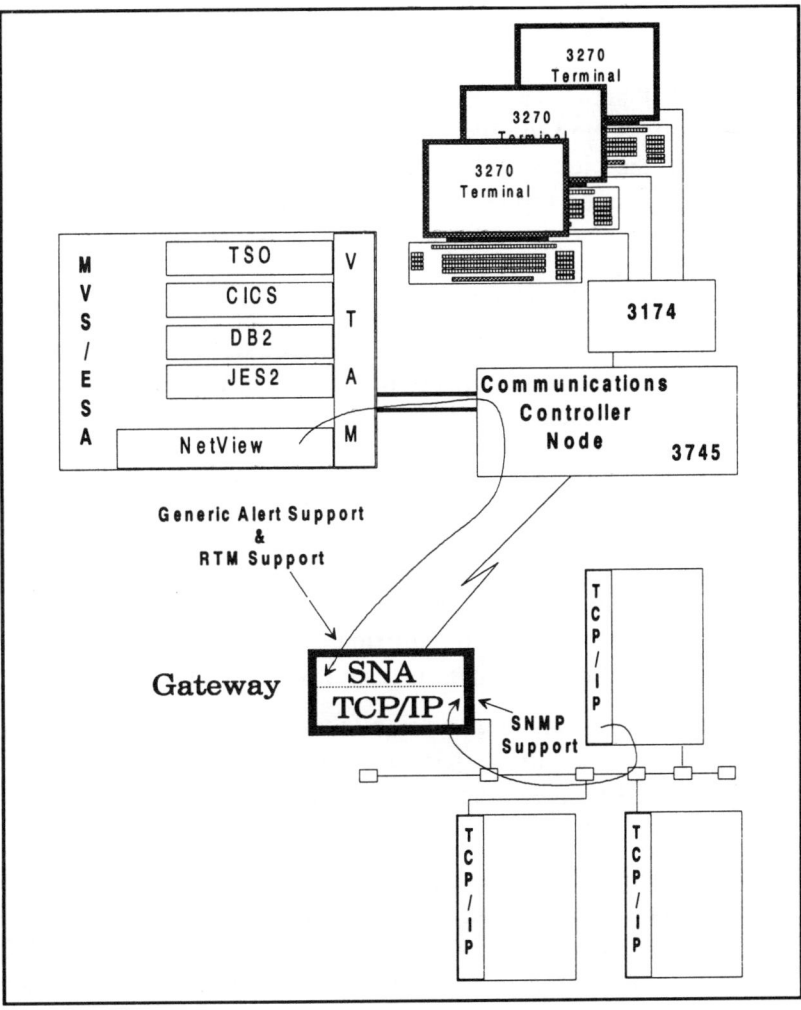

Figure 12.2

Figure 12.2 depicts a gateway that supports NetView management functions and SNMP management functions. The following explores SNMP in greater detail and provides information to understand how network management is achieved in this environment.

12.4 SIMPLE NETWORK MANAGEMENT PROTOCOL (SNMP)

SNMP is the popular way of network management for TCP/IP networks today. It does not work like NetView, nor does it have the same look and feel of NetView. The easiest way to learn SNMP is to not try to compare or contrast it to another type network management tool. This section will present SNMP by breaking the topic down into terms and concepts.

SNMP Introduction

SNMP is used in TCP/IP networks to manage devices such as hosts, network devices like gateways, routers, bridges, and the like. It is best understood by learning the terms and concepts that make up the pieces which allow SNMP to work. Specifically, SNMP is a system whereby events can be reported to network administrators, thus ascertaining the status of a particular device.

SNMP Overview

The basic idea behind SNMP is built upon the client/server model similar to the one discussed with TCP/IP. SNMP uses different names, but the concept is almost parallel. The names used similar to client/server are "applications" and "agents." Five parts of SNMP naming and operation are examined here.

First, the concept of a network element exists. A network element is a device on a TCP/IP based LAN. This may be a UNIX host, VMS host, TCP/IP to SNA gateway, router, bridge or any other valid network host. The term network element is how SNMP lingo generically references these devices. These network elements have "agents" running inside them. These "agents" maintain information about the status of that network element. When the term network element is used it is referring to a device on the LAN.

Second, the term network management station (also called network manager) refers to a device that monitors and controls network elements. Network stations have an "application" that is used to query the network element for information concerning its status.

Third, the term Management Information Base (MIB) is used. An MIB is a database of information about the network element. It is contained in each network element. The kind of network element dictates what information is valid MIB information for that network element. For example, MIB information includes a community name, system interfaces such as token ring or ETHERNET, and statistical information on received and sent TCP segments.

Fourth, the term community is used. A community is a collection of network management stations that have administrative authority over a group of network elements. This is a community. SNMP architecture calls for this type arrangement, and in most cases it is implemented this way. A community name is assigned by a network administrator for the TCP/IP based LAN. If no community name is defined, "public" is the default community name. One purpose behind this is the community name acts somewhat as a security measure. It functions like a password and thereby controls the level of access to network elements.

Fifth, are SNMP message types. Network management stations and network elements communicate via SNMP messages. In most cases, network managers are set up to communicate with network elements in intervals such as every fifteen minutes. SNMP uses five types of messages in this communication process. These message types and their functions are:

- Get Request. This is a specific request from a network manager to a network element requesting a variable or list of variables from that network element's MIB.
- Get Next Request. This is a way whereby a network manager can sequentially read a network element's MIB.
- Get Response. This is sent in reply to a get request, get next request, and set request message.
- Set Request. This is used to set values of one or more variables within a network element.
- Trap. This is used to report events like:
  - Link failures
  - Link functioning
  - Initializing self
  - Message received with incorrect authentication
  - Neighbor not responding

The Structure of Management Information

The Structure of Management Information (SMI) defines data structure and identification schemes that the network managers use in conjunction with the network elements. This is required because in order to read or write an MIB database variable, a way to identify the variable is required.

Hence, a naming tree has been created assigning unique identifiers. Each tree *node* is labeled with a brief text description and integer. A tree node's identifier is also called its Object identifier and is a sequence of integers that begin at the root of the tree (if you will) and follow out to the location of that particular node. Simply put, a numerical structure is used to identify any given node.

The Role of ASN.1

Abstract Syntax Notation One is the OSI language for describing abstract syntax. It is a data type definition language. This means it can describe data types. It is powerful and flexible. It is used to define the structures for managed objects. It is an integral part of what SNMP is built upon.

Concluding Comments

SNMP is an "event" reporting system. Events are reports of a change to the state of a managed object. Status information is exchanged between network managers and agents by way of messages. Network managers communicate with agents located in network elements to ascertain MIB information. This is normally done on a periodic basis, usually every ten to fifteen minutes.

SNMP is dominant in the marketplace. It is generally agreed as being the network management of choice for those implementing TCP/IP networks. Because of such agreement, it is important to know if the network device to be implemented supports SNMP.

12.5 MANAGING INTEGRATED NETWORKS

Network management in SNA is accomplished via NetView. Network management is accomplished in a TCP/IP network via SNMP. Once TCP/IP networks are integrated into SNA, how is network management achieved across such diverse environments? There has to be support for the TCP/IP network under NetView, appearing to NetView as SNA resources.

TCP/IP Management From NetView

The pivotal question to be addressed with regard to this topic is, "Can all TCP/IP LAN hosts be managed from NetView?" The second most important question to ask is, "What type of management information is ascertainable from the TCP/IP LAN hosts from NetView?" Answers to these questions should enlighten the issue. Consider the example in figure 12.3. Here, the TCP/IP hosts can be managed from NetView in the SNA environment.

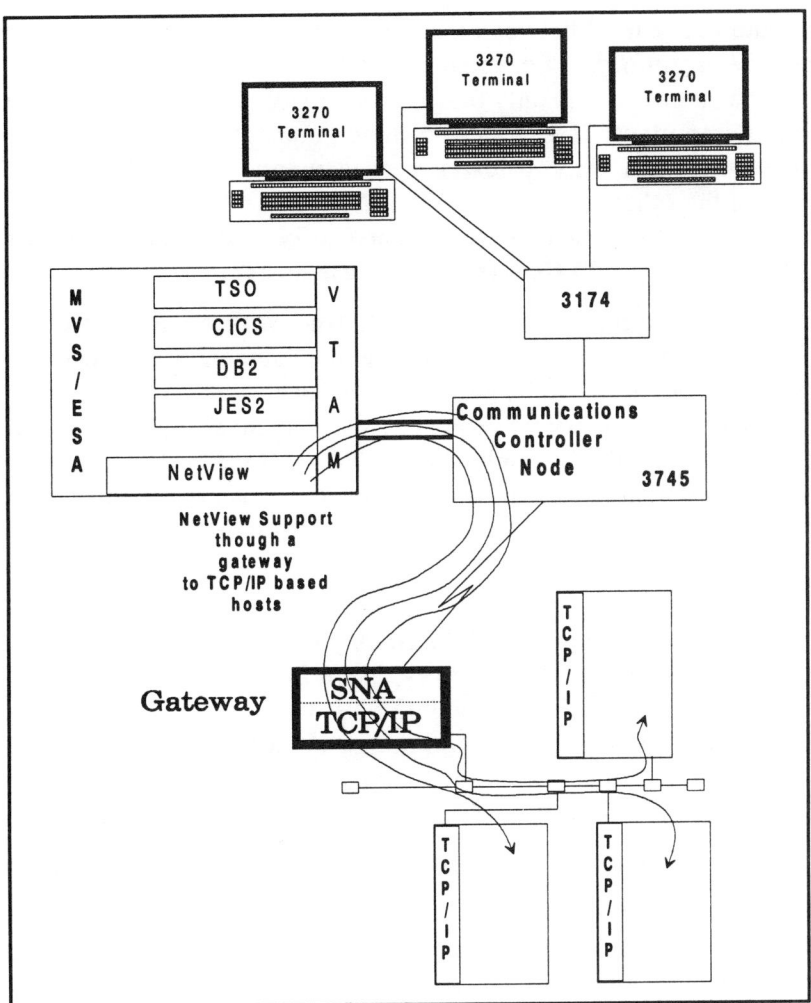

Figure 12.3

First, be aware of the answers given to each question. Consider the first question. A general response to this is, "yes." However, this is not very informative. What does it mean? Does it mean that the TCP/IP LAN hosts will be viewed from NetView as "SNA" devices, or does it mean they will be viewed from NetView as native SNMP type network elements? The former has historically been the answer. And, this being the case, then one must explore what level of "SNA" management support is provided. For example, are NetView *alerts* supported; if so, to what detail? These type inquiries should be made to clarify exactly how a TCP/IP host appears to a NetView operator.

Second, if a gateway is used between the SNA network and the TCP/IP network, some critical questions are in order. For example, "Can NetView view TCP/IP hosts on the LAN, beyond the gateway, or is only the gateway visible from NetView?" The answer to this question is important. If NetView cannot "manage" TCP/IP hosts on the LAN through a gateway, then only gateway management is available, not TCP/IP host management. On the other hand, if the TCP/IP hosts are "manageable" from NetView through the gateway, two other questions need to be asked: At what costs, and what degree of detail is available to NetView from these hosts?

Further clarification should be made as to what network management means. This is another gray area where many vendors define management their own way. If TCP/IP hosts can be managed from NetView, does this mean they can have new releases of software downloaded to them and rebooted? Does it mean only status information is available, such as a link failure or link recovery? Does it mean performance statistics can be gathered? A number of other valid questions exist. This area of integration should not be overlooked because sooner or later it will become important.

Gateway Management

If TCP/IP networks are integrated into SNA via a gateway device, then network management with respect to the gateway itself becomes a variable. For example, assuming a TCP/IP network is integrated into SNA via a gateway, does the gateway have NetView management support? At a minimum it should appear as a PU with available LUs to NetView. In addition, it should be capable of reporting to NetView what type device it has been defined to be. That is a local major node, switched major node, etc.

Beyond NetView is the question of gateway management itself. Valid questions should include:

- Can the gateway be managed remotely via a modem? If so, what management functions are supported?
- Does the gateway have security? If so, what kind? This is an important question, because if it does not, then this device could be the weakest link between both networks.
- Is the gateway manageable from SNMP? If so, what MIB does it support (MIB-I or MIB-II)?
- Does the gateway provide transparent management support from NetView to all hosts on a TCP/IP based LAN? If not, why?

SNA Management From TCP/IP

Practically speaking this is not realistic by today's standards. The problem with this concept is that it would require all resources within an SNA network to be defined by SMI and manageable by MIB information.

This may be doable, but most management at the present time is from NetView managing TCP/IP LAN hosts. Part of the rationale behind this has to do with the architectural nature of SNA and TCP/IP.

12.6 CONCLUSION

Managing integrated networks should not be the last item to consider when the idea to integrate comes to mind. It should be considered and questions asked in the early part of the research phase.

Managing TCP/IP networks is accomplished via SNMP. Once a TCP/IP based LAN is integrated into SNA the question becomes, how is it managed from NetView (assuming it is the network management tool being used)?

Any devices such as gateways that may be used to integrate TCP/IP into SNA should support both SNA network management and TCP/IP management. Additionally, devices such as gateways should provide management capabilities as a means unto themselves.

Acronyms

ACB	Access Control Block
ACF	Advanced Communication Function
ACK	Acknowledgement
ACTLU	Activate Logical Unit
ACTPU	Activate Physical Unit
ANSI	American National Standard Institute
API	Application Programming Interface
APPC	Advanced Program-to-Program Communication
APPN	Advanced Peer-to-Peer Networking
APPL	Application
ARP	Address Resolution Protocol
ARPA	Advanced Research Projects Agency
ASCII	American National Standard Code for Information Interchange
ASN.1	Abstract Syntax Notation One
BIND	SNA BIND command
BGP	Border Gateway Protocol
CCITT	International Telegraph and Telephone Consultative Committee
CLAW	Common Link Access to Workstation
CMIP	Common Management Information Protocol
CMIS	Common Management Information Services
CMOT	Common Management Information Services and Protocol over TCP/IP
CNM	Communciation Network Management
CP	Control Point
CRC	Cyclic Redundancy Check
CSMA/CD	Carrier Sense Multiple Access with Collision Detection
CUA	Common User Access
DARPA	Defense Advanced Research Projects Agency
DCE	Distributed Computing Environment
DDN	Defense Data Network
DEC	Digital Equipment Corporation
DFS	Distributed File Service
DIX	Digital, Intel, and Xerox ETHERNET protocol
DLU	Dependent Logical Unit

Acronyms

DME	Distributed Management Environment
DNS	Domain Name System
DSAP	Destination Service Access Point
DTE	Data Terminal Equipment
EBCDIC	Extended Binary Coded Decimal Interchange Code
EGP	Exterior Gateway Protocol
ESA	Enterprise System Architecture
ESCON	Enterprise System Connectivity
FDDI	Fiber Distributed Data Interface
FTAM	File Transfer, Access, and Management
FTP	File Transfer Protocol
GGP	Gateway to Gateway Protocol
GOSIP	Government Open Systems Interconnection Profile
GTF	Generalized Trace Facility
HDLC	High Level Data Link Control Protocol
IAB	Internet Architecture Board (also known as Internet Activities Board)
IBM	International Business Machines
ICMP	Internet Control Message Protocol
IEEE	Institute of Electrical and Electronic Engineers
IESG	Internet Engineering Steering Group
IETF	Internet Engineering Task Force
IGP	Interior Gateway Protocol
ILU	Independent Logical Unit
IP	Internet Protocol
ISO	International Standard Organization
LAN	Local Area Network
LLC	Logical Link Control
LU	Logical Unit
MAC	Media Access Control
MAN	Metropolitan Area Network
MIB	Management Information Base
MVS	Multiple Virtual Storage
NCCF	Network Communication Command Facility
NCP	Network Control Program
NETBIOS	Network Basic Input Output System

NFS	Network File System
NIC	Network Interface Card
NREN	National Research and Education Network
NSAP	Network Service Access Point
NSFNET	National Science Foundation Network
NTO	Network Terminal Option
NVT	Network Virtual Terminal
OSF	Open Software Foundation
OSI	Open Systems Interconnection
OSPF	Open Shortest Path First
PC	Personal Computer
PDU	Protocol Data Unit
PU	Physical Unit
RARP	Reverse Address Resolution Protocol
RFC	Request For Comment
RIP	Routing Information Protocol
RPC	Remote Proceedure Call
RST	Reset
SDLC	Synchronous Data Link Communication
SLIP	Serial Line Interface Protocol
SMTP	Simple Mail Transfer Protocol
SNA	Systems Network Architecture
SNMP	Simple Network Management
SONET	Synchronous Optical Network
SP	System Product
SPF	Shortest Path First
SSAP	Source Service Access Point
SSCP	System Services Control Point
TCB	Transmission Control Block
TCP	Transmission Control Protocol
UDP	User Datagram Protocol
ULP	Upper Layer Protocol
VM	Virtual Machine
VSE	Virtual Storage Extended
VTAM	Vitual Telecommunication Access Method

Acronyms

WAN	Wide Area Network
X	X Window System
XA	Extended Architecture
XNS	Xerox Network Systems

Glossary

This glossary includes terms used in SNA, TCP/IP, and a networking environment in general. When appropriate, the term is identified with the prevalent environment where it is found.

Abstract Syntax Notation One (ASN.1)—A language used in OSI and TCP/IP networks to define datatypes for use in network management.

Acknowledgement—A response sent by a receiver to a sender indicating successful reception of data. TCP requires acknowledgements, thus insuring a reliable data transfer mechanism.

Active Open—A client operation performed to establish a TCP connection with a server on a target host.

ACTLU—Activate Logical Unit. An SNA command issued to start a session on a logical unit.

ACTPU—Activate Physical Unit. An SNA command issued to start a session on a physical unit.

Address—An identifiable location. A location within memory. A location of a node within a network. A reference to a particular point with a computer or network environment. A way of identifying a network, subnetwork, or node.

Address Mask—A way of omitting certain part of an IP address in order to reach the target destination without broadcasting an address to unnecessary LAN segments or subnetworks. It is also refereed to as a subnet mask. The address mask uses the 32 bit IP addressing scheme, D classification.

Address Resolution—The mapping of an IP address to a hardware address. In the TCP/IP suite of protocols, Address Resolution Protocol (ARP) performs this function.

Advanced Peer-to-Peer Networking (APPN)—Network routing support between two or more APPC systems not directly connected.

Advanced Program-to-Program Communication (APPC)—Data communication at a peer level based on LU6.2 protocols.

Address Space—An identified range of addresses available to an application program.

Agent—An SNMP process, operating in a TCP/IP based host, that responds to both get and set requests; an agent can also send trap messages.

AID key—Attention Identifier Key. A 3270 key that contains a specific code in the inbound 3270 data stream that identifies the source or type of data that follows. A character in the data stream that indicates a user has pressed a key that requires action by the system; examples of AID keys include: Enter, Print, Page Up, Page Down, and Home keys.

API—Application Program Interface. Defined routines that are callable services by a program.

Application Layer—The topmost layer in the OSI reference model that aids in the identification of communicating partners. It performs the following functions: establishes the authority to communicate; supports file services, electronic mail, and print services; and transfers information.

ARPA—Advanced Research Project Agency. This is DARPA's former name. ARPA was an agency funded by the government

ARPANET—Advanced Research Projects Agency Network. The packet switching network that became known as the Internet.

ASCII—American National Standard Code for Information Interchange. ASCII is a character set defining alphanumeric characters; 128 possible binary arrangements exist.

Assigned Numbers—Request For Comment (RFC) documents that specify values used by the TCP/IP protocol suite.

Asynchronous—Also called async. Without a regular time relationship.

Backbone—A term used to refer to a set of nodes and links that are connected and together comprise the core components of a network.

Bandwidth—Refers to the range of frequencies transmitted on a channel. The difference between the highest and lowest frequencies transmitted across a channel.

Baseband—A type of channel where data transmission is carried across only one communications channel. Baseband supports one signal transmission at a time. ETHERNET is an example of baseband technology.

Baseband Signaling—A type of transmission technology used in Local Area Networks. This type transmission is characterized by a continuous encoded signal transmitted over a medium. Only one node at a time may send data over this type transmission technology.

Basic Conversation—A temporary connection between application programs in APPC. It is also an APPC session where the user must provide all information on how data is formatted.

Baud—The number of times per second a signal can change states on a transmission line.

BER—Bit Error Rate.

BIND—In SNA it is a command to activate a session between two logical units.

BIND Image—Session parameters passed in a control initiate (CINIT) request from the SSCP to the primary logical unit.

Bit rate—The rate, typically expressed in seconds, that bits are transmitted.

Block Mode—A string of data recorded or transmitted as a unit. Block mode transmission is the normal transmission mode in an SNA environment.

Bridge—A network device capable of connecting networks using similar protocols.

Broadband—A range of frequencies divided into narrow "bands" each of which can be used for different transmission purposes. Also known as wideband.

Broadband signaling—A type of signaling used in Local Area Networks that use analog signals, implement carrier frequencies, and multiplex more than one transmission at a given instance in time.

Broadcast—Simultaneous transmission of the same data to all nodes connected to the same medium.

Brouter—A network device capable of performing the function of a bridge while simultaneously filtering protocols and/or packets destined for nodes on a different network.

Burst Mode—A transmission mode where data is transmitted in bursts rather than continuous streams.

BSD—Berkeley Software Distribution. This is UNIX based software including support for TCP/IP

BUS—A linear configuration with respect to network topology.

Cache—An implementation of memory that usually operates faster than core or main memory. It is used to speed data and/or instruction transfer because it is designed to store frequently used data and/or instructions.

Carrier Sense—A signal generated at the physical network layer to inform the data link layer that one or more nodes are transmitting on the underlying medium.

Cheapernet—An implementation of ETHERNET where the approximate length of the medium is 200 feet. It utilizes 75 ohm coaxial cable, inexpensive connectors, and requires no transceivers for transmission.

CICS—Customer Information Control System. An IBM licensed program enabling transactions entered at physically remote locations to be processed concurrently, in real time. It has built into it the capability of building, maintaining, and using databases.

Classification—A means of identifying network types.

Glossary

Client—A program that can be invoked by a user; a user being a human or a program. Loosely used to refer to a user.

Client/Server Architecture—A general phrase used to refer to a distributed application environment where a program exists that can initiate a session and a program exists to answer the requests of a client. The origin of this concept is most strongly rooted in the TCP/IP protocols.

Client/Server—Terms used to refer to a peer-to-peer method of operation of applications within hosts. Beyond this definition, it is used to convey different thoughts. Usually a vendor defines its meaning making the word nebulous.

Cluster Controller—An SNA device to which terminals and printers attach. Typically, this is a PU type 2.0 node.

CMIP—Common Information Management Protocol. A network management protocol used natively in an ISO environment. When CMIP is used in a TCP/IP environment it is referred to as CMOT.

CMIS—Common Management Information Service. Management related services provided by CMIP.

CMOT—The implementation of CMIP over TCP/IP, where TCP is used as the transport mechanism.

CMS—Conversational Monitoring System. A component of VM operating system providing interactive time sharing, program development capabilities, and a mechanism for problem solving. CMS operates under the control of the VM control Program (CP).

Control Program (CP)—A component of VM that manages resources such as CMS and components of a single machine so that the appearance of multiple computers is possible.

CNM—Communication Network Management. Managing the distribution of information and control among users of communication systems.

CNM application—IBM's NetView program. An application that interacts with PUs from a network management aspect.

CNM interface—That point of common ground which an access method has with an application program.

Collision—An event that occurs when two or more nodes broadcast on the same network medium at the same time.

Collision Detection—The ability of a device to detect if a collision has occurred.

Compile—To translate a program written in a high-level language into machine language. Thus the program is executable.

Communication Controller Node—A device that contains a Network Control Program (NCP). This type node manages links and routing of data throughout the network.

Connection—A link between two or more entities. Connections may be logical or physical.

Connectionless—Referring to a type of network service that does not send acknowledgements upon receipt of data to the originating source.

Connection Oriented—Referring to a type of network service whereby the transport layer protocol sends acknowledgements concerning the condition of the receipt of data from the source host. This type service provides retransmissions if problems have been determined as a result of data transfer.

Contention—A condition in certain LAN implementations where the Media Access Control (MAC) sublayer permits two or more nodes to start transmission while risking collisions.

Control Point (CP)—Tasks that provide directory and routing functions for advanced peer-to-peer networking (APPN) nodes. A control point provides session and routing services.

Control Unit Terminal (CUT)—A type of protocol used by a 3174 or its predecessor, the 3274, where the controller interprets the data stream. Some terminals that rely on this type data stream include the following: 3178, 3179, 3278 model 2, and a 3279 model S2A. CUT terminals keep screen modifications or whatever operator changes made locally in a buffer until an Attention Identifier key is pressed or the Enter key is pressed, thus passing the buffered data upstream.

CP-to-CP Session—A logical connection (session) between two controlling points, typically in supporting APPN nodes. This session uses LU6.2 protocols. The session is used to exchange required management and other related information.

Cross Domain—A particular term used in SNA referring to the control of resources in more than one domain.

Crosstalk—A term referring to signals that interfered with another signal being transmitted.

CSMA/CD—Carrier Sense Multiple Access with Collision Detection. This is a protocol whereby nodes contend for access to the medium they share and to which they have equal access. It is referred to as a channel access control protocol. This type protocol requires each node to monitor the medium for traffic and permits transmission only when the medium is idle.

CUT mode—An interactive host mode permitting an IBM 3270 personal computer (that has been customized for this mode) to use a session emulating a terminal type used in CUT mode.

DACTLU—Deactivate Logical Unit. An SNA command used to end one or more sessions on a logical unit (PU).

DACTPU—Deactivate Physical Unit. An SNA command used to end a session with a physical unit.

Daemon—A program commonly found in different UNIX environments. It operates unattended performing standard services. This type program can be triggered by time intervals for execution.

DARPA—Defense Advanced Research Project Agency.

Data—A generic reference to alphanumeric characters within a computer or related device.

Data flow control layer—In SNA, that layer where data flow is regulated between half sessions.

Data link—The part of a node that is controlled by a data link protocol. It is the logical connection between two nodes.

Data link protocol—A prescribed way of handling the establishment, maintenance, and termination of a logical link between nodes. Examples of data link protocols include: Token Ring, ETHERNET, SDLC, etc.

Data set—This is how data, programs, etc. are stored under the MVS operating system. Different types of data sets exist; for example, partitioned data sets and sequential data sets.

Data stream—All data and control information sent across a link. In SNA different type data streams exist; for example, 3270 data stream, 5250 data stream, and SNA Character String.

DB2—Data Base 2. IBM's licensed database program which operates under certain operating systems.

Deactivate—An SNA term used to refer to the action taken to remove a device from the state of active.

DDN—Defense Data Network.

Dependent Logical Unit (DLU)—Any logical unit (LU) that requires an SSCP to aid in establishing a LU-LU session. This type LU receives the SNA ACTLU command over a defined link. Also referred to as an SSCP dependent LU.

Destination—A point or location to which data is to be sent.

DIA—In SNA, Document Interchange Architecture. This defines protocols for the exchange of information between office applications.

Destination Address—In an ETHERNET network, this refers to the target node address.

Digital—Referring to a state of on or off; representing a binary 1 or a binary 0.

Distributed Computing Environment (DCE)—An Open Software Foundation (OSF) defined set of technologies supporting distributed computing environments.

Distributed File Service—An Open Software Foundation (OSF) file server technology.

Distributed Management Environment—An Open Software Foundation (OSF) system and network management technology.

Distributed Processing—The act of processing storage, I/O processing, control functions, and actual processing is dispersed among two or more nodes.

Domain—A defined area in SNA where resources reside under a common control. Some resources referred to here include: SSCPs, PUs, LUs, links, link stations, etc.

Domain Name—In a TCP/IP network, a name associated to a host system in a network.

Domain Name System—A service used with the TCP/IP protocol suite to replace the previous method of keeping track with host names, aliases, and internet addresses. The domain name service is a distributed database used to convert node names into internet addresses. The concept behind DNS is decentralizing the naming convention through distributing the responsibility for mapping of names and addresses.

Dotted Decimal Notation—A representation of addressing typically used in expressing internet protocol addresses. For example, 137.1.1.100 is an internet address identifying a network and host.

Double Byte Character Set—A character set where alphanumeric characters are represented by two bytes. Examples of languages where this is used include: Japanese, Chinese, and Korean.

Downstream—In SNA this refers to the direction of data flow. Typically, a host is considered the top of the "stream" and other nodes are downstream from there.

Drop Cable—Typically used in an ETHERNET network. It refers to the cable connecting the node to the transceiver attached to the network backbone.

Dumb Terminal—A nonprogrammable terminal.

Dynamic Link Library (DLL)—A programming module that contains dynamic link routines which are linked at load or execution time.

Glossary

EBCDIC—Extended Binary Coded Decimal Interchange Code. IBM's character set used in SNA. This character set is the foundation where data streams such as 3270, etc. get their components making up a particular data stream.

Emulation—To simulate the real thing.

3270 Emulation—An application program that emulates the functions and 3270 data stream appearing as if it were a genuine 3270 data stream.

Encapsulation—A technique used by layered network protocols where data traveling down the network layers gets headers and trailers added to represent that layer. For example, when data is passed from an application above the TCP layer, TCP adds a header and trailer thus encapsulating the data. Likewise, this datagram is passed to the IP layer where IP wraps an IP header and trailer around the TCP portion, and so on down the network. When this arrives at the target host, the reverse occurs; that is, as the data travels up the layers respective headers and trailers are removed.

End Node—In SNA, an APPN node that only has the capability of being a target or source node. It cannot perform any routing functions.

Enterprise Network—Generally agreed to be a wide area network providing services to all corporate sites. In many instances it has a nebulous meaning, typically defined by the individual or vendor using the term.

ESCD—Enterprise Systems Connection Director.

ESCD Console—Typically, a PS/2 used to perform operator functions and other tasks related to the ESCON director.

ESCM—ESCON manager.

ESCON—Enterprise Systems Connection. Collectively, it refers to IBM's product offerings that include hardware and software. Generally, the term is used to refer to IBM's fiber data channel.

ESCON Channel—A channel using fiber optic cabling as the transmission medium.

ESCON Director—A device used to control and provide connectivity capabilities between ESCON links.

ESCON Environment—A data processing environment using ESCON (fiber optic cabling) as the transmission medium.

ESCON Manager—An IBM licensed program providing host control and communication capabilities for ESCON director connections.

ETHERNET—A data link level protocol. It comprises layers one and two when compared to the OSI reference model. It is a broadcast networking technology.

ETHERNET can be implemented with different media types, such as thick or thin coaxial cable or copper shielded twisted pair cabling as examples. ETHERNET uses CSMA/CD mechanism to access the medium.

ETHERNET Address—A 48-bit address, commonly referred to as a hard address. This address identifies an ETHERNET network interface card (NIC), thus identifying a host hardware address.

Event—An occurrence. For example, an occurrence significant to a specific task.

Explicit Route—In SNA, a set of two or more transmission groups that connect two subarea nodes.

External Storage—Storage accessible to a processor only via I/O channels.

FDDI—Fiber Distributed Data Interface. An ANSI defined standard for high-speed data transfer over fiber optic cabling.

Front end processor (FEP)—Used to refer to a communication controller node.

Frame—Typically, this term refers to data and all TCP/IP headers and trailers including ETHERNET. All this is referred to as a frame.

Frame Relay—A switching mechanism for routing frames as quickly as possible.

FTP—File Transfer Protocol. A TCP/IP based application used for transferring (copying) a file (or multiple files) from one system to another. Part of FTP provides password protection.

Full Screen—A term used to refer to how data is displayed on a terminal. As the term connotes, data is displayed one full screen at a time. This is in contrast to line mode where one line of data at a time is displayed.

Gateway—When used with the Internet, traditionally this term referred to a device that performs a routing function. Now the term refers to a networking device that translates all protocols of one type network into all protocols of another type network.

Gigabyte—One billion bytes. When written in decimal notation this means: 1,073,741,824.

GDDM—An IBM term meaning Graphical Data Display Manager.

GOSIP—Government Open System Interconnection Profile. This is a government standard using the OSI reference model.

Graphical Data Display Manager—A collection of program routines that permit graphics to be displayed.

Heartbeat—A voltage used with ETHERNET and 802.3 based networks.

Glossary

High Level Data Link Control (HDLC)—An international data communication standard that specifies a particular order for a series of bits.

Hop count—The number of bridges data crosses in a token ring network.

Host node—In SNA this is a node containing an SSCP and provides application service support.

Host processor—In SNA, a processor that controls applications in a network.

Host subarea—In SNA, a subarea that contains a processor.

IAB—Internet Activities Board. A group that coordinates the development of the TCP/IP protocol suite.

ICMP—Internet Control Message Protocol. A protocol that works in conjunction with the Internet Protocol (IP) that handles control and error messages.

IEEE—Institute of Electrical and Electronic Engineers.

IEEE 802.2—A data link standard used with the 802.3, 802.4, and 802.5 standards.

IEEE 802.3—A standard defining the physical layer using CSMA/CD with a BUS topology.

IEEE 802.4—A standard defining the physical layer using token passing with a BUS topology.

IEEE 802.5—A standard defining the physical layer using a token passing technology implemented on a ring topology.

IESG—Internet Engineering Steering Group. This is the executive party of the IETF.

IETF—Internet Engineering Task Force. One group that is part of the IAB; it is responsible for short-term engineering needs as they relate to the TCP/IP protocol suite.

IMS—Information Management System. An IBM program offering that is a combination database and data communication system.

Inactive—In SNA, the state of a resource. It means that resource is not operational.

Independent Logical Unit—Technically defined as a logical unit that does not receive an SNA command (ACTLU) over a data link. This type LU can be either primary or secondary. It can also have multiple sessions occurring simultaneously.

Inhibit—A mode that 3270 terminals, and other devices, can get into thus not accepting any interruptions. A reset must be performed.

Initiate—To send a request.

Intelligent Printer Data Stream (IPDS)—This is an all-points-addressable data stream that permits data, images, or graphics at any defined point on the printed page.

Interface—A shared point between two entities, be they software or hardware.

Internet—A collection of networks connected together that span the entire globe. Actually, it is a virtual network. The NFSNET is considered the backbone of the network.

Internet Address—A 32-bit address used to identify hosts and networks.

Interoperability—A case where networks and computer devices of different types are able to communicate effectively.

Interpreter—A program that takes high level language programs and translates them, one line at a time, into machine language. Typically, an interpreter is slower than a compiler because a compiled program is processed prior to execution time, whereas the interpreted program is converted into machine language in real time, immediately before execution.

IOCP—Input/Output Control Program. A program used to define all devices connected to the I/O subsystem.

IP—Internet Protocol. That part of the TCP/IP suite of protocols that handles routing of data.

IRTF—Internet Research Task Force. A group that is part of the IAB. It concentrates on research and development of the TCP/IP protocol suite.

ISPF—Interactive Productivity Facility. An IBM program offering that has full screen editing capabilities.

ISO Reference Model—The networking model created by the International Standard Organization defining seven layers of a network, isolating functions within each layer. It is used as a baseline for comparison/contrast of other network types.

IUCV—Inter-user communication vehicle. This is a facility operating under VM that is used to pass data between VM components and virtual machines operating under VM.

Jam—A way ETHERNET nodes have of communicating to all nodes on the LAN that a collision has occurred.

Jitter—A scenario that can occur with a 10BaseT network where signals are out of phase with one another.

LAN—Local Area Network. A collection of computer related equipment connected in such a way that communication can occur between all nodes connected to the medium.

Learning Bridge—A special type network device. It serves the function of a bridge, but it has the capability to learn what nodes are connected and route data accordingly.

Leased Line—A dedicated communication line between two points. This type line is a constant vehicle for logical communications to occur at all times. Contrast this with switched line.

LEN—Low Entry Networking node. A type of APPN node.

Line mode—In regards to displays, this means one line at a time in displayed. Contrast with Full screen.

Link—A generic term used to refer to a connection between two end points.

Logical—A generic term used to convey an abstract meaning or implementation. It is typically the antithesis of Physical.

Logical Link Control (LLC)—The upper part of the data link sublayer protocol responsible for governing the exchange of data between two end points.

Logical Unit (LU)—In SNA, an end point.

Logon Mode Table (LOGMODE)—An entry in the SYS1.VTAMLST data set that in turn includes entries reflecting particular types of LU session parameters.

Low Entry Networking—In SNA, a particular implementation of 2.1 architecture that permits peer communication between two nodes.

Low Entry Networking Node—LEN Node. A 2.1 architected node using LU6.2 but not capable of routing and other functions performed by a network node.

MAC—Media Access Control. The lower half of the data link sublayer. It is responsible for framing data and controlling the physical link between two stations.

Mainframe—A general term, normally used to refer to IBM's largest hardware architected machines. For example, the 3090 and 4300 series machines would fit this category. The ES/9000 processor line would fit this category as well.

Major node—In SNA this is a set of VTAM resources which can be activated and/or deactivated as a single group.

Medium Access Unit (MAU)—A device for central connection of nodes operating in a network.

Menu—A list of choices presented in a preformatted pattern.

Microcode—IBM's term used to refer to firmware. It is a set of instructions inside a programmable read only memory chip.

Modem—A device that converts digital signals into analog signals and vice versa.

Modem eliminator—A device that functions as two modems, but in fact is merely providing a service for data terminal equipment (DTE) and data communication equipment (DCE).

Multiple-Domain Network—In SNA, a network with more than one host node.

Multihomed Host—A host attached to two or more networks.

Multiplex—To simultaneously transmit multiple signals over one channel.

Multitailed—In SNA, a term used to refer to a communications controller node attached to more than one host.

MVS—IBM's Multiple Virtual Storage operating system.

National Education and Research Network (NREN)—A high capacity network planned to be a future backbone network for the Internet.

National Science Foundation (NFSNET)—A network that is part of the Internet.

NCCF—Network Communications Control Facility. A part of IBM's NetView product offering used in network management.

NCP—Network Control Program. An IBM program operating on a communications controller node. It is software that performs routing and data flow control functions.

NETBIOS—Network Basic Input Output Operating System. An IBM, and compatible, network programming interface.

NetView—IBM's software product offering used in management of SNA environments. NetView consists of software components such as Network Problem Determination Aid (NPDA), Network Logical Determination Manager (NLDM), and the Network Communications Control Facility (NCCF). NPDA is a hardware monitor. NLDM is a session monitor. NCCF is a command line providing support for various commands such as VTAM, etc.

Network—A collection of computers and related devices connected in such a way so that effective communication occurs.

Network Accessible Unit (NAU)—In SNA this is an addressable point. Different types of NAUs exist; for example, SSCPs, CPs, PUs, and LUs.

Network File System (NFS)—Sun Microsystem's protocols that permit clients to mount remote directories onto their own local file system, thus appearing to be local.

Network Interface Card (NIC)—A generic reference for a networking interface board.

Network Information Center (NIC)—A centralized administration facility used with the Internet.

Network Management—Reference to the control mechanism of a network. This may include monitoring, activation, and deactivation.

Network Virtual Terminal (NVT)—A basic set of protocols governing virtual terminal emulation.

Node—A generic term used to refer to varying types of networking devices.

Node type—In SNA, nodes characterized by capabilities, function, PU architecture, or LU support.

Non-SNA—Meaning not a native SNA device.

Optical Fiber—Glass or plastic cable used as a communications medium.

Open Shortest Path First (OSPF)—An internet routing protocol that can route traffic via multiple paths using network topology.

Open Software Foundation (OSF)—A group of computer, and computer related vendors, collaborating to produce technologies for multivendor interoperation.

Open Systems Interconnection (OSI)—A set of ISO standards relating to data communications.

Operator Information Area—An SNA term referring to the 25th line on a 3270 terminal whereby symbols represent the status and state of the terminal with respect to the SNA environment.

Packet—In TCP/IP networks, this refers to that data passing between the internet layer and the data link layer. Technically, a packet includes an IP header, TCP header, and data. The term is also used in a generic sense referring to a defined portion of data transferred throughout the network.

Parallel Channel—IBM's name for a link that transmits data in parallel format. Contrast with ESCON.

Partitioned Data Set (PDS)—A method used for storage under the MVS operating system. A PDS consist of a directory and members. The members in turn consist of records, which is the actual data.

Path—In SNA this refers to a route from one point to another.

Peer—In SNA, a corresponding node.

Peer-to-Peer Communications—Reference to data communications between two nodes using LU6.2 sessions, whereby either node can initiate a conversation.

Peripheral node—In SNA, a network device that uses local addressing for routing rather than network addressing.

Glossary

Physical Unit (PU)—Software implemented in such a way so that particular hardware takes on certain characteristics.

Point-to-Point—Direct data transmission between two points without intervention from other devices in any way.

Point-to-Point Protocol (PPP)—This protocol has the ability to provide host-to-network and router-to-router connections over synchronous and asynchronous lines.

Port—In TCP/IP, a number used to identify applications. In general, a port is referred to as an entry or exit point.

Primary Logical Unit—In SNA, the LU that initiates the SNA BIND command.

Processor—A central processing unit.

Protocol—A set of rules governing behavior or method of operation.

Protocol Conversion—Changing one type protocol (way of performing a task) to another type protocol (way of performing a task).

Protocol Data Unit (PDU)—A generic term used to refer to a unit of data, headers, and trailers at any layer in a network. This term is frequently used in a TCP/IP environment.

Proxy—A mechanism where a system functions for another system when responding to protocol requests.

RACF—Resource Access Control Facility. IBM's security software product offering. RACF identifies and verifies users attempting to gain access to the system.

Remote Job Entry (RJE)—The ability to submit jobs via a terminal attached through some device in the SNA, or non-SNA, network.

Remote Procedure Call (RPC)—A specific protocol that permits calling a routine that executes a server; the server returns output and return codes to the caller.

Remote Spooling Communications Subsystem (RSCS)—An IBM software product that operates under the VM operating system. It supports command entry, provides spool file transfer capability, and messages between VM users.

Request/Response Unit—In SNA, a generic term used to refer to a request unit or a response unit.

Requests for Comment (RFC)—A set of documents containing TCP/IP protocols. They comprise the TCP/IP protocol suite and are available at the Network Information Center.

Request Unit—In SNA, a message containing request or function management information.

Response Unit—In SNA, a message acknowledging a request unit.

Repeater—A network device that regenerates signals so the length of a network can be extended.

Resolver—A software package that provides a client the support to access the Domain Name System database(s).

Resource—Generally used to refer to application programs, however it may be used in a general sense to refer to devices such as hardware. A resource can be referred to as being local, remote, network, or other characterizations.

Response time—The amount of time between the end of an inquiry to the beginning of the response.

Reverse Address Resolution Protocol (RARP)—A protocol included in the TCP/IP protocol suite that allows a TCP/IP node to acquire its IP address by performing a broadcast on the network.

RIP—Routing Information Protocol. A protocol used by the Berkeley BSD UNIX operating systems for exchanging information pertaining to routing. Typically, it is used when a small number of computers are in use.

RISC/6000—IBM's line of processors and workstations that are based on RISC processors. They use the Advanced Interactive Executive (AIX) operating system, which is an implementation of UNIX.

Rlogin—A remote login service provided with the Berkeley BSD UNIX operating system. The service is similar to TELNET application in the TCP/IP protocol suite.

Routine—A program, or part of a program, that serves a specific purpose; normally this purpose is calling another routine to perform a function.

Routing—A process of determining which path is to be used for data transmission.

Routing table—A list of valid paths through which data can be transmitted.

RS-2332-C—A physical layer specification for connecting devices.

SAA—Systems Application Architecture. IBM's architecture, announced in March 1987, that defines a Common User Access (CUA), Common Programming Interface (CPI-C[using the C language]), and the Common Communications Support (CCS) components.

SAP—Service Access Point.

Secondary ESCON Manager—An ESCON manager whereby it receives a command from the primary ESCON manager via intersystem communication.

Secondary Logical Unit (SLU)—The requesting end of a dependent logical unit.

Segment—Parts of a network; typically ETHERNET LANs are divided into parts. These parts are commonly called segments.

Serial—A description of events explaining that the occurrence of events is one after another. Contrast to parallel.

Server—An application that answers requests from clients. The term is dominant in the TCP/IP networking environment. A server can also perform specific functions such as: print, file, terminal, communications, etc. In this sense, a server is used generically.

Session—In SNA, a logical connection between two end points. Different types of sessions exist and are required for SNA functions.

Simple Mail Transfer Protocol (SMTP)—In TCP/IP, an application including a client and server providing EMAIL services for all hosts with TCP/IP software installed and enabled.

SLIP—Serial Line Internet Protocol. A protocol for using internet protocol over serial lines, such as a switched telephone line. SLIP seems to be slowly being replaced by PPP.

SNA—Systems Network Architecture. IBM's proprietary networking protocol announced in 1974. It is very prevalent worldwide and considered a reputable industry standard.

SNA character string (SCS)—A particular data stream used in SNA consisting of EBCDIC control codes, end user data, and transported via a request/response unit.

SNA Distribution Services (SNADS)—An IBM set of rules defining asynchronous service for receiving, routing, and sending EMAIL in a multinetwork environment.

Socket—In TCP/IP a socket is an addressable point that consists of the IP address and the TCP or UDP port number. Basically, it provides application access to TCP/IP protocols.

Source Routing—A method of delivery (routing) determined by the source node.

Source—The originating entity.

Subarea—In SNA, a part of a network that consists of attached peripheral nodes, associated resources, and as defined by SNA, a subarea node. Interestingly, no area nodes exist, only subarea nodes.

Subchannel—That part of a channel address identifying a particular device on a channel.

Subnet—In TCP/IP, part of a TCP/IP network identified (isolated) by a portion of the internet address.

Subnet address—In TCP/IP, that part of the IP address that identifies the subnetwork.

Glossary

Subnet Mask—A way to exclude networks from having a broadcast on certain networks, isolating broadcasts to the desired network(s).

Subroutine—A set of instructions that are executed by a call from another program.

Swapping—A process that moves all program contents from internal to external storage and vice versa.

Switched connection—A data link connection that is similar to a telephone call. The link is established on demand. Thus the reference to a switched line. Contrast a leased line.

Synchronous Data Link Control (SDLC)—A code-transparent and serial bit-by-bit data transfer over a physical link.

Synchronous Data Transfer—The physical transfer of data between two nodes that are clocked, or timed, and a predictable time relationship exists.

SYSGEN—The process of selecting and configuring parts of an operating system where the results are a customized operating system configured to meet specific site requirements.

System Services Control Point (SSCP)—In SNA, a focal point for managing the configuration and network resources. An SSCP exists in a host node, containing a PU 5.

Tera—A numeric quantity, when expressed in bytes, one terabyte is denoted as: 1,009,511,627,766.

TCP—Transmission Control Protocol. A transport layer protocol that is part of the TCP/IP protocol suite. TCP provides a reliable data stream mechanism performing retransmissions when a positive acknowledgement is not returned to the source from the destination node.

TCP/IP—The acronym for Transmission Control Protocol/Internet Protocol. TCP/IP is an upper layer networking protocol. It is client/server based at the application layer.

10Base2—An uncommon reference to ETHERNET. It literally means 10 megabits per second, using baseband signaling, with a contiguous cable segment length of 100 meters and a maximum of 2 segments.

10Base5—A reference to ETHERNET referring to 10 megabits per second, using baseband signaling, with 5 continuous segments not exceeding 100 meters per segment.

10Base-T—A general reference to ETHERNET meaning 10 megabits per second, using baseband signaling, and twisted pair cabling.

Telenet—This is a public, packet switched network utilizing X.25 protocol. It is operated by GTE.

TELNET—A TCP/IP application using TCP as a transport mechanism. It consists of a client and server. All TCP/IP protocol suites have this application because it is part of the definition of what makes TCP/IP what it is.

Terminal Server—A network device that provides physical access for dumb terminals. Most terminal servers have an abbreviated TCP/IP suite of protocols to permit dumb terminal remote logon and other services on the TCP/IP network.

Terminator—A resistor that must be on the ends of a thick and thin-net ETHERNET network. A terminator absorbs spent broadcasts on the network.

TFTP—Trivial File Transfer Protocol. This is a mechanism for remote logons similar to TELNET; but it uses UDP as a transport layer protocol.

Throughput—The amount of data that can be successfully moved across a medium or processed within a certain time period.

Time Sharing Option (TSO)—IBM's product that offers interactive development for users. It is actually a time sharing subsystem.

Token Ring—An IBM developed lower layer networking protocol using a token passing method controlling data traffic. It is connection oriented at a data link level.

Topology—The configuration of network devices. Examples include: BUS, Star, Ring, Dual Ring, etc.

Traffic—A generic term used to describe the amount of data on a network backbone at a given period in time.

Transceiver—A network device required in baseband networks. It simply takes a digital signal and puts it on the analog baseband medium. Transceivers are devices that sense collisions.

Type 2.1 node—A node using peer protocols.

UDP—User Datagram Protocol. A transport layer protocol in the TCP/IP protocol suite. It does not perform retransmissions. Contrast to TCP.

UNBIND—In SNA, the command to deactivate a session between logical units.

Varyonline—In SNA this means to put a resource in an active state.

Varyoffline—In SNA this means to put a resource in an inactive state.

Virtual—Appearing to exist, but in reality the appearance is achieved by functions or processes.

Virtual Machine—An IBM operating system that supports operating systems running under its control.

Virtual Storage Extended (VSE)—An IBM operating system designed for users who need an S/390 or S/370 architected machine. It is best suited in small to intermediate data centers. It provides spooling, utilities, networking control, transaction processing, batch processing, and interactive processing as well as other functions.

Well Known Port—In TCP/IP, an address for an expressed purpose generally agreed upon by TCP/IP users.

Wide Area Network (WAN)—The term usually refers to a network spanning large geographic distances.

Workstation—This term connotes different meanings to different individuals. For example, it could be used to refer to a PC, an RISC based processor, or even a dumb terminal. At best its meaning is arbitrary.

X.400—A protocol defining standards for electronic mail in an open network.

X.500—A protocol defining standards for directory services in an open network.

X Series—A collection of standards widely accepted; included are data communication protocols.

XNS—Xerox Networking Standard. The Xerox corporation network protocols. These protocols are similar to TCP/IP, but they are different.

X Window—A software protocol developed at MIT for a distributed windowing system.

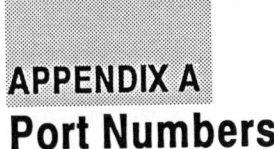

APPENDIX A
Port Numbers

TCP and UDP transport mechanism use Well Known Ports. These port names reflect specific applications of wide implementation and usage. Ports are the end points, an addressable entity to create a logical connection. Also known as service contact ports, these ports provide services to callers (requesters) of a particular service. The following list includes the port's decimal number as it is known, the name of the reference associated with a specific port, and a brief description of what each port provides. The list is not exhaustive; it is intended to provide the reader with a reference for common ports used in TCP/IP networks.

Decimal	Name	Description
0		Reserved
1	TCPMUX	TCP Port Service Multiplexer
2-4		Unassigned
5	RJE	Remote Job Entry
7	ECHO	Echo
9	DISCARD	Discard
11	USERS	Active Users
13	DAYTIME	Daytime
15		Unassigned
17	Quote	Quote of the Day
19	CHARGEN	Character Generator
20	FTP-DATA	File Transfer (Data)
21	FTP	File Transfer Protocol
23	TELNET	TELNET
25	SMTP	Simple Mail Transfer
27	NSW-FE	NSW User System FE
29	MSG-ICP	MSG-ICP
31	MSG-AUTH	MSG Authentication
33	DSP	Display Support Protocol
35		Any Private Printer Server
37	TIME	Time
39	RLP	Resource Location Protocol
41	GRAPHICS	Graphics

Decimal	Name	Description (Continued)
42	NAMESERVER	Host Name Server
43	NICNAME	Who Is
49	LOGIN	Login Host Protocol
53	DOMAIN	Domain Name Server
67	BOOTPS	Bootstrap Protocol Server
68	BOOTPC	Bootstrap Protocol Client
69	TFTP	Trivial File Transfer
79	FINGER	Finger
101	HOSTNAME	NIC Host Name Server
102	ISO-TSAP	ISO TSAP
103	X400	X.400
104	X400SND	X.400 SND
105	CSNET-NS	CSNET Mailbox Name Server
109	POP2	Post Office Protocol version 2
110	POP3	Post Office Protocol version 3
111	SUNRPC	SUN RPC Portmap
137	NETBIOS-NS	NETBIOS Name Service
138	NETBIOS-DGM	NETBIOS Datagram Service
139	NETBIOS-SSN	NETBIOS Session Service
146	ISO-TP0	ISO TP0
147	ISO-IP	ISO IP
150	SQL-NET	SQL-NET
153	SGMP	SGMP
156	SQLSRV	SQL Service
160	SGMP-TRAPS	SGMP TRAPS
161	SNMP	SNMP
162	SNMPTRAP	SNMPTRAP
163	CMIP-MANAGE	CMIP/TCP Manager
164	CMIP-AGENT	CMIP/TCP Agent
165	XNS-COURIER	Xerox
179	BGP	Border Gateway Protocol

APPENDIX B
RFCs

TCP/IP continues to be an evolving protocol suite. It is based on Request For Comments (RFCs). These RFCs are maintained at the Network Information Center in Chantilly, VA. RFCs are submissions of protocols designed and implemented by researchers and individuals as well. RFCs have become and continue to contribute to the standard which TCP/IP is built upon. The following list includes RFC #'s and RFC title, and when possible the author of the RFC has been included. The list is not exhaustive, but it provides significant information for those who need a beginning point of reference for additional details in a particular area.

RFC #	RFC Title	Author
768	User Datagram Protocol	Postel, J. B.
791	Internet Protocol	Postel, J. B.
792	Internet Control Message Protocol	Postel, J. B.
793	Transmission Control Protocol	Postel, J. B.
821	Simple Mail transfer Protocol	Postel, J. B.
822	Standard for the format of ARPA Internet Text Messages	Cocker, D.
823	DARPA Internet Gateway	Hinden, R. M. & Sheltzer
826	ETHERNET Address Resolution Protocol	Plummer, D. C.
854	TELNET Protocol Specification	Postel, J. B. Reynolds, J. K.
856	TELNET Binary Specification	Postel, J. B. Reynolds, J. K.
857	TELNET Echo Option	Postel, J. B. Reynolds, J. K.
877	Standard for the Transmission of IP Datagrams over Public Data Networks	Korb, J. T.

Appendix B

RFC #	RFC Title	Author (Continued)
885	TELNET End of Record Option	Postel, J. B.
919	Broadcasting Internet Datagrams	Mogul, J. C.
922	Broadcasting Internet Datagrams in the Presence of Subnets	Mogul, J. C.
937	Post Office Protocol version 2	Butler, M.
		Postel, J. B.
		Chase, D.
		Goldberger, J.
		Reynolds, J. K.
950	Internet Standard subnetting Procedure	Mogul, J. C.
		Postel, J. B.
952	DOD Internet Host Table Specification	Harrenstien, K.
		Stahl, M. K.
		Feinier, E. J.
959	File Transfer Protocol	Postel, J. B.
		Reynolds, J. K.
974	Mail Routing and the Domain Name System	Partridge, C.
1001	Protocol Standard for a NETBIOS Service on a TCP/UDP Transport: Concepts and Methods, Network Working Group	
1002	Protocol Standard for a NETBIOS Service on a TCP/UDP Transport: Detailed Specification, NetBIOS Working Group	
1013	X Window System Protocol, Version 11	Scheifler, R.
1014	XDR: External Data Representation Standard	SUN Microsystems, Inc.
1033	Domain Administrators Operations Guide	Lottor, M.

APPENDIX C
UNIX File Structure

This appendix is for users new to the UNIX operating system needing a basic understanding of file structures. Before depicting UNIX file structure, background information is presented.

UNIX is prevalent in the marketplace today. It accommodates multiple users and can operate on a PC or very large processors supporting hundreds of users. UNIX is an interesting operating system because it has many different implementations. For example, UNIX System V is AT&T's version of UNIX, HP-UX is Hewlett Packard's version of UNIX, SUN Microsystems has their own version of UNIX, IBM has their Account Interactive Executive (AIX) version of UNIX, and the list goes on. Different vendors typically have their own versions of UNIX.

This means UNIX is not all the same. UNIX, at a programming level differs by vendor version; ironically, the UNIX operating system is not as "open" as many think. It is open, to a degree; the question is to what degree. The point is just because an application operates on vendor A's version of UNIX does not necessarily mean that same application (without modifications) will operate on vendor B's version of UNIX. Hence, openness is relative; it is matter of degree.

Before examining UNIX file structures, a brief perspective of UNIX is valuable for newcomers to UNIX. Like the majority of operating systems, UNIX has a command interpreter. It is a UNIX utility and responsible for generating the system prompt users see on a display. It also causes the UNIX operating system to execute valid commands when entered at the user prompt. Three prominent command interpreters exist in the UNIX environment. These interpreters are also called shells. These interpreters are: Bourne Shell, C Shell, and Korn Shell. They provide different functions, and the prompt seen on the user display differs depending on which shell is currently in use. Most shells include features and functions such as:

Appendix C

- Interactive Processing. Provides communication between the user and the UNIX operating system.
- Background Processing. Managing processes to be executed in background mode, without interrupting the interactive users.
- Shell Scripts. This is a combination of commands (user selected), arranged in such a way so that execution at a later time is possible. This is similar to a batch file in the DOS operating system.
- Programming Language. Shells support varying language constructive capabilities. These language constructs allow the user to create a shell script to perform complex functions when executed.
- Input/Output redirection. To demystify this concept for those unfamiliar with I/O redirection, consider this. Many programs are designed to interact with users (humans), meaning accept input from users. With I/O redirection, files can receive input from another source such as a file, then send the output to another destination such as a printer.
- Pipes. This is simply a way to connect individual programs providing simple functions and realize the synergy from combining multiple programs providing customized operations without customizing programs each time a need changes.

Regardless of the shell, file structure in popular UNIX operating environments includes a directory and file(s). Figure C.1 depicts two examples; the first is multiple directories, each having multiple files. The second is an example of a root directory with multiple directories, and the last directory includes a list of filenames.

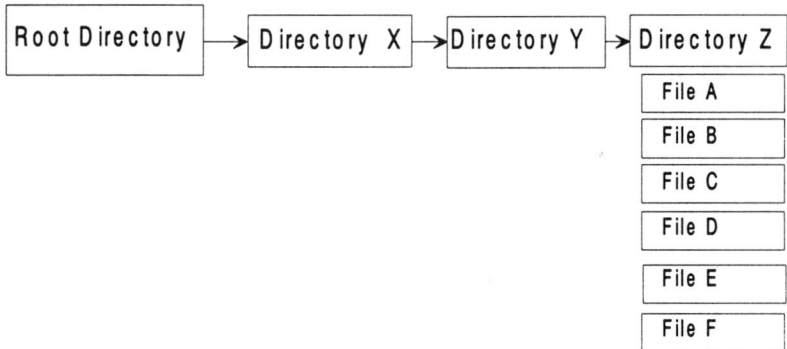

Figure C.1

The examples in figure C.1 are true in most vendors' versions of UNIX. Additional information for those new to UNIX includes understanding the concept of a PATH name. Two type path names exist. First, a fully qualified path name indicates the root directory and all directories (subdirectories) that lie in the "path" to the directory containing a particular file. Directories in a path are separated by a slash (/). A path beginning with a slash indicates the path starts with the root directory. Consider the following example of a path beginning with the root directory.

`/marketing/products/support/gateways/modelXYZ`

This example indicates the root directory by the slash (/) on the far left, a marketing directory, support directory, gateways directory, and a specific product, namely modelXYZ.

Another type path is called a partially qualified path. This type path identifies the current working directory and a filename in that directory. Consider the following:

`gateways/modelXYZ`

Other information about the UNIX operating system is available. A credible book on this topic is: *Illustrated UNIX System V: Complete Command Reference with Tutorial*, by Robert Felps, ISBN# 155622-187-8.

APPENDIX D
MVS File Structure

This appendix is for users new to the MVS operating system. It provides basic information about file structures in a MVS environment.

MVS is a popular operating system in SNA. It stores data in a variety of ways. Common reference to data storage in MVS is called a Data Set. Multiple types of data sets exist, but two are commonly used by programmers and users alike.

The first type data set is called a partitioned data set (PDS); it is also referred to as a parmlib by some. Regardless the name, a PDS is similar to a directory with files. Figure D.1 depicts a partitioned data set. Notice that records are located beside each member. Records are the data that is stored.

Directory of members			
Member A	Record	Record	Record
Member B	Record	Record	Record
Member C	Record	Record	Record
Member D	Record	Record	Record
Member E	Record	Record	Record

Figure D.1

Appendix D

A second commonly used data set is known as a sequential data set. This is similar to a file. A sequential data set resides in a directory whose name is the same as the user logon id. Figure D.2 is an example of a sequential data set. Notice beneath the sequential data set name are records. These records are data that comprise the data set.

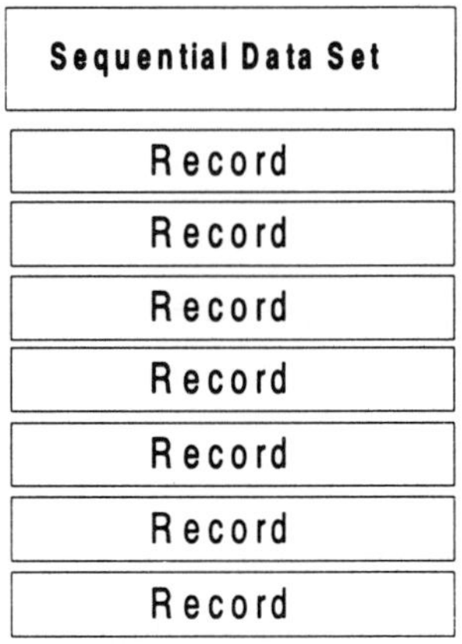

Sequential Data Set
Record
Record
Record
Record
Record
Record
Record

Figure D.2

In the MVS environment the concept of record format exists. Three typical record formats and a brief description are:

- Fixed length. This means all records in a data set are the same length, in bytes. Consider figure D.3 showing fixed length records.

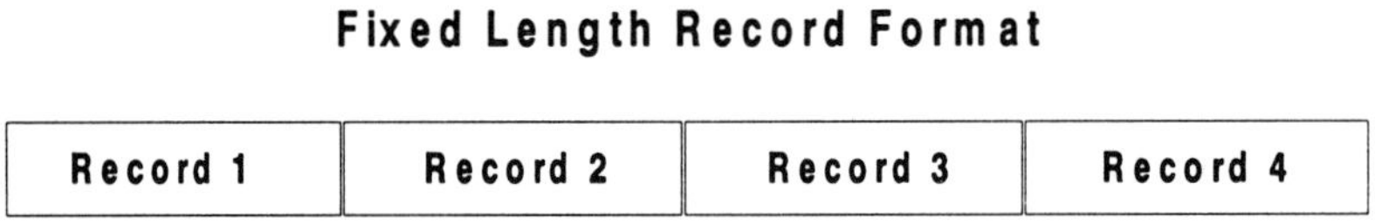

Fixed Length Record Format

Record 1	Record 2	Record 3	Record 4

Figure D.3

- Variable length. These type records vary in length; some may be longer than others. Consider figure D.4 showing variable length records.

Variable Length Record Format

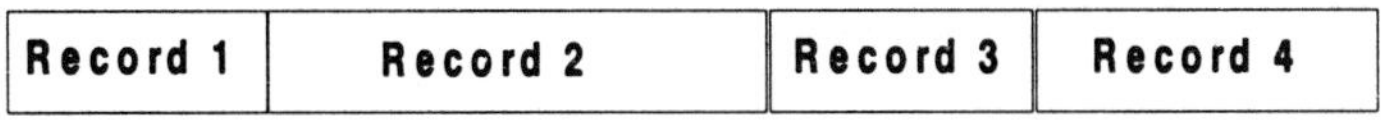

Figure D.4

- Unspecified length. This type record has no prescribed length in terms of size. Consider figure D.5 showing a record with an unspecified length.

Unspecified Length Record Format

Record 1	

Figure D.5

Other types of data sets exist in an MVS environment, but those are not the topic here. This appendix is a reference for users not familiar with partitioned or sequential data sets.

APPENDIX E
VM File Structure

This appendix is for users new to the VM operating system. It provides basic information about file structures in a VM environment. VM is also a popular operating system in SNA. It stores data differently than MVS, however.

System Directory

The VM operating system was covered previously, but additional information is needed here to aid in the understanding of data storage under VM. As stated previously, each guest operating system under VM "thinks" it is the only operating system in the machine. Each guest operating system has access to only those physical system resources defined for it in the VM system directory. The system directory operates under CMS and is maintained by an operator with administrative privileges. Some administrative functions include: adding a directory for a newly defined user, changing the status of a user's capabilities, and/or changing a user's password. Other administrative functions include: generating a list of users, shutting down the system to perform maintenance, and other site dependent reasons.

Disks

Each physical VM disk (disks in the IBM world are also known as volumes) is partitioned into groups of tracks called minidisks. Each Conversational Monitoring System (CMS) disk volume has a master file directory containing names of all files on that physical disk. When a user accesses a particular minidisk the name(s) that person may access are paged into a user file directory residing in virtual storage. See figure E.1.

Appendix E

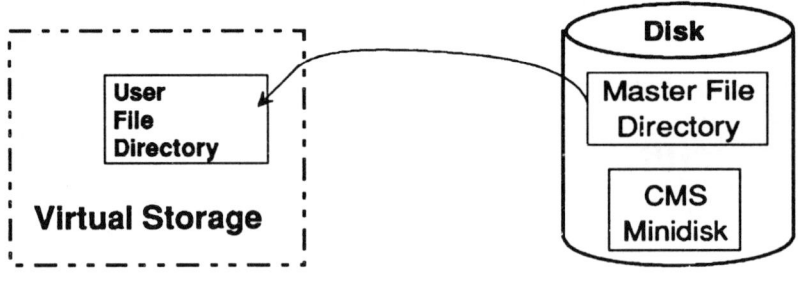

Figure E.1

Consequently, to a user it appears each minidisk has its own directory of filenames.

When a user updates a CMS file, or creates a new file, information about this file is updated in the master file directory on the CMS disk volume and the user file directory in virtual storage.

Minidisks are available to CMS users in two modes: Read only and read/write. This applies to files, collectively, on a minidisk—not a file by file basis. For example, if a user has read only privileges, a file cannot be updated, but it can be browsed, copied, or executed. On the other hand, if a user has read/write privileges for a particular minidisk, each time the user updates a file the user file and master file directory are updated immediately. Other users having read only access to that particular minidisk are not notified about the change(s).

Typically, CMS users are allowed read/write access to only one minidisk, called their "A" disk. All others are read only minidisks. Each minidisk is known by a letter, hence the maximum number of minidisks available to a user at one particular time is twenty-six.

File Identification

A file is the fundamental unit of data in a CMS environment. Even though VM is a virtual machine supporting multiple preferred guest (MPG) operating systems, CMS disk files cannot be read or written to using other operating systems. CMS files are categorized by:

- Filename
- File type
- File mode

VM File Structure

A filename is part of what gives a CMS file its identity. Its uniqueness helps in the identification process. The file type is a naming convention used to group files according to some common characteristic. For example, COBOL, ASSEMBLER, or EXECUTABLE. The file mode is an identifier consisting of two characters. First, the file mode indicates to CMS in which virtual minidisk the file resides. Second, the file mode is used to assign certain access characteristics to a file. For example, the number one (1) could represent a certain type file, whereas the number two (2) could represent another type file. Consider figure E.2.

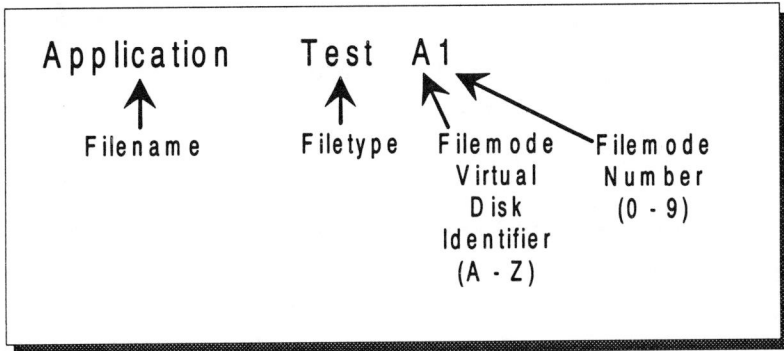

Figure E.2

Records

The constituent parts of a file are records. A record can be spoken of with regard to length. Records can be a fixed or variable length. In CMS, records constitute a line of data. If a file contains a fixed length record format, then it would appear as figure E.3 shows.

```
Fixed Length Record Format
        This is an example ■■
        used to convey ■■■■
        the ■■■■■■■■■■■■■
        concept of a fixed■■■
        file format ■■■■■■■■■
        in ■■■■■■■■■■■■■■
        a CMS file ■■■■■■■■
```

Figure E.3

Appendix E

Figure E.3 shows a file where CMS fills trailing positions in a record with blanks. The advantage of this is fixed length records increase processing speeds; however, the disadvantage is disk space is not used efficiently.

Variable length records appear as figure E.4 shows.

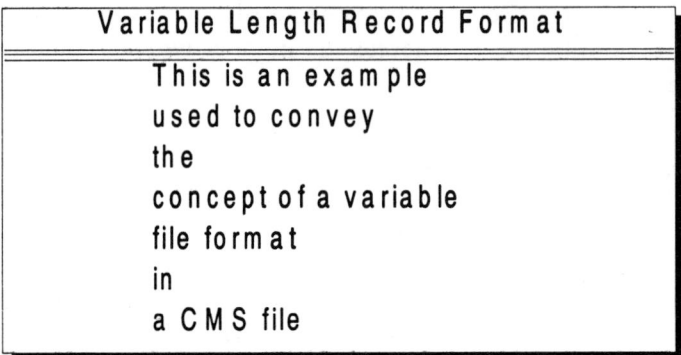

Figure E.4

In variable length record format, CMS stores up to the last significant character only. In actuality, this amounts to less overhead than fixed length record format. However, the negative side of this format is processing time per record is increased.

VM file structure was architected around the VM operating system. Even though multiple preferred guests can execute simultaneously on a VM machine, they each have their own file structures, respectively.

APPENDIX F
VMS File Structure

Virtual Memory System (VMS) is the Digital Equipment Corporation's operating system for its Virtual Address Extension (VAX) range of computers. File structure in VMS is a combination of directories and files.

All files on a disk reside in a directory. Directories are specified by square brackets [ ]. On each disk, the top level directory is called the master file directory (MFD).

When a DIRECTORY command is entered with no qualifiers, the following is displayed:

- The disk where the directory and file are located
- The directory name
- Filenames, types, and version numbers
- The total number of files in the directory

For example, if the DIRECTORY command was entered at the system prompt, an example such as the following appears:

```
$ DIRECTORY                    (and the Enter key is pressed)
Directory Hardware: {Test}     (this is displayed)
test1.txt;2                    (this is displayed)
test2.txt;4                    (this is displayed)
test3.txt;7                    (this is displayed)
Total of 3 files               (this is displayed)
```

According to a digital glossary, a file is "A set of data elements arranged in a structure significant to the user." A file is any named, stored program or data, or both, to which the system has access.

In VMS files are identified by:

- Filename
- Type
- Version Number

Filenames are created by a user, normally having significant meaning to the user. A file will normally describe what kind of data the file consists of; however, this does not have to be the case. The following are examples of file types:

- DAT—A data file
- DIR—A directory file
- TXT—A text file
- C—An input source file for a C compiler
- PAS—An input source file for a Pascal compiler

When a file is initially created, it is assigned version number 1 by VMS. Thereafter, anytime a file is edited VMS increases that version by 1.

A full file specification consists of information VMS needs to locate a particular file. This may require node specification if the VMS system is networked. Consider:

```
NODE::Device:[directory]filename.type;version number
```

In the example above the NODE refers to the host where the file is located. The Device reference indicates the disk or tape drive it is located on. The directory name, filename, file type, and latest version number follow.

In the VMS environment, logical names may be assigned to files. A logical name is a specified name for any portion or all of a file specification. This is a method of abbreviation that can be used instead of having to enter the directory name, filename, file type, and version number. A table maintains the correlation between logical names and the directory, filename, and file type.

APPENDIX G
Helpful Resources of Information

The following is a brief list of magazines, newsletters, and other sources that have continually provided credible information regarding those topics discussed within this book.

Business Communications Review
BCR Enterprises, Inc.
950 York Road
Hinsdale, IL 60521
(800) 227-1234

ComputerWorld
Box 9171
375 Cochituate Road
Framingham, MASS 01701-9171

Data Communications
McGraw Hill, Inc.
McGraw Hill Building
1221 Avenue of the Americas
New York, New York 10020
(212) 512-2000

Datamation
275 Washington Street
Newton, MA 02158
(617) 558-4281

Enterprise Systems Journal
Cardinal Business Media
10935 Estate Lane
Suite 375
Dallas, TX 75238
(214) 343-3717

IBM Internet Journal
Cardinal Business Media
10935 Estate Lane
Suite 375
Dallas, TX 75238
(214) 343-3717

IBM Systems Journal
IBM
P. O. Box 3033
Southeastern, PA 19398

INFO WORLD
155 Bovet Road
Suite 800
San Mateo, CA 94402
(415) 572-7341

LAN Magazine
600 Harrison Street
San Francisco, CA 94107
(415) 905-2587

Network World
161 Worcester Road
Framingham, MASS 01701-9172
(508) 875-6400

Open Systems Today
CMP Publications
600 Community Drive
Manhasset, NY 11030

RS/Magazine
Computer Publishing Group, Inc.
1330 Beacon Street
Brookline, MA 02146
(617) 739-7001

SNA Perspective
Communications Solutions, Inc.
2071 Hamilton Avenue
San Jose, CA 95125-9842

UNIX Review
Miller Freeman, Inc.
600 Harrison Street
San Francisco, CA 94107
(415) 905-2200

APPENDIX H
Vendor Listing

The following is a brief list of vendors supplying network devices that can be used in some manner of implementation to integrate TCP/IP and SNA. This list does not include terminal emulation suppliers intentionally; however, some vendors listed do provide terminal emulation software. The list is divided into categories: Bridges & Routers and Gateways. Vendor names are listed with telephone numbers.

BRIDGES & ROUTERS

3COM Corporation
1-800-NET-3COM

Andrew Corporation
1-800-733-0331

ASCOM Timeplex Inc.
1-800-755-TLAN

Cabletron Systems, Inc.
(602) 332-9400

Cisco Systems
(800) 473-4776

EICON Technology
(514) 631-2592

Fibronics International Inc.
(508) 778-0700

Harris Adacom Networking Services
(214) 386-2186

IBM Corporation
(800) 426-2255

Interlink Computer Sciences Inc.
(800) 422-3711

OpenConnect Systems
(214) 484-5200

Optical Data Systems
(214) 234-6400

Proteon Inc.
(508) 898-2800

RAD Data Communications
(201) 529-1100

RETIX
(800) 255-2333

Synoptics Communications Inc.
(800) PRO-NTWK

VitaLink Communications Corp.
(510) 745-1100

WELLFLEET Comunications Inc.
(617) 275-2400

GATEWAYS

3COM Corporation
1-(800) NET-3COM

Brixton Systems, Inc.
(617) 661-6262

InterLink Computer Sciences
1-(800) 422-3711

Harris Adacom Networking Services
(214) 386-2000

McDATA Corporation
(303) 460-9200

OpenConnect Systems
(214) 484-5200

APPENDIX I
MS-DOS TO UNIX COMMAND CROSS REFERENCE

The following table lists MS-DOS and UNIX commands that perform similar functions. It is advisable to look up the module for each of the UNIX commands listed to gain a complete understanding of the command.

MS_DOS Command	UNIX Command	Description
CHDIR (CD)	cd	Change directory
CLS	tput clear, clear	Clear terminal screen
COMMAND	sh, ksh, csh	Command interpretors (user shells)
COMP	diff, cmp, comm	Compare files
COPY	cp, cpio, tar, dd	Copy a file or group of files
	cat	Concatenate files
DATE	date	Display and change system date. Only super-user can change the date on UNIX.
DIR	ls	List directory contents
EDLIN	ed, ex	Line editor
ERASE, DEL	rm	Remove/delete files
FIND	grep, egrep, fgrep, nawk, sed	Search for text in files
MKDIR (MD)	mkdir	Make a directory
MORE	pg	Display files one screen at a time
PRINT	lp	Print files in background(spooling)
RENAME	mv	Move/rename files
RMDIR (RD)	rmdir	Remove a directory
SET	set	Set value of shell variable
SORT	sort	Sort contents of files
TIME	date	Display and change system time
TYPE	cat, tail, head, nawk, sed	Display contents of a file

APPENDIX J
VMS TO UNIX COMMAND CROSS REFERENCE

The following table lists VAX VMS and UNIX commands that perform similar functions. It is advisable to look up the module for each of the UNIX commands listed to gain a complete understanding of the command.

VAX/VMS Command	UNIX Command	Description
SET DEFAULT	cd	Change directory
SHOW DEFAULT	pwd	Display present working directory.
CLS	tput clear, cls	Clear terminal screen
CREATE	touch	Create an empty file.
	sh, ksh	Command interpretors (user shells)
	diff, cmp, diff3, comm	Compare files
COPY	cp, cpio, tar, dd	Copy a file or group of files
	cat	Concatenate files
SHOW TIME	date	Display and change system date
DIR	ls	List directory contents
	ed, ex	Line editor
EDT	vi	Screen editor
DELETE, PURGE	rm	Remove/delete files
	grep, egrep, fgrep, nawk, sed	Search for text in files
	mkdir	Make a directory
	pg, more, less	Display files one screen at a time
PRINT	lp	Print files in background(spooling)
SHOW QUEUE	lpstat	Display print queue.
RENAME	mv	Move/rename files
DELETE/DIR	rmdir	Remove a directory
	sort	Sort contents of files
TYPE	cat, tail, head, nawk, sed	Display contents of a file
Symbols	alias x="command"	Setting up symbols (aliases)

205

APPENDIX K
vi QUICK REFERENCE

This appendix provides quick reference information on the **vi** editor.

vi Command Table   This table provides a quick reference to the motion and four most used operators combined with the motions.

Unit of Text	Delete	Change	Copy/(yank)	Filter	Indent
Character					
Current	x	r	yl	NA	NA
Previous	X	hr	yh	NA	NA
Next	lx	lr	lyl	NA	NA
Word					
Beginning next	dw	cw	yw	NA	NA
End current	de	ce	ye	NA	NA
Beginning previous	db	cb	yb	NA	NA
Up to next ip\(dg	dW	cW	yW	NA	NA
Previous ip	dB	cB	yB	NA	NA
Line					
Current	dd	cc or S	yy or Y	!!	>>
Beginning of	d0	c0	y0	NA	NA
End of	d$ or D	c$ or C	y$	NA	NA
Previous	dk	ck	yk	!k	>k
Next	dj	cj	yj	!j	>j
Forward to c	dfc	cfc	yfc	NA	NA
Back to c	dFc	cFc	yFc	NA	NA
Sen/Para/Sec					
Previous sentence	d(	c(	y(	!(	>(
Next sentence	d)	c)	y)	)!	>)
Previous paragraph	d{	c{	y{	!{	>{
Next paragraph	d}	c}	y}	!}	>}
Previous section	d[[	c[[	y[[	![[	>[[
Next section	d]]	c]]	y]]	!]]	>]]

APPENDIX K

Unit of Text	Delete	Change	Copy/(yank)	Filter	Indent
Screen					
Beginning of	dH	cH	yH	!H	>H
Middle of	dM	cM	yM	!M	>M
End of	dL	cL	yL	!L	>L
Searches					
Previous pat	d?*pat*	c?*pat*	y?*pat*	!?*pat*	>?*pat*
Next pat	d/*pat*	c/*pat*	y/*pat*	!/*pat*	>/*pat*
Marks					
Line marked m	d'*m*	c'*m*	y'*m*	!'*m*	>'*m*
Character marked m	d'*m*	c'*m*	y'*m*	!'*m*	>'*m*
Buffer					
Beginning of	d1G	c1G	y1G	!1G	>1G
End of	dG	cG	yG	!G	>G
Line number x	dxG	cxG	yxG	!xG	>xG

Customizing Options   The **ex/vi** editor has many options that you can set to customize how the editor functions.

Index

1401, 46
3172, 50
3172 interconnect controller, 50
3172 IP routing, 127
3172 offload, 108
3172 model 003 offload, 108
3174, 50
3270, 15
3270 communications controller, 50
3270 emulation, 130, 131
370/ESA architecture, 47
370/XA architecture, 47
3745 communications controller, 50
3COM Corporation, 115, 131
5250, 15
5250 emulation, 130, 131
604, 46
650, 46
6611, 118
6611 Network Processor, 118
701, 46
702, 46

Activate Logical Unit, 77
Activate Physical Unit, 77
Activation, 80
ACTLU, 77
ACTPU, 77
Address classes, 27
Address Resolution Protocol, 25
Advanced Peer-to-Peer Networking, 72
Agent, 150
AID key, 17, 138, 139
Alerts, 148
APPC in TCP/IP, 89
Apple ids, 80
Application, 150
Application definition, 80

Application ids, 80
Application Program Interface, 70
Application services, 70
Application support layer, 70
APPLIDs, 80
APPN, 72
APPN nodes, 74
ARP, 25
ARPA, 21
ARPANET, 11
ASCII, 14
ASN.1, 24, 152
Asynchronous link, 98

BIND, 80
Block Mode, 137
Block Oriented, 17
Blueprint, 69
Brain based, 144
Brains, 143
Bridge, 6
Bridge types, 119
Bridges, 119
Brixton Systems, 115
Broadcast technology, 6
Bugs, 41

Cascading, 60, 61
CCS, 65
Channel gateway, 131
Chaos, 104
Character Mode, 137
Character oriented, 15
Cisco Systems, 117
Class A, 27
Class B, 27
Class C, 27
Class D, 27

Index

Class E, 27
CLAW, 127
CLAW driver, 127
Client/server, 14
CLPA, 123
Cluster controller, 59
CMIP, 24
CMIS, 24
CMOT, 24
CNM, 62
CNM facility, 62
Common Communications Support, 65
Common Link Access Workstation, 127
Common Link Pack Area, 123
Common Programming Interface, 65
Common transport semantics, 71
Common User Interface, 65
Communication controller node, 73
Communications software, 53
Computer gridlock, 93
Concepts, 144
Connection oriented technology, 6, 25
Connectionless oriented, 25
Control Point, 75
CP-CP, 77
CPI, 65
Creating a LAN, 92
CUI, 65

DARPA, 11, 21
Data link layer, 2
Data link protocols, 3
Data representation, 14
Data set, partitioned, 141
Data streams, 15
Data translation, 101, 111
DB2, 55
DCA, 22
DCE, 41
DDN, 22
Deactivation, 80

Dependent Logical Unit, 76
Dependent LU, 76
DEVICE statement, 124
Disorganization, 104
Disparities, 135
DLU, 76
DNS, 24
DOS/VSE, 54
Dotted decimal notation, 27

EBCDIC, 15
EGP, 118
Eicon Technology, 117
Encapsulation, 118
End node, 73
Enterprise system connection architecture, 48
Escape mode, 139
ESCON, 48, 77
Establishment controller, 50
/etc/services, 28
ETHERNET, 30, 79
Event reporting system, 152
Ex editor, 138

Factors beyond integration, 97
Factors of integration, 98
FDDI, 78
Fiber Distributed Data Interface, 78
Fibronics International Inc., 117
File structures, 140
Firmare, 52
Forces driving integration, 13
Frame relay support, 130
FTP, 14, 36
FTP commands, 37

Gateway, 5, 114
Gateway, as IBM defines, 115
Gateway access via menus, 130
Gateway history, 114
Gateway interface options, 131

Gateway management, 154
Gateway Protocols, 25
GATEWAY statement, 124
Gateway vendors, 115
GDS, 16
GEN, 79
Generation, 79
Generic Alerts, 148
GGP, 118

Hair-split, 100
Hard media, 113
Hardware architectures, 16
Hardware gateway, 130
Hardware gateway support, 131
Harris Adacom, 131
Harris Adacom Networking Services, 115
Hierarchical, 71
Historical snapshot, 83
History of gateways, 114

I/O GEN, 80
I/O subsystem, 80
I/O supervisor, 52
IBM Corporation, 117
IBM gateway, 115
IBM PC, 83
IBM's 6611, 118
IBM's networking blueprint, 69
IBM's RISC/6000, 128
ICMP, 25
IGP, 118
IGRP, 118
IIA, 16
Illusion, 144
ILU, 77
Initiate, 35
Input mode, 139
Integration, factors beyond, 97
Integration, the term, 136
Integration, what is it?, 111
Integration by gateway, 99, 127

Integration by SNA host, 121
Integration planning, 132
Integration requirements, 136
Integration via gateway, 19
Integration via SNA host, 19
Integration via TCP/IP host, 18
Intelligent door keeper, 79
Interlink, 117
internet, 29
Internet, 29
Internet Control Message Protocol, 25
Internet Protocol, 25
Invoke, 35
IP, 25
IP addressing, 27
IP routing on a 3172, 127
ISO, 1
ISPF editor, 138

JES2, 55

Kerberos, 24
Knowledge, 144

LAN, creating, 92
LAN Magazine, 117
LAN Times Buyers Guide, 117
LANs, when they are needed, 84
LANs, which LAN is best, 84
Layer 0, 113
Layer 7, 5
Learning curve, 97
LEN node, 73
LINK statement, 124
LinkMaster 6100 Series, 131
LinkMaster 7100 Network Controller, 131
Logical Unit, 75
LOGMODE, 80
LOGMODE table, 80
Logon Mode Table, 80
Low Entry Networking node, 73
Lower layer protocols, 4

Index

LU definition, 79
LU-LU, 77
LU0, 76
LU1, 76
LU2, 76
LU3, 76
LU4, 76
LU6.1, 76
LU6.2, 16, 76
LU7, 76
Luminiferous ether, 30

MAU, 9
Management Information Base, 150
McDATA Corporation, 115, 131
Media Access Unit, 9
Media types, 113
Memory, 51
Methods of integration, 120
MIB, 150
Microcode, 52
Models, 49
MPG, 53
Multicasting, 27
Multiple language support, 131
Multiple preferred guest, 53
Multiple routes, 63
Multiprotocol Routing, 118
MVS, 51, 140

NAU, 75
Navigating MVS, 140
NCCF, 62
NCP, 55
NCP GEN, 80
NetView, 81, 145
Network Accessible Unit, 75
Network Communications Control Facility, 62
Network Control Program, 55
Network devices, 5, 112
Network element, 150

Network islands, 13
Network layer, 4
Network Layer 0, 113
Network Logical Data Manager, 148
Network mangement, 145
Network management station, 150
Network manager, 150
Network node, 73
Network Packet Switched Interface, 56
Network Problem Determination Aid, 62
Network Terminal Option, 64
Networking, 83
Networking blueprint, 69
NEWS, 41
NFS, 24
NFSNET, 29
NIC, 29
NLDM, 148
NPDA, 62
NPSI, 56
NTO, 64

OCS II, 129
Offload Server, 127
Offload feature, 108
OpenConnect Systems Inc., 115, 129
OpenConnect's FTP Server, 129
OpenLook, 42
Operating environments, 140
Operating systems, 51
Origins of X, 40
OSI reference model, 1,2
OSPF, 118

Paging, 52
Palo Alto, CA, 30
Parallel channels, 77
Parallel links, 63
PARC, 30
Partitioned data set, 141
PC hardware, 91
PCs verses PS/2s, 91

Peer technology, 9
Peripheral node, 73
Personnel training, 144
Physical layer, 2
Physical Unit, 75
Physical Unit Control Point, 75
Planning integration, 132
PLU, 76
Presentation layer, 5
Primary Logical Unit, 76
Printers, 50
Processor architecture, 49
Processors, 48
Protocol conversion, 100, 101, 111
Protocol problems, 111
Protocol selection, 88
PU statement, 79
Public, 151
PUCP, 75
Pure integration, 137
PUs, types of, 75

RARP, 25
Raw telnet, 34
Real storage, 51
Reality, 104, 143
Remote bridge, 137
Remote control, 81
Remote TCP/IP LANs, 95
Repeater, 6, 120
Response Time Monitor, 149
RETIX, 117
Reverse Address Resolution Protocol, 25
RFC, 29
RFC states, 29
RFC status, 29
RIP, 25, 118
RISC/6000, 128
Router, 6, 116
Router vendors, 117
Routing, the act of, 118

Routing, types of, 118
RPC, 24
RTM, 149

S/360, 45
S/370 architecture, 47
S/390 architecture, 48
SAA, 64
SCE, 48
SCS, 16
SDLC, 78
SDLC gateway, 131
Secondary Logical Unit, 76
Sequential data set, 141
Series, 49
Session, 64
Session layer, 5
Session types, 77
Short-sighted, 101
SLU, 76
SMI, 151
SMTP, 14, 39
SMTP commands, 39
SNA, 11, 12
SNA, 1975, 58
SNA, 1977, 60
SNA, 1979, 63
SNA, 1980's, 64
SNA, 1987, 64
SNA, 1990-1992, 66
SNA & APPN, 71
SNA characteristics, 15
SNA concepts, 73
SNA data flow control, 68
SNA data link control, 67
SNA data link protocols, 17
SNA definitions, 79
SNA layers, 66
SNA nodes, 73
SNA path control, 67
SNA physical control, 67

Index

SNA presentation services, 68
SNA software architectures, 16
SNA terminology, 73
SNA transaction services, 68
SNA transmission control, 67
SNALink, 125
SNMP, 24, 145, 147
SNMP management, 150
SNMP messages, 151
Sockets, 28
Soft media, 113
Software gateway, 130
SSCP, 75
SSCP-LU, 77
SSCP-PU, 77
SSCP-SSCP, 77
SSP, 56
Structure of Management Information, 151
Subarea host node, 73
Subnetwork layer, 71
SUN Microsystems, 41
SuperNet Communication System, 131
Swapping, 52
Synchronous Data Link Control, 78
Synoptics Communications Inc., 117
SYS, 142
SYS1, 142
SYS1 data set, 142
System control element, 48
System Services Control Point, 75
System Support Program, 56
Systems Application Architecture, 64
Systems management, 70

T2.0 PU, 75
T2.1 PU, 75
T4 PU, 75
T5 PU, 75
Tasks, 124
TCP, 25

TCP/IP, 11, 12
TCP/IP addressing, 26
TCP/IP applications, 14
TCP/IP characteristics, 14
TCP/IP components, 22
TCP/IP history, 21
TCP/IP offload feature, 126
TCP/IP Socket Interface for CICS, 125
TCP/IP to SNA gateway, 131
TCP/IP's strengths, 31
Technological enginge, 83
Technological flux, 115
TELNET, 14, 33,
TELNET commands, 35
Terminal emulation, 19
Terminal models, 49
Terminal server, 131
Terminals, 49
TFTP, 24
The 1980's, 83
Time Sharing Option, 55
TN3270 Client, 34
Token ring, 78
Token ring gateway, 131
Topologies, 7
Training, 101
Training, optional, 144
TRANSLATE statement, 124
Transport layer, 4
Trap, 151
TSO, 55
Tunneling, 118
Types of Bridges, 119
Types of links, 77
Types of media, 113
Types of PUs, 75
Types of sessions, 77

UDP, 25
UNIX, 143
Upper layer protocols, 4

Vary online, 81
VBUILD, 79
VBUILD statement, 79
Vi editor, 138
Virtual network, 114
Virtual storage, 51
Virtual Telecommunications Access
  Method, 54
Vitalink Communcations
  Corporation, 117
VM, 52
Volume Table of Contents, 142
VSE, 54
VTAM, 54
VTAM GEN, 79
VTAM V. 4 R. 1, 66
VTOC, 142

Well-known ports, 28
Wellfleet, 117
What is integration?, 111

X, 14, 23, 39
X application, 42
X functions, 43
X layers, 42
X library, 42
X protocol, 42
X toolkit, 42
X user interface, 42
X/Open management protocol, 70
X.25 support, 130
X.25, 79
Xerox, 30

Other Books from Wordware Publishing, Inc.

Computer Aided Drafting
Illustrated AutoCAD (Release 11)
Illustrated AutoCAD (Release 12)
Illustrated AutoLISP
Illustrated AutoSketch 2.0
Illustrated Generic CADD Level 3

Database Management
Illustrated dBASE III Plus
Illustrated dBASE IV 1.1
Illustrated Force 2
Illustrated FoxPro 2.0

Desktop Publishing
The Desktop Studio: Multimedia with the Amiga
Illustrated PFS:First Publisher 2.0 & 3.0
Illustrated PageMaker 4.0
Illustrated Ventura 3.0 (Windows Ed.)
Illustrated Ventura 3.0 (DOS/GEM Ed.)
Illustrated Ventura 4.0

General and Advanced Topics
111 Clipper Functions
The Complete Communications Handbook
Financial Modeling using Lotus 1-2-3
Graphic User Interface Programming with C
Illustrated DacEasy Accounting 4.2
Illustrated Novell NetWare 2.x/3.x Software
Integrating TCP/IP into SNA
Learn P-CAD Master Designer 6.0
Novell NetWare: Adv. Tech. and App.
Programming On-Line Help with Turbo C/C++
Understanding 3COM Networks

Integrated
Illustrated Enable/OA
Illustrated Framework III
Illustrated Microsoft Works 2.0
Illustrated Q&A 3.0 (2nd Ed.)
Illustrated Q&A 4.0

Programming Languages
Illustrated Borland C++ 3.1
Illustrated C Programming (ANSI) (2nd Ed.)
Illustrated Clipper 5.0 (2nd Ed.)
Illustrated QBasic for MS-DOS 5.0
Graphics Programming with Turbo Pascal
Illustrated Turbo C++
Illustrated Turbo Debugger 3.0
Illustrated Turbo Pascal 6.0

Spreadsheet
Illustrated Excel 4.0 for Windows
Illustrated Lotus 1-2-3 Rel. 2.2
Illustrated Lotus 1-2-3 Rel. 3.0
Illustrated Quattro

Systems and Operating Guides
Illustrated DR DOS 6.0
Illustrated MS-DOS 5.0
Illustrated UNIX System V
Illustrated Windows 3.1

Word Processing
Illustrated Microsoft Word 5.0 (PC)
Illustrated WordPerfect 1.0 (Macintosh)
Illustrated WordPerfect 5.1
Illustrated WordPerfect for Windows
Illustrated WordStar 6.0
WordPerfect Wizardry: Advanced Techniques and Applications

Call Wordware Publishing, Inc. for names of the bookstores in your area
(214) 423-0090

Other Books from Wordware Publishing, Inc.

Popular Applications Series
Build Your Own Computer
Cost Control Using Lotus 1-2-3
Creating Newsletters with Ventura
Database Publishing with Ventura
Desktop Pub. with Word 2.0 for Windows
Desktop Pub. with WordPerfect for Windows
Learn AmiPro 3.0 in a Day
Learn AutoCAD in a Day
Learn AutoCAD 12 in a Day
Learn C in Three Days
Learn CorelDRAW! in a Day
Learn DataPerfect in a Day
Learn dBASE Programming in a Day
Learn DOS in a Day
Learn DrawPerfect in a Day
Learn Excel for Windows in a Day (Ver. 3.0/4.0)
Learn FoxPro 2.0 in a Day
Learn Freelance Graphics for Windows in a Day
Learn Generic CADD 6.0 in a Day
Learn Harvard Graphics 3.0 in a Day
Learn Lotus 1-2-3 Ver. 2.4 in a Day
Learn Microsoft Assembler in a Day
Learn Microsoft Works in a Day
Learn Norton Utilities in a Day
Learn Novell NetWare Software in a Day
Learn OS/2 in a Day
Learn Pacioli 2000 Ver. 2.0 in a Day
Learn PageMaker 4.0 in a Day
Learn PAL in a Day
Learn Paradox 4.0 in a Day
Learn Paradox for Windows in a Day
Learn Pascal in Three Days
Learn PC-Paintbrush in a Day
Learn PC-Tools 8.0 in a Day

Popular Applications Series Cont.
Learn PlanPerfect in a Day
Learn Q&A in a Day
Learn Quattro Pro 4.0 in a Day
Learn Quicken in a Day
Learn Turbo Assembler Prog. in a Day
Learn Ventura 4.0 in a Day
Learn Windows in a Day
Learn Windows NT in a Day
Learn Word 2.0 for Windows in a Day
Learn WordPerfect 5.2 for Windows in a Day
Learn WordPerfect in a Day (2nd Edition)
Mailing Lists using dBASE
Moving from WordPerfect for DOS to
    WordPerfect for Windows
Object-Oriented Prog. using Turbo C++
Presentations with Harvard Graphics
Programming Output Drivers using
    Borland C++
WordPerfect Macros
WordPerfect 6.0 Survival Skills
Write Your Own Programming Language
    using C++

At A Glance Series
FoxPro 2.5 at a Glance
FoxPro for Windows at a Glance
Lotus 1-2-3 for Windows at a Glance
Microsoft Windows at a Glance
Paradox for Windows at a Glance
Quattro Pro 4.0 at a Glance
Quattro Pro for Windows at a Glance
Word 2.0 for Windows at a Glance
WordPerfect 5.2 for Windows at a Glance

Call Wordware Publishing, Inc. for names of the bookstores in your area
(214) 423-0090

Regional Books from Wordware Publishing, Inc.

100 Days in Texas: The Alamo Letters
by Wallace O. Chariton

Classic Clint: The Laughs and Times of Clint Murchison, Jr.
by Dick Hitt

Country Savvy: Survival Tips for Farmers, Ranchers, and Cowboys
by Reed Blackmon

Critter Chronicles
by Jim Dunlap

Dirty Dining: A Cookbook, and More, for Lovers
by Ginnie Siena Bivona

Don't Throw Feathers at Chickens: A Collection of Texas Political Humor
by Charles Herring, Jr. and Walter Richter

Exploring the Alamo Legends
by Wallace O. Chariton

From an Outhouse to the Whitehouse
by Wallace O. Chariton

The Great Texas Airship Mystery
by Wallace O. Chariton

Kingmakers
by John R. Knaggs

Rainy Days in Texas Funbook
by Wallace O. Chariton

Recovery: A Directory to Texas Substance Abuse Treatment Facilities
Edited by Linda Manning-Miller

San Antonio Uncovered
by Mark Louis Rybczyk

Spirits of San Antonio and South Texas
by Docia Schultz Williams and Reneta Byrne

Texas Highway Humor
by Wallace O. Chariton

Texas Politics in My Rearview Mirror
Waggoner Carr and Byron Varner

Texas Tales Your Teacher Never Told You
by Charles F. Eckhardt

Texas Wit and Wisdom
by Wallace O. Chariton

That Cat Won't Flush
by Wallace O. Chariton

That Old Overland Stagecoaching
by Eva Jolene Boyd

They Don't Have to Die
by Jim Dunlap

This Dog'll Hunt
by Wallace O. Chariton

To The Tyrants Never Yield
by Kevin R. Young

A Trail Rider's Guide to Texas
by Mary Elizabeth Sue Goldman

Unsolved Texas Mysteries
by Wallace O. Chariton

Call Wordware Publishing, Inc. for names of the bookstores in your area
(214) 423-0090